Cullen Montgomery Baker, Reconstruction Desperado

Cullen Montgomery Baker

RECONSTRUCTION

DESPERADO

Barry A. Crouch and Donaly E. Brice

LOUISIANA STATE UNIVERSITY PRESS

BATON ROUGE AND LONDON

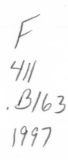

F
411
.B163
1997

Designer: Erin Kirk New
Typeface: New Caledonia
Typesetter: Impressions Book and Journal Services, Inc.
Printer and binder: Thomson-Shore, Inc.

Library of Congress Cataloging-in-Publication Data

Crouch, Barry A., 1941–
   Cullen Montgomery Baker, reconstruction desperado / Barry A.
Crouch and Donaly E. Brice.
      p.   cm.
   Includes bibliographical references and index.
   ISBN 0-8071-2140-1 (cloth : alk. paper)
   1. Baker, Cullen Montgomery.   2. Reconstruction—Arkansas.
3. Reconstruction—Texas.   4. Outlaws—Arkansas—Biography.
5. Outlaws—Texas—Biography.   6. Murderers—Arkansas—Biography.
7. Murderers—Texas—Biography.   8. Arkansas—History.   9. Texas—
History—1846–1950.   I. Brice, Donaly E.   II. Title.
   F411.B163   1997
976.4′06′092—dc21
[B]   97-6677
                                                              CIP

For Joan and Clare

Contents

Illustrations

———◆———

Acknowledgments

———•———

IT HAS BEEN A CHALLENGE to write this biography about a post–Civil War desperado who gained fleeting national fame but then receded into the regional history and folklore of Texas. Many individuals assisted in this venture. Like the authors, these people had only a vague conception of what information would be useful, but they applied their talents and expertise to our quest with unfailing generosity. They readily revealed their treasures and pointed the way to more. In light of their extraordinary efforts, we thank these individuals for helping us to discover the "real" Cullen Montgomery Baker.

Many friends and colleagues contributed to this book in a variety of ways. The late Walter Novotsky listened to our ideas about desperadoes ad infinitum. Joseph S. Kelley, Jr., provided computer expertise. Keith Cheshire drew original maps reproduced in this volume. Donna Perreault copyedited the manuscript with a discerning eye. Junious Hargrave lent emotional support. Patrick Williams read the manuscript at a crucial juncture and provided a thorough critique. Larry Madaras applied his historical experience to the final version as did several other people in Lockhart, Texas. Les E. Abrahamson kindly sent us published essays on Baker of which we were not aware. Sources of great inspiration include Bill Cecil-Fronsman, Carl M. Moneyhon, Robert J. Robertson, and Richard B. McCaslin. In the history department at Gallaudet University, Washington, D.C., John V. Van Cleve and John S. Schuchman gave constant support to this project, as did Robert L. Williams in the psychology department there. Michael R. Karchmer, dean of graduate studies at Gallaudet University, aided this work by facilitating numerous travel grants. We owe an extraordinary debt to Sally W. Dunn, who organized the research trips.

We salute the National Endowment for the Humanities, which awarded Crouch a 1992 summer research grant to investigate throughout Baker country: northeastern Texas and Arkansas. In order to observe and fully understand the region where Baker became famous, both of us traveled to this area endeavoring to locate materials. Texas towns we worked in include Sherman, Bonham, Paris, Clarksville, New Boston, Linden, Jefferson, Queen City, Atlanta, and Bloomburg (the site of the annual Cullen Montgomery Baker County Fair). In Linden, Rebecca Montoya of the Cass County Title Company showed us where John Baker's homestead had been located and made it possible for us to pursue leads in the General Land Office. And in Jefferson, Katherine Ramsay Wise, owner of the charming Wise Manor, showed us her file on Baker, which led us to additional newspaper articles.

In Arkansas, on a farm outside the town of Doddridge, we spent a delightful afternoon with S. G. Nichols and his wife. Nichols guided us to the graves of William (1813–1888) and Elizabeth (1821–1876) Foster, Baker's in-laws. He knew about the Baker saga and showed us the place where Baker was killed. In Texas, Jerry and Dorothy Orr of Georgetown very helpfully supplied critical background information on Thomas Orr, Jerry's grandfather. We must also praise the assistance we received from a number of courthouse clerks across northeast Texas. They answered all our questions and led us to relevant records. Similarly, loyal librarians generously shared with us their knowledge of Baker and the region.

We are indebted to many reference specialists throughout the Lone Star State. The staff of the archives division of the Texas State Library, where Brice works, were unfailing in their support and encouragement of this project. They guided us to material we would otherwise have overlooked and made research in their depository a delightful and invigorating experience, especially for Crouch. Christine Woodrow of New Boston, Texas, gathered superb background information on Thomas U. Taylor's collection of data for his Baker manuscript, and she supplied us with copies. The archivists at the Center for American History at the University of Texas, Austin, graciously answered our inquiries and steered us to useful sources.

Two more information specialists deserve special mention. Susan M. Davis, the interlibrary loan coordinator at Gallaudet University, expended great energy in finding materials not readily accessible. Through her diligence, we were able to obtain most of the previously published information on Baker and a considerable amount of additional material. Another person who gave invaluable assistance is Michael T. Meier of the Old Military Records division of the National Archives. He pointed us to records of which we were totally unaware and demonstrated their usefulness. At a critical point in this study, he made it possible for us to research original military papers not ordinarily available to the public.

Several members of Crouch's family deserve special thanks. One man who helped to instigate this biography is Crouch's son, "Bear." He knew something of Baker because he had read the Louis L'Amour western entitled *The First Fast Draw*, which makes use of the Baker legend. From Bear's response to this book our manuscript grew, and we thank Bear for his diverse reading interests. In addition, Patsy Conn, her four children (Patrick, Denise, Dana, and Dale), and their families have been sources of inspiration. Robert B. Crouch shared his enthusiasm for this project and gave much encouragement. Jennifer and Dale Sorghardt, along with their children, David and Katherina, listened more than they probably wanted to about desperadoes. Naomi Mirman was always supportive.

Finally, we acknowledge our deep gratitude to our wives. Crouch's wife, Joan, has been the ideal supporter of this work. Although her expertise lies elsewhere, she cheerfully learned the history of the distant Texans who people this work. In fact, Joan assimilated the manuscript's information in a wonderful way and met with equanimity her husband's frequent research trips to Texas. Brice's wife, Clare, equally promoted this project. It was she who inclined us toward the Arkansas connection (her family originated there). Both Joan and Clare immersed themselves in our search for Cullen Montgomery Baker and gave us the benefit of their wisdom and encouragement. Because of them, this book became a reality.

Abbreviations Used in Notes

AAAG	Acting Assistant Adjutant General
AC	Assistant Commissioner (head of the Freedmen's Bureau in each state where it was established)
AG	Adjutant General
AGO	Adjutant General's Office
AHQ	*Arkansas Historical Quarterly*
BRFAL	Bureau of Refugees, Freedmen, and Abandoned Lands
CFAH	Center for American History, University of Texas, Austin
DT	Department of Texas
ECBTHC	Eugene C. Barker Texas History Center. Part of the CFAH.
GC	General Correspondence
GLO	General Land Office, Austin
GP	Governor's Papers
JSH	*Journal of Southern History*
JTK	Joel T. Kirkman
LR	Letters Received

MCR	Manuscript Census Returns
NA	National Archives
NR	Narrative Reports
OR	Operations Reports
RG	Record Group
SwHQ	*Southwestern Historical Quarterly*
TSL	Texas State Library, Austin
USACC	U.S. Army Continental Commands, 1821–1920
WGK	William G. Kirkman

Cullen Montgomery Baker, Reconstruction Desperado

Introduction

———————◆———————

DESPERADOES HAVE LONG BEEN perversely revered as heroes of American history by students of American culture. Ever since the nineteenth-century press promoted Jesse James, John Wesley Hardin, and Billy the Kid as the Robin Hoods of America's lower classes, desperadoes have become fixed in the national imagination. These social outcasts challenged the prevailing order and performed daring and violent acts, which usually involved robbing banks and trains. Legend has it that they distributed the proceeds of their work to those in need and often demonstrated an abiding concern for family and class. While it fuels good stories, most of this kind of folklore on desperadoes is untrue and unsubstantiated. But such legends are gradually constructed and carefully nurtured.

Although much historical writing has recounted the exploits of desperadoes and outlaws in the later years of the nineteenth century, little work has focused on those who appeared in the era immediately following the Civil War. The most publicized gunfights and cowboy sagas occurred decades later. Nevertheless, the postwar years witnessed a rise in gang violence. The frequent connection between the desperadoes and Ku Klux Klan is notable, although the Klan was not always connected with outlaw violence.[1] In the Southwest, before many of the names in western outlaw and lawmen history became familiar, one desperado in particular was known: Cullen Mont-

1. On this idea see Louis S. Gerteis, "A Border War," *Reviews in American History,* XVII (December, 1989), 559–65.

gomery Baker, who terrorized northeast Texas, southwest Arkansas, and occasionally northwest Louisiana to promote a defeated dream.

The phenomena of guerrilla warfare and social banditry during the Civil War, especially in Missouri and Kansas, have been extensively studied, but little attention has focused upon the postwar period. At that time communities used the ruthlessness of outlaw gangs to mask the Ku Klux Klan's later activities. These bands harassed the Union army, Freedmen's Bureau agents, and unionists; and they terrorized with a view to punishing the local black population. Group violence, whether of the desperado or Klan variety, played a definite role in defeating the implementation of Reconstruction ideas in "Baker country": that region where Texas, Arkansas, and Louisiana border one another.[2]

One interpretation of these guerrilla outlaws, declares James M. McPherson, portrays them as "defenders of a rural order of yeomen farmers against the encroachments of a capitalist market economy represented by Yankee soldiers and Unionists during the Civil War, and by banks and railroads afterward." The desperadoes "took no prisoners, killed in cold blood, plundered, and pillaged (but almost never raped or killed white women)." They became, according to Michael Fellman's psychological profile of Missouri during the war, examples of the "noble guerrilla" and "noble outlaw." Many, however, were "psychopathic killers, nihilistic lovers of violence," McPherson contends, and the "war gave quasi-official sanction to their atavistic impulses." Their exploits became "ugly, dirty, and vicious."[3]

2. *Ibid.*, 564; Michael Fellman, *Inside War: The Guerrilla Conflict in Missouri During the American Civil War* (New York, 1989); Gary L. Cheatham, " 'Desperate Characters': The Development and Impact of the Confederate Guerrillas in Kansas," *Kansas History*, XIV (Autumn, 1991), 144–61; James M. McPherson, "Wartime," *New York Review of Books*, April 12, 1990, pp. 33–35; David Thelen, *Paths of Resistance: Tradition and Dignity in Industrializing Missouri* (New York, 1986); Thurman Sensing, *Champ Ferguson: Confederate Guerilla* (Nashville, 1942); Richard S. Brownlee, *Gray Ghosts of the Confederacy: Guerrilla Warfare in the West, 1861–1865* (Baton Rouge, 1958); Kevin H. Siepel, *Rebel: The Life and Times of John Singleton Mosby* (New York, 1983); W. Wayne Smith, "An Experiment in Counterinsurgency: The Assessment of Confederate Sympathizers in Missouri," *JSH*, XXXV (1969), 361–80. Perhaps the most neglected and yet the most incisive perceptions (which Fellman ignored) are found in the two pieces by Don R. Bowen, "Guerrilla War in Western Missouri, 1862–1865: Historical Extensions of the Relative Deprivation Hypothesis," *Comparative Studies in Society and History*, XIX (January, 1977), 30–51, and "Counterrevolutionary Guerrilla War: Missouri, 1861–1865," *Conflict*, VIII (1988), 69–78.

3. McPherson, "Wartime," 34–35. The banks and railroads were also seen as "soulless forces of capitalist transformation" that demonstrated no mercy. This Marxist interpretation may be

Two major problems confront historians when they write about a desperado active during the Reconstruction years; both are intertwined with myth-making. First, in the popular literature, especially at the local level, Reconstruction in Texas is still seen as a time when rapacious carpetbaggers implicated government in a multitude of sins. As Randolph B. Campbell recently demonstrated, this view grossly distorts the facts. Carpetbaggers and blacks constituted but a small percentage of officeholders and delegates to constitutional conventions during the period from 1867 to 1874.[4] The second problem concerns the direction that standard legends of outlaws have taken. Stories have transformed these gunmen into protectors of the people and avengers against the opposition during Reconstruction.

In the 1920s, Thomas U. Taylor wrote that the "careers of Cullen M. Baker, Ben Bickerstaff, Bob Lee, John Wesley Hardin, and Bill Longley [all desperadoes] bear a striking resemblance to each other in their first stages." They lay the primary cause of their postwar difficulties at the feet of the former slaves, who were "often encouraged by scalawags and carpetbaggers." Baker was "driven to his first deed" by freedmen; Hardin had to defend himself against "a burly black giant"; Lee protected his home "against similar forces"; and Longley was making his Evergreen neighborhood (Lee County) safe for white people. In "normal times," Taylor surmised, "these men would have been normal men." All this is patent nonsense.[5]

Born in Parker County in 1858, Taylor visited Baker territory in 1874, where Baker's deeds and career were "on everybody's tongue, old and young." Taylor returned to the area and interviewed many of Baker's associ-

---

considerably overdrawn. For the life of a native Alabamian yeoman farmer who began his robbing career in Texas and exemplifies McPherson's thesis, see William Warren Rogers, Jr., "Violence and Outlawry in the New South: Rube Burrow's Train Robbing Days in Alabama, Mississippi, and Florida" (M.A. thesis, Auburn University, 1979). Another Alabamian, whose career closely paralleled that of Baker but who enjoyed a more respectable reputation than that gunman, is the subject of William Warren Rogers and Ruth Pruitt, *Stephen S. Renfroe, Alabama's Outlaw Sheriff* (Tallahassee, 1972).

4. Randolph B. Campbell, "Carpetbagger Rule in Reconstruction Texas: An Enduring Myth," *SwHQ*, XCVII (1994), 587–96. Carpetbaggers accounted for about 20 percent of all officeholders.

5. [Thomas Ulvan Taylor], "Bill Longley and His Wild Career," *Frontier Times*, III (June, 1926), 17. Taylor wrote under the sobriquet "the Frontier Native." The writer blames blacks for the evolution of these individuals into killers, but there is no evidence to substantiate such a damning claim. In the case of John Wesley Hardin, his first homicide did stem from a personal dispute with a black man. Hardin claimed self-defense.

ates, schoolmates, acquaintances, and relatives. He was approximately seventy-eight years of age when he penned his Baker manuscript, which has since become the most commonly used reference on Baker's life. "Everyone agreed," wrote Taylor, that Thomas Orr's 1870 biography was "violently partisan, ex parte, and unjust." A "bitter enemy" of Baker, Orr should never have written his history, according to Taylor. The latter did not "esteem" any of Baker's "misdeeds," but claimed to present them as though for a court.[6]

Others besides Taylor have tirelessly promoted the Baker legend. One fan suggested that he was the "biggest bad wolf of all the bad men in the Southwest." His exploits, if widely publicized, "would have made Jesse James and all the gunmen of pioneer days pale into insignificance." No "cigarette-puffing, silk-shirted machine-gun-toting public enemy of modern times" could compare with him in "sheer nerve, cold courage, or dogged endurance." Not "a bandit in the true sense of the word," Baker fancied himself as a champion of the Lost Cause. Robbing, pillaging, plundering, and stealing "when necessary," Baker simultaneously "acquired a sort of Robin Hood glamour and was looked upon by many as a hero and benefactor."[7]

One of the more fascinating, original, and truly fantastic efforts to explain Baker was the 1979 publication of Traylor Russell and Robert T. Russell. These two brothers maintained, without any evidence, that Baker suffered from schizophrenia. It would have been easy for nineteenth-century biographers to "fail to notice, even to a small degree, the complexities of reasons that motivate certain aberrant behavioral patterns." Thus they explain why Orr's account "contains no direct reference to a distinct mental disorder." Complacently, they conclude that Baker was a "thief, a rebel, a murderer, and a sadist," as well as a "lover, a father, a gentleman, and a humorist."[8]

Baker, according to the Russells, "recognized that he suffered from an unexplainable disorder," which he called "my afflictions." In view of this supposed schizophrenia, Baker's crimes can be categorized in three ways:

6. T. U. Taylor, "Swamp Fox of the Sulphur or Life and Times of Cullen Montgomery Baker," *ca.* 1936 (Typescript in ECBTHC), 137; James Marten, *Texas Divided: Loyalty and Dissent in the Lone Star State, 1856–1874* (Lexington, 1990), 102–103. The T. U. Taylor Papers, deposited at the CFAH, reveal how Taylor approached his Baker project.

7. J. K. Bivins, "Cullen Baker, Civil War Desperado," in *Memoirs* (N.p., privately printed [1945]), 21. A copy is in the TSL.

8. Traylor Russell and Robert T. Russell, "'If I Had Killed Jesus Christ . . . ,'"; *Some Die Twice* (Waco, 1979), 2. Thomas Orr may not have attempted to explain Baker psychologically, but he did comment on Baker's strangeness. From the evidence the Russells present, Baker seems to fit the profile of a psychopath, not a schizophrenic.

his murder of United States government officials, exemplars of "Reconstruction bureaucracy"; his murderous acts based upon personal revenge and retaliation; and finally those murders he committed simply for "pleasure and sadism." For his actions against the government, the Russells absolve Baker. And they rationalize that when he was motivated by revenge and retaliation, his acts were "provoked by others; and in the lawless, unregulated western frontiers, retribution and justice were often obtained only by violent, personal methods." However, the Russells do not defend his killing for pleasure.[9]

Later writers gave Baker's image a more realistic evaluation. William L. Richter contended that Baker was "typical of the [postwar] bandit chieftains." A murderer before the war and a Confederate deserter, Baker established an outlaw school where he "taught his recruits the fine points of using a six-shooter and the virtues of shooting all prisoners or wounded soldiers in the head." He became a kind of Robin Hood among the citizens because he distributed his ill-gotten booty to them. Baker gained fame, Richter concludes, "in spite of his frequent murders of Texans who dared to associate his name with any crime whatsoever." His "psychotic drive to kill finally became obvious even to the most ardent Confederate flag-wavers."[10]

James Marten labeled Baker the "epitome of a violent, pragmatic disloyalist" and the "most famous Texas guerrilla." His "war-time pragmatism" led to "at least limited approval for his deeds in his self-appointed role as a local 'regulator.'" A "majority of the residents in Baker's territory probably did not condone his crimes," Marten contends, but "his post-war 'regulating' of Unionists, northerners, and freedmen did atone to a certain extent for his war-time behavior, and he became something of a hero in the eyes of at least a few of his neighbors." Marten theorizes that the "informal, violent, potentially lucrative life of a 'Confederate' partisan" suited Baker.[11]

Another enduring myth associated with Baker concerns his prowess with a six-gun. He has been credited with being the originator of the fast draw—

9. *Ibid.*, 2.

10. William L. Richter, "'The Revolver Rules the Day!': Colonel DeWitt C. Brown and the Freedmen's Bureau in Paris, Texas, 1867–1868," *SwHQ*, XCIII (January, 1990), 317; *The Army in Texas During Reconstruction, 1865–1870* (College Station, Tex., 1987), 145; "The Army in Texas During Reconstruction, 1865–1870" (Ph.D. dissertation, Louisiana State University, 1970), 223–25.

11. Marten, "Drawing the Line: Dissent and Disloyalty in Texas, 1856 to 1874" (Ph.D. dissertation, University of Texas, Austin, 1986), 264–67; *Texas Divided*, 103. Marten also believes that men like Baker "relished the chaos spawned by the war" (*Texas Divided*, 105).

that is, to "slap leather" more quickly than his opponent, draw his six-gun, and fire with a steady aim. This myth argues that he thus bested his opponents with a revolver. Although it is untrue, this wonderful tale has become a standard part of the Baker saga.

Baker knew how to use a six-gun, and he used one often, especially to murder blacks and Yankees in the years following the Civil War. However, the documentary record shows that he shot and killed only defenseless people by ambush or through surprise. There is not one shred of documentary evidence that Baker ever faced down anyone or had to quickdraw as we have come to envision such an event from old television shows like *Gunsmoke* or from Jack Paladin in *Have Gun, Will Travel*. The record belies those Baker chroniclers who suggested that he pioneered this technique. Their own evidence, which is flimsy at best and nonexistent at worst, renders Baker as a coward, a back-shooter, an alcoholic, and a hate-filled man who "loved" to kill outsiders or those who sullied his reputation. Unfortunately, he personified and acted on what many white southerners felt during the postwar era.

Dubbed "the Swamp Fox of the Sulphur," Baker has fascinated and intrigued writers for more than one hundred years. In fact, his persona has been so compelling that it has even been made the subject of a novel. The late Louis L'Amour immortalized him in the early western novel *The First Fast Draw* (1959). Too often in western desperado history, Baker has been adulated even though he killed innocent people. He was probably much like the character of Billy the Kid as drawn by Larry McMurtry in his novel *Anything for Billy* (1988): essentially a coward, a bully, and a cold-blooded murderer of defenseless individuals—in short, a sociopath.[12]

12. Louis L'Amour, *"The First Fast Draw"* (New York, 1959); Larry McMurtry, *Anything for Billy* (New York, 1988). Almost every writer comments about Baker's quick-draw method but fails to verify that he ever used it. McMurtry's portrayal of "The Kid" is far from the historical truth. See Robert M. Utley, *Billy the Kid: A Short and Violent Life* (Lincoln, Nebr., 1989); and *High Noon in Lincoln: Violence on the Western Frontier* (Albuquerque, 1987). Baker probably did murder more people than Billy, as the latter seems only to have been directly responsible for four deaths. For the Kid's image, see Stephen Tatum, *Inventing Billy the Kid: Visions of the Outlaw in America, 1881–1981* (Albuquerque, 1982). Two short biographical sketches of Baker, one laudatory and the other derogatory, demonstrate the division of opinion about his life: Ed Bartholomew, "Cullen Montgomery Baker," in *The Biographical Album of Western Gunfighters* (Houston, 1958), n.p.; Denis McLoughlin, "Cullen M. Baker," in *Wild and Woolly: An Encyclopedia of the Old West* (Garden City, N.Y., 1975), 27–28. See also the sketch in Walter Prescott Webb and H. Bailey Carroll, eds., *The Handbook of Texas* (2 vols.;

Much of the saga has depended on fiction and exaggeration and has succeeded in obscuring the real Baker. Indeed, fiction has been much kinder to the Swamp Fox than life was. L'Amour and several of Baker's biographers have attributed traits and attitudes to him that he did not possess. Although fiction writers may represent historical characters as they please, they risk creating popular misconceptions about their subjects. L'Amour at least concludes accurately that "Cullen Baker was an unreconstructed rebel who carried on a lone fight, and those who read a book written by Thomas Warren will tell you that Cullen was a drunken murderer and a thief," an apt description of the real Baker.[13]

The most interesting aspect of L'Amour's story is that it says nothing about the freeing of the slaves or the recognition of black rights. His is basically a race-free tale, for Baker is never connected with the freedmen in any manner. Yet almost every other writer directly attributes many of Baker's difficulties to his hatred of the former slaves. In addition, L'Amour, like most other writers, has portrayed Reconstruction as a time of carpetbag rule and scalawag treachery: in cahoots with the army, these outsiders and rebels are said to have plundered and raped the prostrate South. This interpretation has been out of favor for three decades now; but until recently, Baker chroniclers have followed that line and viewed his presence and violence as necessary reactions to Reconstruction.[14]

The majority of those who have written about Baker (exceptions include Smallwood, Richter, and Marten) have perpetuated similar stereotypes and

Austin, 1962), I, 98. For general background, see Emerson Hough, *The Story of the Outlaw: A Study of the Western Desperado* (New York, 1905); Frank Richard Prassel, *The Great American Outlaw: A Legacy of Fact and Fiction* (Norman, Okla., 1993).

13. Richard N. Current, "Fiction as History: A Review Essay," *JSH*, LII (1986), 77–90; L'Amour, *The First Fast Draw*, 155. The character Thomas Warren was in real life Thomas Orr. A schoolteacher who married a woman Baker desired to betroth, Orr assisted in killing Baker and later, in 1870, wrote a biography of him: Thomas Orr, *Life of the Notorious Desperado Cullen Baker, from His Childhood to His Death, with a Full Account of All the Murders He Committed* (Little Rock, 1870). The Orr book is rare but is included as an appendix to Ed Bartholomew, *Cullen Baker: Premier Texas Gunfighter* (Houston, 1954).

14. L'Amour, *The First Fast Draw*, 54, 65–66. A quick and succinct summary of historiographical changes for the Reconstruction era is Eric Foner, "The New View of Reconstruction," *American Heritage*, XXXIV (October/November, 1983), 10–15. A more detailed analysis is contained in his "Reconstruction Revisited," *Reviews in American History*, X (December, 1982), 82–100. A superb overview is Foner's *Reconstruction: America's Unfinished Revolution, 1863–1877* (New York, 1988). For Texas, see Barry A. Crouch, " 'Unmanacling' Texas Reconstruction: A Twenty-Year Perspective," *SwHQ*, XCIII (January, 1990), 275–302.

exaggerated tales, many of which originated with Taylor, who relied almost solely upon oral testimony. They have described Baker's life with embellished accounts, but much of the same material is recycled.[15] Only fairly recently have writers begun to challenge these old and prevailing interpretations. But even they have made little effort to track down new information relating to the Swamp Fox. No one has hitherto attempted a fully documented biography of Baker that reveals the sources for re-creating his life. The present work aims to fill this gap.

The years following the Civil War were a trying time for all concerned. Union occupation dismayed the South and led to outrages against the army and the Freedmen's Bureau. In the early stages of Reconstruction, there was general violence. Reports arrived at military headquarters that pro-Union citizens were unsafe and that if an election were held, individuals who had supported the Union during the war could not be elected. During this period of conservative control of the state government in Texas, the focus of desperado activity was stealing and cattle rustling. Occasionally, blacks became the victims of violence, but not so frequently as when they became voters.

Into this drama stepped Cullen Montgomery Baker, whose organized violence quickly attracted local, state, and even national attention. White southerners resented the North, detested army occupation, and despised

15. Until 1995, the most recent additions to the Baker literature were Yvonne Vestal, *The Borderlands and Cullen Baker* (Atlanta, Tex., 1978); Russell and Russell, *Some Die Twice;* and James Smallwood, "Swamp Fox of the Sulphur," *True West,* XXXVIII (October, 1991), Pt. 1, pp. 20–23; (November, 1991), Pt. 2, pp. 38–41. Only Smallwood added to existing knowledge. Now Baker sympathizers can include in their ranks Billy Cox, "Cullen Montgomery Baker: Scourge of the Red River Country," *Old Time Chronicle* (June, 1995), 6–10 (kindly sent us by Les E. Abrahamson of Texarkana, Texas); and Robert W. Teel (the great-great-grandson of Cullen Montgomery Baker), *Cullen Montgomery Baker: Champion of the Lost Cause* (Huntsville, Ala., 1995). These latter two sources, bereft of a chronological framework, add nothing new to the Baker story. They perpetuate the same old myths about Reconstruction and rely heavily (as do most other sources) on the reminiscences collected by Taylor. Thus, they represent Baker as a Texas Robin Hood opposed to the evil Thomas Orr, who had the effrontery to write a biography of his enemy. On the subject of reminiscences, Don E. Fehrenbacher has concluded that "although they may at times be reasonably accurate and may reveal facts not previously known, [they] are, as a category, the least reliable of primary sources because of what time does to memory and because of the enormous variation in their quality." The "interpretative weight" placed on recollective material "should be compatible with its estimated credibility" ("The Making of a Myth: Lincoln and the Vice-Presidential Nomination in 1864," *Civil War History,* XLI [December, 1995], 290).

those who came among them to implement the new order (Freedmen's Bureau agents and Union army personnel) along with those whites who had remained loyal to the United States during the war. Baker terrorized and killed people committed to change, and his actions encouraged the rise of outlaw bands and indirectly assisted the formation of the Ku Klux Klan.

Baker's name appears often in contemporary accounts, and less frequently in modern histories of Reconstruction, as the leader around whom Texas outlaws and renegades coalesced. In one instance, a Freedmen's Bureau agent reported that Baker, Benjamin F. Bickerstaff, Bob Lee, Jack English, Dick Johnson, Sam Dixon, plus "several more desperadoes of that class are banded together" and "recently murdered six or seven white men." Reports of these occurrences, confirmed by other agents, local citizens, and army post commanders, were repeatedly made. These "desperate men" rode through the streets of various towns with "not a soul to molest" them.[16]

One contemporary observer claimed that following the war, northeast Texas was "on the eve of Revolution." Gangs, calling themselves "Ku Klux," committed all kinds of atrocities "upon the Colored people." The citizens "look over and see these outrages with perfect complacency," wrote a government official, "which demonstrates the fact that the community is to blame for these outrages and should be held responsible for them." There was so much violence that it became impossible to provide a description of every incident. Citizens, whether desperadoes or Klan members, committed brutalities upon the freedmen and freedwomen, according to Freedmen's Bureau agent T.M.K. Smith in Marshall, Texas, and they "kill[ed] negroes from the pure love of killing."[17]

Loyal blacks and whites could not be protected. The occupation army had neither the manpower nor the financial resources. The "melancholy

16. DeWitt C. Brown (Agent, Paris, Tex.) to C. S. Roberts (AAAG), June 1, 1868, AC, OR, B-155, in Texas, BRFAL, RG 105, NA.

17. T.M.K. Smith (Agent, Marshall, Tex.) to Charles A. Vernou (AAAG), July 31, 1868, AC, OR, S-268, and Brown to Vernou, August 16, 1868, AC, LR, B-202, both in Texas, BRFAL, RG 105, NA. After a particularly outrageous confrontation, whites often gave barbecues to "assure the colored population that they would be protected from violence provided they would conduct themselves in proper manners" (S. L. Love to Mrs. S. V. Young, August 9, 1868, in Burton and Young Family Papers, Southern Historical Collection, University of North Carolina, Chapel Hill). For more on this practice, see Barry A. Crouch, "Self-Determination and Local Black Leaders in Texas," *Phylon*, XXIX (December, 1978), 353. For a continuation of the practice into the 1890s, see Lawrence C. Goodwyn, "Populist Dreams and Negro Rights: East Texas as a Case Study," *American Historical Review*, LXXVI (1971), 1435–56.

fact," wrote one historian of the army, is that "no amount of troops could have prevented assaults on Negroes when the crimes took place on remote stretches of country roads by disguised men." In the tri-state region where Baker intimidated the citizens, there was no necessity to operate in disguise. There residents knew who had committed these outrages because the men had grown up and claimed kin in these communities. Afraid of retribution, people refused to provide information and consequently "made it difficult for the Army to protect those who did agree to testify." [18]

For the most part, white people in this southwestern region, whether they had supported the Confederacy or held secret unionist loyalties, were afraid to report Baker's activities. He killed both blacks and whites, and his attitude toward people continually changed; no one could be sure of what he felt about them. Baker seems to have exerted some strange psychological and physical control over the citizens in his region of operation. A few whites did assist the military in attempting to capture Baker, and blacks served as army guides whenever Baker was sought. As a general rule, however, his tremendous influence restricted the information to be gained about him from the locals.

By late 1868, the "New Rebellion," as the New York *Tribune* referred to it, had become national news. The newspaper reported much of the same information various Bureau agents had relayed to their respective headquarters a year earlier. Conditions had considerably deteriorated from the previous year, and gang violence stalked the region. The *Tribune* stated that "for some time past the Eastern portion of the State [of Texas] has been infested by a number of bands of reckless outlaws whose principal occupation seems to be to kill defenseless and unoffending Union men and industrious negroes." Encouraged and led by men such as Baker and other desperadoes, they had "become a terror to law and order loving people" in the area. These guerrillas, "fed, secreted, and encouraged by a large number of the people throughout the country," received so much assistance that the authorities were foiled in every attempt at their capture. Local cooperation in concealing and aiding these outlaws made it difficult to gather reliable in-

---

18. James E. Sefton, *The United Army and Reconstruction, 1865–1877* (Baton Rouge, 1967), 224. For Texas, this is amply confirmed in Richter, *The Army in Texas,* and Robert W. Shook, "Federal Occupation and Administration of Texas, 1865–1870" (Ph.D. dissertation, North Texas State University, 1970). Shook summarized his ideas in "The Federal Military in Texas, 1865–1870," *Texas Military History,* VI (Spring, 1967), 3–53. Richter's and Shook's interpretations about the army's involvement in Reconstruction are quite dissimilar.

formation. The area was "in a terrible condition; the people evince a spirit of lawlessness and resistance to civil law, and only await an opportunity to repeat what has just taken place could they be assured their lives would not be in danger." Law and order had "ceased to exist," and men like Baker, "cold blooded assassins," were "big men" in the area even though they had murdered men, women, and children.[19]

A Cincinnati *Commercial* correspondent wrote that in east Texas one could not pick up a paper without reading of murder, assassinations, and robbery, yet "not the fourth part of the truth has been told; not one act in ten is reported." Travelers often heard of "fresh murders and violence." Numerous problems, from the powerlessness of the civil authorities to the insufficient numbers of the military, continued to weaken the government "while hell has transferred its capital from pandemonium to Jefferson, and the devil is holding high carnival in Gilmer, Tyler, Canton, Quitman, Boston, Marshall and other places in Texas."[20] It was a second civil war, but the occupation authorities did not always realize that fact.

Before the Civil War, there is no indication that Baker had any strong feelings about slavery or blacks. But as Bill Cecil-Fronsman has forcefully demonstrated in his book on common whites, a desire to maintain the old order was pervasive among men like Baker. His father, John Baker, had made his way among slaves, free Negroes, and an antebellum system where everyone knew his place and status.[21] But the eruption of the war changed everything. Although the social structure and class roles were not reversed, they had been drastically altered. Baker, who often killed indiscriminately, found government personnel and blacks easy targets. He may have seen both these groups as agents of unacceptable change.

19. New York *Tribune*, September 29, 1868, p. 1. In " 'The Revolver Rules the Day!' " Richter writes that the "bandit chief" Baker "spoke of his fight against the bureau and the army as a 'New Rebellion,' and collectively labeled his Yankee enemies, 'abolitionists' " (317–18). There is absolutely no evidence that Baker ever referred to his actions as a "New Rebellion." Such a view was probably beyond his ken.

20. *Alabama State Journal* (Montgomery), January 30, 1869, quoted in James Smallwood, "When the Klan Rode: White Terror in Reconstruction Texas," *Journal of the West*, XXV (October, 1986), 1; Allen W. Trelease, *White Terror: The Ku Klux Klan Conspiracy and Southern Reconstruction* (New York, 1971), 138.

21. Bill Cecil-Fronsman's *Common Whites: Class and Culture in Antebellum North Carolina* (Lexington, 1992) is a superb portrayal. See also Stephanie McCurry, "The Politics of Yeoman Households in South Carolina," *Divided Houses: Gender and the Civil War*, ed. Catherine Clinton and Nina Silber (New York, 1992), 22–38.

Baker may also have been a de facto Klansman. He provided support for that organization in numerous ways. As a desperado who challenged the authority of the Freedmen's Bureau and the United States army, he demonstrated to civilians across the South that terror and violence could be used as an effective weapon against those recently freed from slavery. Baker and his gang determined to show town and country folk that intimidation and cruelty would put blacks back into their place. Whether local citizens paid him for his services or remunerated him in other ways, Baker gave community leaders a lesson in the use of coercion.[22]

One Bureau agent in Arkansas captured the nature of Baker's (and other desperadoes') appeal when he wrote that such characters are as "essential to the ends and aims of the citizens of this part of the country as hounds are to a hunter. Through such instrumentalities the chivalry govern the lower grades of society even more effectually than they could by legal enactments[,] by narrating their deeds of valor to the ignorant freedmen who recount them by their evening firesides with horror and consternation." If the government could spend thousands to protect United States citizens in foreign countries, one writer plaintively asked, why could "she not protect her soldiers [and citizens] in her own territory?"[23]

22. Stanley F. Horn, in *Invisible Empire: The Story of the Ku Klux Klan, 1866–1871* (Boston, 1939), writes that the "name and garb of the Ku Klux were used by independent bandits, notably by a desperate character named Cullen Baker who was described by the newspapers as a man 'who has probably caused more excitement and committed more crimes than any man in modern times' " (259). In her pro-Klan polemic *Authentic History: Ku Klux Klan, 1865–1877* (New York, 1924), Susan Lawrence Davis blames the army for the majority of the violence as it "committed many more depredations and outrages than were committed by either white or black natives" (246). See also William Peirce Randel, *The Ku Klux Klan: A Century of Infamy* (Philadelphia, 1965). An interesting novel that concentrates on the Klan in Texas is Laura Krey, *And Tell of Time* (Boston, 1938). Whites also used the justification that local Republican Party groups, such as the Union League, led to the formation of the Klan. Melinda Meek Hennessey, in "To Live and Die in Dixie: Reconstruction Race Riots in the South" (Ph.D. dissertation, Kent State University, 1978), writes that the "Loyal, or Union, League especially angered whites throughout the South, for the League sought to organize blacks within the Republican party, but the effectiveness of this Republican tactic was never as complete as Democrats claimed. Democrats, however, used the Loyal League as a justification for their organizations such as the Klan" (78). A solid account is Michael W. Fitzgerald, *The Union League Movement in the Deep South: Politics and Change During Reconstruction* (Baton Rouge, 1989).

23. V. V. Smith (Agent, Lewisville, Ark.) to Jonathan E. Bennett (AAAG), November 30, 1867, in AC, NR, LR-1593, Box 11, Arkansas, BRFAL, RG 105, NA; WGK (Agent, Boston) to

Several outlaws (Bickerstaff, Lee, and Longley) apparently consorted with Baker. Heroes to many, they abhorred the government's intrusion during Reconstruction and the freeing of the slaves. Citizens silently supported men such as Baker by giving information and assistance. Another Arkansas Bureau agent summarized the essence of feelings in the area in which Baker operated when he wrote, "Yet there are many that admire and laud him as a brave man as 'he only *kills yankees and niggers*' and [they] would imitate him if an opportunity presents itself." Those residents who feared Baker and his ilk endured his depredations and hoped they would not be harmed. If they spoke out against him, terrifying results followed.[24]

But was Baker really this imposing? L'Amour describes Baker as six feet, two inches tall, weighing about 200 pounds, lean, and "with the face of a man who had known much trouble and little of softness or loving—the face of a man born to struggle and the hard ways." In actuality he was not nearly so impressive. At five feet, nine inches, as described in a reward circular, Baker weighed about 160 pounds. Pale complected, with dark blue eyes and sandy hair, he had very long hands. A gruff voice and slow speech pattern suggest that Baker did not present a menacing physical appearance or cultural refinement, although sympathizers would argue otherwise. With his ordinary looks, it is not surprising that others failed to recognize him.[25]

A few other varied descriptions of Baker deserve mention. When R. H. Watlington first met him in December, 1866, Baker "appeared to be about thirty-five years of age, medium size and height, yellow complexion, long sandy hair, and beardless." He was a man of few words except when under the influence of liquor. Two years after this encounter, when Watlington again met Baker, he did not immediately recognize the Swamp Fox. "From

---

JTK (AAAG), July 25, 1867, pp. 14–16; WGK to Thomas Latchford (Commander, Jefferson, Tex.), July 26, 1867, pp. 16–18, both in Vol. 67, Texas, BRFAL, RG 105, NA.

24. Smith to Bennett, February 8, 1868, Vol. 109, pp. 383–86; March 4, 1868, Vol. 109, pp. 392–98; Smith to C. C. Ballard (Post Commander, Washington, Ark.), March 5, 1868, Vol. 109, pp. 387–89; Hiram F. Willis (Agent, Rocky Comfort, Ark.) to Bennett, February 29, 1868, Vol. 179, pp. 42–43, all in AC, Arkansas, BRFAL, RG 105, NA. Italics ours.

25. L'Amour, *The First Fast Draw*, 5; Taylor, "Swamp Fox of the Sulphur," 49. There is also a copy in TSL and one in the Texarkana Public Library. For background on this manuscript, see A. L. Burford to the Texarkana Library, October 18, 1965, in Special Collections, Texarkana Public Library. Almost every writer quotes verbatim the reward circular describing Baker's physical characteristics that Governor E. M. Pease of Texas issued; Proclamation, $1,000 Reward, Cullen Baker, October 18, 1867, Executive Record Book (Pease), 82, TSL. No photograph of Baker seems to exist.

the sallow, thin, hatchet-face, taciturn man of yore, to this bold, outspoken, red face," Baker's every "feature [was] deeply stamped with the marks of dissipation." The *Texas Republican* described Baker as "a small man, all muscle, of about 140 pounds weight, with light hair and gray eyes."[26] While the military's 1867 description of the "brigand" Baker largely agrees with the others mentioned, it adds some details about his appearance on the road. By this account he rode a fine black mule, and his "chubby build" was dressed in the "garb of the country, home spun"; he carried a double-barreled shotgun with several revolvers, traveled alone or with one or two comrades, and was "addicted to hard drink."[27]

Individuals like Baker may have appeared all over the post–Civil War South. Other than studies of the Klan, however, history has largely neglected organized violence. The southwestern region still evinced characteristics of a frontier society where defense of honor could and should be upheld through killing. After all, self-defense was a recognizable argument and accepted by all judicial institutions, from local courts to the state supreme court. With the proper argument, a white person who killed could walk away a free individual. In contrast, blacks had no rights, a fact that society impressed upon them again and again, so men like Baker could do largely as they pleased. He only once had to face a judge, and this case involved a white.[28]

26. R. H. Watlington, "Memoirs" (Typescript in TSL), 31, 84. There is also a copy at the CFAH. The original is in the Texarkana Public Library.

27. S. H. Starr (Commander, Mount Pleasant Post) to H. A. Swartwout (AAAG), October 20, 1867, in DT, LR, S-148, USACC, RG 393, NA. The military's estimation of Baker's age corresponds with that of the 1850 census.

28. Richard Maxwell Brown, *No Duty to Retreat: Violence and Values in American History and Society* (New York, 1991); Brown, "Western Violence: Structure, Values, Myth," *Western Historical Quarterly*, XXIV (February, 1993), 5–20; Brown, *Strain of Violence: Historical Studies of American Violence and Vigilantism* (New York, 1975); W. Eugene Hollon, *Frontier Violence: Another Look* (New York, 1974); Werner J. Einstadter, "Robbery-Outlawry on the U.S. Frontier, 1863–1890: A Reexamination," in *Violent Crime: Historical and Contemporary Issues*, ed. James A. Inciardi and Anne E. Pottieger (Beverly Hills, 1978), 21–37; George C. Rable, *But There Was No Peace: The Role of Violence in the Politics of Reconstruction* (Athens, Ga., 1984); Herbert Shapiro, *White Violence and Black Response: From Reconstruction to Montgomery* (Amherst, 1988). On Texas specifically, see Bill O'Neal, "Violence in Texas History," *Texas: A Sesquicentennial Celebration,* ed. Donald W. Whisenhunt (Austin, 1984), 353–69; Crouch, "A Spirit of Lawlessness: White Violence; Texas Blacks, 1865–1868," *Journal of Social History*, XVIII (1984), 217–32; Gregg Cantrell, "Racial Violence and Reconstruction Politics in Texas, 1867–1868," *SwHQ*, XCIII (1990), 333–55. For Louisiana, see Gilles Vandal,

Why study a desperado such as Baker? Baker's contemporary Thomas Orr called him the "great man slayer, Federal fighter and negro killer, of the south-west, and, indeed, the unsurpassed desperado of modern times." According to Frank Triplett, a nineteenth-century chronicler of outlaws, Baker fascinates, attracting both supporters and detractors. While Baker was often viewed as "a man more sinned against than sinning," and a "gallant gentleman, a patriot and a hero," Triplett believed he was a "brutal and ferocious" murderer. Although Baker had a "spirit of tyrannical brutality," Triplett theorized, "at heart [he] was a coward, and did not desire a fair combat."[29]

After Baker's death in early 1869, the Jefferson *Times* stated that the "future novelist, in search of facts as a foundation for a thrilling romance, will find no more fruitful theme than that of the life, exploits, and death of Cullen M. Baker."[30] Baker's life was hardly one of "thrilling romance," but his activities need to be reexamined in the light of the changed historiography of Reconstruction. In many respects, Baker's support from the local citizenry is somewhat remarkable considering the way he treated many of them. Precisely what Baker attempted to accomplish, whom he influenced, and what resulted from his gang's depredations needs to be investigated from a newly informed perspective and through a variety of sources.

The problem with drawing a realistic and complete portrait of Baker is that few primary materials exist relating to his early life. This deficit is not surprising as outlaws like Baker generally did not leave behind a corpus of private papers. Thus, for the years prior to Reconstruction, we have had to rely upon various accounts of other investigators, who were not always accurate. As a result of these writers' different politics or proclivities, Baker has appeared in various guises. Some writers have even portrayed Baker as heroically attempting to deliver the South from the grip of congressional Reconstruction, the corruption of carpetbaggers and scalawags, and the impudence and laziness of the newly freed slaves.

" 'Bloody Caddo': White Violence Against Blacks in a Louisiana Parish, 1865–1876," *Journal of Social History*, XXV (Winter, 1991), 373–88; "Black Violence in Post–Civil War Louisiana," *Journal of Interdisciplinary History*, XXV (Summer, 1994), 45–64.

29. Orr, *Life of the Notorious Desperado*, 86. Frank Triplett, "Cullen Montgomery Baker," in *History, Romance and Philosophy of Great American Crimes and Criminals* (New York, 1884), 434–35, 442. The same phrase, "more sinned against than sinning," has often been used to defend the murderous ways of John Wesley Hardin.

30. *Texas Republican* (Marshall), January 15, 1869, p. 3. Also quoted in Taylor, "Swamp Fox of the Sulphur," 136.

This book is not about the honor of an individual imbued with the principles of the Old South, of the sort Bertram Wyatt-Brown and Edward Ayers have described in their outstanding works.[31] Only in the sense that defeated southerners needed to avenge the loss of the Confederacy, in whatever way, did "honor" become part of the code of the "New South." Cullen Montgomery Baker, basically a common white whose personal life demonstrated nothing but loss and failure, conducted himself before the war as a drifter, a killer, and an individual without social or moral responsibility. During the war, his commitment to the South was ephemeral and fleeting, but subsequently he became a hero because he killed "yankees and niggers."

In contrast to foregoing accounts, ours strives to unearth and validate the facts about Baker, this dispossessed former Confederate soldier. He was born in Tennessee and grew up in the wilds of east Texas amidst violence and feuds. Parental supervision may have been absent, although this cannot be firmly established. Baker came from a hard-working and seemingly normal family; his parents worked together to make a life for themselves in a frontier society where violence abounded. They may have attempted to raise their sons and daughters with ethical values. If so, these principles passed Baker by, for he became, by most accounts, a cold-blooded killer.

Pursuing the facts about Baker has been an exercise in detection. When we started this project, we had only vague perceptions about the Swamp Fox. As we expanded our investigation to encompass the extent of Baker's alleged activities, the paucity of documentary material became exceedingly clear. What we have concluded about Baker's place in history is opposed to the local, county, and regional literature on him. When one dares to explore the opposite side of an entrenched idea, the results are sometimes surprising and even disappointing. Our conclusions on Baker exemplify this phe-

---

31. Bertram Wyatt-Brown, *Southern Honor: Ethics and Behavior in the Old South* (New York, 1982); Bruce A. Rosenberg, *The Code of the West* (Bloomington, 1982); Edward L. Ayers, *Vengeance and Justice: Crime and Punishment in the 19th-Century South* (New York, 1984), 9–33; Ayers, "Legacy of Violence," *American Heritage,* XLII (October, 1991), 103–109; Ayers, *The Promise of the New South: Life After Reconstruction* (New York, 1992). Honor, as distinguished from dignity (a northern concept), became ritualized and was synonymous with respect. For a combined religious/secular perspective on honor see Edward R. Crowther, "Holy Honor: Sacred and Secular in the Old South," *JSH,* LVIII (November, 1992), 619–36. For how honor connected and reinforced itself in all slave societies and then engendered violence in the aftermath of slavery's removal, see Orlando Patterson, *Slavery and Social Death: A Comparative Study* (Cambridge, Mass., 1982); Patterson, *Freedom in the Making of Western Culture* (New York, 1991), Vol. I of Patterson, *Freedom,* 2 vols. to date.

nomenon. In brief, Baker's local reputation far exceeds anything that he deserves.

To maintain that Baker was some kind of social avenger, it is necessary to accept the old shibboleths about Reconstruction. But once these ideas have been invalidated, there is little left to sustain the continued vilification of the Republicans and their allies, the few carpetbaggers in politics, and the former slaves. It became necessary for us to investigate a variety of manuscript and secondary sources at the local and county levels because so many subscribed to those now-obsolete views. They frequently cast Texas Reconstruction as a time of repression, oppression, and shame. In fact, the newer perceptions about Reconstruction continue to have little influence upon county and local history writing, and the same ideas that first emerged at the turn of the twentieth century are almost endlessly repeated.

We had two methodological objectives in writing about the life of Baker. First, we extensively canvassed the extant secondary material at all levels to ascertain what had been written. Second, we combed local, state, and national archives for new Baker materials. Thus, as we wrote about Baker, we juxtaposed past writings with what contemporary documentary evidence demonstrates. We have tried to indicate clearly what materials we relied upon and what interpretations and possible conclusions can be drawn.

Cullen Montgomery Baker's life has been shrouded in myth and sometimes in plain falsehood. His character and deeds continue to fascinate writers of all persuasion. Certainly some of Baker's exploits must be apocryphal, but enough evidence remains to suggest that he did create fear and loathing among citizens of the region where he operated. Regardless of their veracity, the various stories that circulated about him inflamed his reputation, and his fame and/or infamy consequently spread throughout the Southwest in the post–Civil War years. It is now time to sort out the life from the legend of this obscure desperado.

ONE

The Making of a Killer

———————•———————

IN 1869, the year Cullen Montgomery Baker died, H. C. Mack wrote *Texas: Information for Emigrants,* which claims that the extent of lawlessness in post–Civil War Texas was exaggerated by the northern press. However, Mack admits that a "few famous characters" such as "Cullan" [Cullen] Baker, Benjamin F. "Bickerstoff" [Bickerstaff], Bob Lee, and their followers, were "charged with conduct calculated to injure the reputation of the State" and sully its heritage. Bickerstaff and Lee committed themselves to "partisan warfare with the Federal soldiery," and Baker "engaged in a kind of personal melee with neighbors and acquaintances, all [of] which excitement result badly for the country."[1]

Blaming the occupation army for the wrongs of Reconstruction, Mack targets Bickerstaff and Lee as being "responsible for the initiative movements in getting up the unfortunate state of things that grew out of these conflicts of the soldiers and civilians." He dismisses Baker as a minor figure. The "Baker disturbances," he declares, "cannot properly be classed" with those of Bickerstaff and Lee, "for these last acted under a sense of self protection and were certainly most wretchedly provoked by their enemies, while Baker had in view the avenging of pretended personal wrongs and

1. H. C. Mack, *Texas: Information for Emigrants* . . . (Franklin, Tenn., 1869), 141, 143. Mack collected the material for his account "from personal observation and from conversation and correspondence with men of intelligence who have visited the different portions of the state."

might more consistently be charged with the commission of crimes."[2] Mack was misinformed about the extent of Baker's activities.

Piecing together the family background and the early years of Cullen Montgomery Baker is a difficult task. Little is known about his parents, and most writers have dismissed them as largely irrelevant. Endlessly repeated stories exist about Baker as a young boy, but where they came from nobody seems to know. Some, reiterated here, will provide a context for understanding the mature Baker. The family established themselves in a sparsely populated section of Texas that attracted a large migration from the upper South. The Bakers themselves had come from Tennessee; in Texas, they struggled to survive.

Cullen Montgomery Baker's father, John, was born in South Carolina between 1805 and 1808, and later migrated to Tennessee; but why or when is unknown. Cullen's mother only lived about five years or so after the family arrived in Texas. Previous writers have suggested that her name was Nancy, but Nancy Parker was actually his stepmother. His natural mother, whose name according to Al Eason was Elizabeth, died between 1844 and 1846.[3] During his formative years, Cullen allegedly did not have much parental supervision. Maybe this deficit explains those stories that he wandered

2. *Ibid.*, 143.

3. MCR, Fifth Census (1830), Weakley County, Tennessee, p. 337. In the 1830 Tennessee census, John is listed as married (the wife's name is not provided), and the couple has a female child under five (again, no name); Seventh Census (1850), Cass County, Texas, p. 780; Eighth Census (1860), Cass County, Texas, p. 108, Records of the Bureau of the Census, RG 29, NA; Carl W. Breihan, "Cullen Baker—First of the Gunfighters," *The West*, VII (July, 1967), 16–19, 42–47; Breihan, "Cullen Baker," in his *Great Gunfighters of the West* (San Antonio, 1962), 66; Al Eason, "Cullen Baker—Purveyor of Death," *Frontier Times*, XL (August–September, 1966), 6; Ed Bartholomew, *Cullen Baker: Premier Texas Gunfighter* (Houston, 1954), 22; James Smallwood, "Swamp Fox of the Sulphur," Pt. 1, *True West*, XXXVIII (October, 1991), 20; Frank Triplett, "Cullen Montgomery Baker," in his *History, Romance, and Philosophy of Great American Crimes and Criminals* . . . (New York, 1884), 435; Yvonne Vestal, *The Borderlands and Cullen Baker* (Atlanta, Tex., 1978), 12. Thomas Orr, in *Life of the Notorious Desperado Cullen Baker, from His Childhood to His Death, with a Full Account of All the Murders He Committed* (Little Rock, 1870), 3, says the couple married in 1832. The 1850 MCR, Cass County, Texas, 780, counts four children in the Baker household, but the 1860 census, p. 108, includes only John and a son, R. J., age fourteen. Smallwood, Vestal, Orr, and Triplett credit the Baker family with seven or eight children. Although the name of this source is unknown, one individual reminisced that John Baker died when "Cullen was small"; quoted in Myreline Bowman, *People of Cass County: Atlanta, Queen City, Texas* (Atlanta, Tex., 1973), Pt. I, 225.

alone through the woods, practicing with his rifle and pistol, searching for a purpose.

Little information exists about Baker's mother. She was apparently born in 1813 near Winchester in Franklin County, Tennessee, and allegedly descended from one of the "best families" in that state. (Here again, Baker aficionados may be confusing mother with stepmother.) Described as the "most pious of women," she was a Presbyterian. She was married to John at age seventeen, and Mrs. Baker and her husband were viewed as a "God-fearing young couple," "solid, respectable people," and were "well thought of"—although it is impossible to ascertain who made this evaluation. John, a "respectable farmer," did not find the opportunity he sought in the Volunteer State.[4]

Born in Weakley County, Tennessee, near the Kentucky line on the Obion River, on June 22 or 23, 1835 (perhaps 1836 or 1837), Cullen Montgomery Baker was the second of three children, and the only son, of John and his first wife. Sometime between September and December, 1839 (Cullen was four), the family endured a hard and trying trek to Spanish Bluffs in Red River County, Texas, northeast of DeKalb. Even legends about Baker as a child have been perpetuated. Eason, a pro-Baker writer, stated that the innocent "lad playing in the back of the wagon was destined to become one of the most feared killers the West has ever known."[5]

Precisely why John Baker uprooted his family and moved to Texas is unknown. Apparently this man with a roving nature found the state attractive. A vast uninhabited area awaited cultivation and became a major drawing

4. Robert W. Teel (Baker's great-great-grandson) to Donaly E. Brice, August, 1993, in author's possession. This paragraph also condenses numerous comments by Baker biographers.

5. MCR, Seventh Census (1850), Cass County, Texas, p. 780, RG 29, NA, lists Cullen's age as thirteen. As his birthday had passed, this information suggests that he was born in 1837, not 1835, as most writers have indicated. Of course, the census enumerator could have been mistaken. On the marriage certificate with Martha Foster (July 1, 1862) Baker's age is listed as twenty-six, which would make his birth year 1836 (Teel to Brice, August, 1993). There is also a minor dispute about Baker's birthday: some say June 22, others claim June 23. We have used June 22, 1835, as Baker's date of birth as it is the most frequently cited by those writing in the nineteenth century. Smallwood, "Swamp Fox," Pt. 1, 20, says June 22 or 23. See, in particular, Eason, "Cullen Baker," 6; T. U. Taylor, "Swamp Fox of the Sulphur or Life and Times of Cullen Montgomery Baker," *ca.* 1936 (Typescript in ECBTHC), 1; Breihan, "Cullen Baker," 66; Breihan, "First of the Gunfighters," 16; Bartholomew, *Cullen Baker,* 21–22; Orr, *Life of the Notorious Desperado,* 3–5. Vestal, in *The Borderlands,* 12, places the Baker settlement at "Spanish Bluffs on the Red River north of present day Clarksville."

card for immigrants. Between 1821 and 1846, more than 100,000 people migrated to Texas. Whether John was a failure in his community, or suffered due to the Panic of 1837, or felt more general economic pressure, the family left Tennessee. Clearly, low land prices in what became the Lone Star State lured those seeking new opportunities or escaping old obligations. By 1840, wrote Mark E. Nackman, the Texas population contained "appalling numbers of adventurers, desperadoes, and bankrupts ready to take advantage of the country's land grant policy."[6]

Land certainly attracted John Baker to the isolation of east Texas. Long before the Republic of Texas liberalized its homestead policies, Baker had made his decision to move west. It is well-nigh impossible to ascertain precisely what the Bakers brought with them to this virgin region, but it is certain the parents had the capacity for hard work. To be sure, in whatever section of the Texas wilderness they might have decided to locate, an enormous amount of labor would have had to be expended to carve out a farm. John Baker brought little but his family to Texas, but it is clear from the later records that he aspired for more. Perhaps he wanted to leave his family an economic legacy.

The Bakers initially settled in the Spanish Bluff section, a pioneer settlement in Red River County (organized 1836). Their farm was located a few miles north of what became Boston, Texas, now in Bowie County. Red River encompassed 5,000 square miles; 180 miles long and 90 miles wide, it contained all or parts of 29 future counties. Because of Red River's vast size, transportation to the county seat was difficult and costly, so John Baker signed a petition to create at least one additional county from this unmanageable polity. Baker and other citizens also petitioned for the establish-

6. Mark E. Nackman, "Anglo-American Migrants to the West: Men of Broken Fortunes?; The Case of Texas, 1821–46," *Western Historical Quarterly*, V (October, 1974), 452. See also Richard Lowe and Randolph Campbell, "Heads of Families in Antebellum Texas: A Profile," *Red River Valley Historical Review*, V (Spring, 1980), 68–80. The migration can be traced in Terry G. Jordan, "The Imprint of the Upper and Lower South on Mid-Nineteenth-Century Texas," *Annals of the Association of American Geographers*, LVII (December, 1967), 667–90; Jordan, "Population Origins in Texas, 1850," *Geographical Review*, LIX (January, 1969), 83–103; Jordan, "A Century and a Half of Ethnic Change in Texas, 1836–1986," *SwHQ*, LXXXIX (April, 1986), 385–417; and the older, but still useful, Barnes F. Lathrop, "Migration into East Texas, 1835–1850," *SwHQ*, LII (July, 1948), 1–31; Lathrop, *Migration into East Texas, 1835–1860: A Study from the United States Census* (Austin, 1949). For other background material see Marilyn McAdams Sibley, *Travelers in Texas, 1761–1860* (Austin, 1967), 152–70.

ment of an additional district land office because the original structure was located in a remote, swampy, insect-infested area, almost inaccessible.[7] Baker was clearly a concerned community member.

But what John Baker did besides eking out a living cannot be ascertained. He may not have realized the perils inherent in such a remote region, but it soon became the scene of a local war that may have driven the family to a new location. (After the move, Cullen would begin to make his mark.) John Baker must have had compelling reasons to leave his original settlement, given his allegiance to the area. Although we cannot know for certain why the family relocated, there was unquestionably much friction in the area.

Writing from the Red River region, R. K. Clark, a lawyer and immigrant from Tennessee, informed his sister that "society is bad here at present in most places," and that a "great many mean people [are] here." He did not "consider this a material objection to the county as it is so in all new countrys and time will cure the evil." He believed that with the land and resources available, this country would "certainly make a good population in a few years." And just as Clark had predicted, time did make it possible for communities to appear. By 1850, when information begins to surface about this area, many settlements had emerged in this section of Texas.[8]

This region received immigrants and settlers from the United States as early as 1819. After the 1840s influx of migrants from the upper South, the 1850s brought more slaveholders from the Deep South. Bowie County seems to have quickly come under the sway of this latter group. That they found the rich bottomlands of the Red River attractive is evidenced by the fact that slaves were a majority of the county's population in both 1850 and 1860. Although Tennesseeans may have originally predominated in the Cass County region, they soon confined themselves to settling the eastern part of it close to the Arkansas line. This is where John Baker made his mark and his son grew to manhood. The Baker homestead would not have been ad-

7. "Citizens of Red River County to Create a New County," [1840]; "Citizens of Red River District Concerning Site of District Land Office," n.d., both in Memorials and Petitions, RG 100, TSL; H. P. N. Gammel, comp., *The Laws of Texas, 1822–1897* (10 vols.; Austin, 1898), II, 97–99; Barbara Overton Chandler and J. Ed Howe, *History of Texarkana . . . and . . . Bowie and Miller Counties Texas—Arkansas* (Texarkana, 1939), 19; Gifford White, "The First Settlers of Bowie and Cass Counties" (Typescript in TSL); *1840 Citizens of Texas* (2 vols.; St. Louis, 1984), II, 139; Walter Prescott Webb and H. Bailey Carroll, eds., *The Handbook of Texas* (2 vols., Austin, 1952), I, 198, 483, II, 452.

8. R. K. Clark (Paris, Lamar County) to Mrs. Harriet Stephens, November 17, 1844, rpt. in J. E. Pirie, "A Letter from Lamar County in 1844," *SwHQ*, LIII (July, 1949), 66–67.

vantageous to slave labor. The land and tax records demonstrate that John Baker was a yeoman farmer without slaves.

Bowie and Cass Counties were similar in size. Bowie encompassed 873 square miles; Cass was but 92 square miles larger. The topography of Bowie County, located between the Red and Sulphur Rivers, included rich bottomlands and abundant forests of pine, cedar, and white oak. Cass County, fed by Red River tributaries, contained pine, hardwoods, and gum, plus a variety of sandy and alluvial soils. In 1850, Bowie County had an aggregate population of 2,912, divided between 1,271 whites and 1,641 slaves. Cass County, much larger, had 4,991 inhabitants: 3,089 whites and 1,902 slaves. A decade later, Bowie contained 5,052 people: 2,401 whites and 2,651 slaves. Cass's total population was 8,411: 4,936 whites and 3,475 slaves. By 1850, Bowie County's slave population constituted 56 percent of the total, while in Cass County whites composed 62 percent of all inhabitants. In 1860, slaves still retained a majority in Bowie although their percentage dropped three points, which is exactly the percentage by which they increased in Cass County.[9]

Into the 1850s and early 1860s, Bowie and Cass Counties increased their cultivated acreage. By 1857, Bowie had 266,970 acres assessed at $298,300 and Cass had 459,062 acres valued at $807,760. The slaves in their midst were collectively worth $815,460 and $1,656,980, respectively. On the eve of the Civil War, both sections had added to their assessed agricultural acreage and town growth had significantly begun. Bowie had 176 town lots and Cass 433. The 1858 *Texas Almanac* suggested that the two counties were experiencing growth. In Bowie, "churches, schools, and society in general" had appeared, and few counties were "in advance" of this area. As for Cass, attention was paid to schools and churches, and "the society" was "good."[10]

In the two decades before the Civil War, a rather loosely knit society had begun to form in frontier communities such as Bowie and Cass Counties. In

9. Jordan, "Population Origins," 89, 92; Webb and Carroll, eds., *Handbook of Texas*, I, 198 and 306; Francis A. Walker, *A Compendium of the Ninth Census* (1870) (Washington, D.C., 1872), 63–66. The slave figures in Randolph B. Campbell, *An Empire for Slavery: The Peculiar Institution in Texas, 1821–1865* (Baton Rouge, 1989), 264, differ from the 1850 and 1860 census returns.

10. *The Texas Almanac for 1857* (Galveston, 1856), 52–53, 68–69; *The Texas Almanac for 1858* (Galveston, 1857), 34–35, 41, 45, 56–57, 59; *The Texas Almanac for 1859* (Galveston, 1858), 215; *The Texas Almanac for 1862* (Galveston, 1861), 31.

Bowie, town life centered on Boston, which by 1860 may have had eight hundred residents. Jefferson was the first county seat of Cass, but Linden became the county's center when Marion County was formed and Jefferson became its official center. It would be the small settlements, however, of Forest Home and Courtland that attracted Cullen Baker and perhaps occasionally his family. There, communities were isolated, fragmented, and not especially close-knit.

In 1840, the legislature of the Texas Republic separated Bowie County from Red River. DeKalb, originally to be called Aurora, served as the county seat during 1840–1841, but Boston eventually became the official center. Much of this section was the "dumping ground of the States" and a "refuge of all the bold and lawless spirits of the entire frontier," according to Nackman. It was about this time, 1839–1844, that two internecine wars ranged throughout the northeastern region of Texas. The Regulator-Moderator war, whose origins were in Shelby County, south of the Baker homestead, continued intermittently for a few years, as did the Rose-Potter feud, which was nearer to where the Bakers lived.

The conflicts involved political chicanery, traffic in forged land certificates, cattle and horse theft, robbery, murder, the intimidation of witnesses, and other violence. All sides were populated by characters who had unsavory reputations. One faction supported justice rendered by an established legal system, whereas their opponents favored a vigilante approach. Whether these clashes actually moved far enough north to encompass the area where the Bakers lived is unknown, but all the evidence indicates that violence escalated throughout the region. Charles Dickens, in _American Notes_, took notice of these feuds. C. L. Sonnichsen said that "hell itself could hardly have promoted a better crop of wickedness." [11]

Although the Baker family was industrious and self-reliant, according to T. U. Taylor, the confrontations between the various bands forced them to move. Ed Bartholomew asserts that, living close to the warring factions, Cullen "learned the meaning of hate, fear and death." Frank Triplett, like

11. MCR, Seventh Census (1850), Cass County, Texas, p. 780, RG 29, NA; White, "The First Settlers,"; _1840 Citizens of Texas_, II, 139; Taylor, "Swamp Fox of the Sulphur," 2–3; Bartholomew, _Cullen Baker_, 23; Orr, _Life of the Notorious Desperado_, 4–5; C. L. Sonnichsen, _Ten Texas Feuds_ (Albuquerque, 1957), 14, 63; John W. Middleton, _History of the Regulators and Moderators and the Shelby County War in 1841 and 1842, in the Republic of Texas_ (Fort Worth, 1883); Webb and Carroll, _Handbook of Texas_, I, 709, 765; 901; Webb and Carroll, _Handbook of Texas_, II, 232, 401, 458, 503–504.

Bartholomew, argues that a youngster such as Cullen growing up among this bloodshed became inured to its effects. He contends that "this anarchy and triumph of violence over law and order could not but have its effect— and that no good one either—upon the minds of the youth of the country, who were daily accustomed to scenes of blood and riot, and who were thus rendered callous to the enormities which should have horrified them." [12]

The Baker household uprooted itself in 1843 or 1844, when Cullen, a "natural slouch and ruffian" according to Triplett, was eight or nine years old. They moved forty miles south to the Sulphur Fork bank of the Red River in what became Cass County, just west of the Arkansas state line. John prospered and bought land. (Whether he earlier owned land is unknown.) Baker is listed in the 1850 census as having real property valued at $540. His first wife, Cullen's mother, apparently died after the 1843–1844 move. John returned to Tennessee in 1846, and on December 7 in Weakley County married Nancy Parker. (She was dead by 1860.) One child, a boy named R. J., was born to the couple in 1847. Nothing is known about him. [13]

During Cullen's formative years, his father desired title to the land he had settled and worked hard to legalize his ownership. Although illiterate (Cullen himself was semiliterate), he discovered the Texas congress had created a headright system. Family men who had migrated to the Republic of Texas before October 1, 1837, could receive a 1,280-acre grant and single men 640 acres. Families who arrived between October 1, 1837, and January 1, 1842, could claim 640 acres. Charles Graham surveyed the land in April, 1844. John, after fulfilling the three-year Republic residency requirement, applied for a headright grant in February, 1850. In 1854, Baker borrowed $1,000 from Graham and gave the surveyor 100 acres as a lien on the property. [14]

12. Taylor, "Swamp Fox of the Sulphur," 2–3; Triplett, "Cullen Montgomery Baker," 437. Interestingly, this is the same argument used about how the excessive violence on television today translates into violence in everyday life.

13. MCR, Seventh Census (1850), Cass County, Texas, p. 780, RG 29, NA; Byron and Barbara Sistler, *Early West Tennessee Marriages* (Nashville, 1989), I, "Grooms," 12; Breihan, "Cullen Baker," 66; Breihan, "First of the Gunfighters," 16; Bartholomew, *Cullen Baker*, 23; Triplett, "Cullen Montgomery Baker," 436–37; Orr, *Life of the Notorious Desperado*, 4–5; Boyd W. Johnson, "Cullen Montgomery Baker: The Arkansas-Texas Desperado," *AHQ*, XXV (Autumn, 1966), 230. Eason, "Cullen Baker," 6, claims the move was made to the same area but on the "bluff side of Baker Creek, a feeder stream of the Sulphur River."

14. Cass County, No. 115, Classification Unconditional, 640 Acres, John Baker, February 18, 1850, GLO; Deed Record, "H," November 12, 1850, filed April 6, 1854, pp. 306–307, Cass

John Baker, to ensure his land title, had his 640 acres surveyed again in early 1855 by the county surveyor, Thomas Heath. His ostensible purpose was to correct Graham's earlier survey. In 1860, not long before he was removed as governor, Sam Houston issued a letter patent assigning Baker the right and title to the land. His acreage was located in Cass County about one and one-half miles south of the Sulphur River and twenty-two miles northeast of the county seat, Linden. John Baker farmed the same land until 1862. Originally valued at $640, its value increased over the years. In the early 1850s, John began to acquire livestock, farm machinery, and produce manufactures out of the household.[15]

John Baker emerges from the 1850 and 1860 agricultural censuses as a stockraiser and herder rather than as a cultivator. In 1850, Baker had 30 acres of improved land and 560 unimproved valued at $540. He had farm implements worth another $90. His livestock consisted of 6 horses, 17 "milch cows," 6 "working oxen," 40 other cattle, and 60 hogs, collectively valued at $810. He raised 250 bushels of Indian corn, 20 bushels of peas and beans, and the same amount of sweet potatoes. The milk from his cows produced an impressive 300 pounds of butter. His homemade manufactures were worth $50, and he had slaughtered animals that year valued at $60. A decade later, with the added burden of worrying about his son Cullen, Baker's fortunes declined.[16]

In the year before the advent of the Civil War, John Baker had improved acreage of 35 and listed 600 acres of unimproved land, all valued at $1,000. His farm machinery value had dropped to $75. He owned but 3 horses, 3 more milk cows, 3 oxen (decrease of 3), 23 other cattle (down 17), and 23 pigs (decrease of 37), valued at $700 (reduction of $110). He raised 150

County Courthouse; Gammel, comp., *The Laws of Texas,* II, 35–36; Nackman, "Anglo-American Migrants to the West," 450, n. 20; W. Eugene Hollon, *The Southwest: Old and New* (New York, 1961), 125. Today, title insurance would replace the lien on the land.

15. Survey Field Notes, North and South, John Baker, File No. 164; Land Grant to John Baker, September 26, 1860, Vol. 30, No. 431; Vol. 31, No. 279, both in GLO; Deed Record, "U," pp. 325–27, Cass County Courthouse; Cass County Tax Rolls, 1840, 1844, TSL. For observations on the Red River valley and adjoining areas, see William E. Sawyer, "A Young Man Comes to Texas in 1852," *Texana,* VII (Spring, 1969), 17–37; Melinda Rankin, *Texas in 1850* (Boston, 1850). John Baker signed his name with an X. The survey field notes demonstrate how nineteenth-century surveyors used any natural element, rocks, trees, and streams, to establish land boundaries.

16. Seventh (1850) and Eighth (1860) Censuses, Schedule 4, Productions of Agriculture, Cass County, Texas, RG 29, NA.

bushels of Indian corn, doubled his output of peas and beans, quintupled his harvest of sweet potatoes, and added 5 bushels of Irish potatoes. He produced only one-third of the butter as previously. Home manufacturing had declined more than half, and he placed a value of $100 on the animals he slaughtered.[17]

Although it is not statistically relevant, let us compare Baker with twenty-five of his neighbors. Baker's thirty improved acres seem meager compared with those owned by farmers around him. His unimproved land and the farm's value lagged considerably behind the majority. His ownership of farm machinery placed him in the group's middle, but he was near the top in horse, cow, swine, oxen, and "other cattle" ownership. (He owned no mules.) Overall, Baker was near the middle in livestock worth. His production of corn, peas, beans, and Irish and sweet potatoes placed him in the middle of the pack. He was in the top third in butter output and home-made manufactures and near the bottom in value of animals slaughtered.[18]

John Baker never increased his acreage, but he did add to his animal stock. By 1862, although he now had 75 head of cattle, the state valued them at only $375. He apparently paid off the lien to Graham. His personal and real property had grown to a worth of $1,875. In 1862, he paid the princely sum of $4.75 in state taxes and $1.87 to the county. John may have died that year because his name disappears from the tax rolls. There is no will or other evidence to indicate to whom he bequeathed the land and the farm. In fact, after 1862 John Baker disappears completely from the historical record. Most likely he left his estate to his eldest daughter rather than to Cullen owing to the latter's increasingly unstable behavior and his propensity for finding trouble.[19]

John Baker's farmstead seems to be typical of those cultivated by southern plain folk. He focused upon grazing cattle and grew food instead of money crops. He lived in a section where he should have been relatively compatible with his neighbors, as 53 percent of the 1850 Texas non-slaveholding farmers

17. *Ibid.*
18. *Ibid.*
19. Cass County Tax Rolls, 1846–1878, TSL. For background see Rex Wallace Strickland, "Anglo-American Activities in Northeastern Texas, 1803–1845" (Ph.D. dissertation, University of Texas, Austin, 1936), 64–317; Barbara Susan Overton Chandler, "A History of Bowie County" (M.A. thesis, University of Texas, Austin, 1937), 16–29; Chandler and Howe, *History of Texarkana*, 16–24. We searched the records of the Cass County Courthouse in Linden extensively but found no will.

in his region were born in the upper South; the 1860 percentage dropped to 43 percent. But slavery was well entrenched in this section. Bowie County had more slaves than Cass County, but Cass had two of the nine largest slaveholders in 1860 Texas.[20]

But what about young Cullen Baker? Orr, his first biographer, wrote that the boy was "noted for his shrewd, quick-witted and noticeable character, which far surpassed that of others boys who were growing up to manhood with him." Possessed, Orr declares, with a "natural relish for frontier life," Cullen "usually devoted his leisure hours in the forest with no other companion than his favorite rifle, pursuing various species of wild game which was found in almost any portion of the Red River country." To most Baker writers, this pursuit denotes a leniency in parental supervision. In Orr's view, "his opportunities for sporting and gaming were unsurpassed by any boys of his age" as a consequence of his autonomy, a not particularly convincing argument.[21]

Contradictory perceptions of Baker as a teenager emerge. He now began to attract the attention of the local community. One image he projected was that of a "hard-working, self-reliant, inoffensive boy." Old settlers claimed he was "noted for kindness, intelligence, and bravery." Other than these

20. John Solomon Otto, "The Migration of Southern Plain Folk: An Interdisciplinary Synthesis," *JSH*, LI (May, 1985), 183–200; Richard G. Lowe and Randolph B. Campbell, *Planters & Plain Folk: Agriculture in Antebellum Texas* (Dallas, 1987), 48–49; Campbell and Lowe, *Wealth and Power in Antebellum Texas* (College Station, Tex., 1977), 32–106; Campbell, *An Empire for Slavery*, 274–76. Although there are J. Bakers listed in both the 1850 and 1860 Cass County slave schedules who owned five and nine slaves, respectively, it most certainly was not Cullen's father. The 1850 Baker had three males (ages fifty, twenty-seven, and six) and two females (ages thirty and twenty-two). The 1860 Baker had seven females (all age twenty) and two males (age eighteen); Seventh Census (1850), Cass County, Texas, p. 272; Eighth Census (1860), Cass County, Texas, pp. 189–90, RG 29, NA. The Cass County tax rolls for 1850 and 1860 list John, Cullen's father, as owning no slaves. Although a remote possibility, there is no contemporary evidence to support the fact that John Baker was a slave holder. If he had owned them, it might explain his son's later antagonism toward freedmen and blacks in general. This argument has been advanced to explain the social bandits in Missouri by Don R. Bowen, "Guerrilla War in Western Missouri, 1862–1865: Historical Extensions of the Relative Deprivation Hypothesis," *Comparative Studies in Society and History*, XIX (January, 1977), 30–51; and "Counterrevolutionary Guerrilla War: Missouri, 1861–1865," *Conflict*, VIII (1988), 69–78.

21. Orr, *Life of the Notorious Desperado*, 5. In their essay, "If I Had Killed Jesus Christ . . . ,' " in *Some Die Twice* (Waco, 1979), Traylor and Robert Russell declared that "in the woods," Cullen "learned the ways of evasion, concealment, attack, and counter-attack and the 'hit-run-and-hide' technique that he was to use in years to come when he continually had to elude his hundreds of pursuers" (3).

vague characterizations, there is little information available on the young Cullen Baker, but here, claims a Baker admirer, his "fame as a fighter first began." Numerous stories abound about his early exploits. In one caricature, Cullen is described as "delicate," "sallow-faced," and an "independent-looking chap," who often went shoeless. A scantly educated, restless loner, Baker became known for his outlandish behavior.[22]

If one of the often-repeated stories in the Baker saga is true, then Cullen early exhibited questionable judgment. When he was twelve, Cullen purportedly accompanied his father to Jefferson, stole a horse belonging to a local businessman, and rode it to death. His father paid four bags of corn (all that he had) in compensation. After this, Cullen became increasingly quarrelsome, troublesome, a solitary character, and a "scrapper and fighter." Triplett describes him as a "vulgar ruffian" who loved the outdoors, isolation, and quiet. But unlike the quest "of the noble old pioneer, Boone," Baker's "was not inspired by any love for nature in her silent moods, but was rather the skulking of the wild beast from the haunts of man."[23]

An assessment of Baker's character in his boyhood and teen-age years is almost impossible to validate, as we have only the writings of Baker chroniclers upon which to draw. Some stories seem outrageous. For example, his riding a horse to death would never have been accepted or tolerated. A horse was an important asset to a farmer and even to a businessman in that time and place. Farm and city boys understood this fact. What might have possessed the young Baker to perform this cruel act probably can never be ascertained. In earlier accounts, writers fail to perceive its overall importance and easily dismiss it as a boyish prank. If it is true, this story suggests that something was askew in Baker's young mind.

Many of those who have focused upon Baker's life believe a certain incident at a gristmill, variously dated during the late 1840s or early 1850s, had a major influence upon his developing character. At the mill he was taunted and jeered by a group of boys for his dress. The family's clothes, homemade

22. Russell and Russell, *Some Die Twice,* 3; Taylor, "Swamp Fox of the Sulphur," 1; Breihan, "Cullen Baker," 66–67; Breihan, "First of the Gunfighters," 16–17; Smallwood, "Swamp Fox," Pt. 1, p. 20; Bartholomew, *Cullen Baker,* 23. Chandler and Howe, *History of Texarkana,* 23, state that at age fifteen, Baker, "could manage with dexterity five yoke of oxen"; Russell and Russell, *Some Die Twice,* 3, claim that Baker handled oxen with "skill and confidence" and a bull whip like "an expert."

23. Triplett, "Cullen Montgomery Baker," 437; Taylor, "Swamp Fox of the Sulphur," 1; Bartholomew, *Cullen Baker,* 24; Breihan, "Cullen Baker," 66; "First of the Gunfighters," 16; Orr, *Life of the Notorious Desperado,* 4–5.

"both from necessity and for convenience," wrote Eason, caused Baker's "first trouble" and "altered his whole life." Baker offered no resistance, but Mr. Vaughn (the miller) urged him to defend himself. Challenging the local bully, a fellow named Atkinson (or Adkinson), Baker would have stomped him to death except that the miller intervened. One Baker biographer claims the story "was told throughout the neighborhood and his skill and reputation as a fighter was established." [24]

After the gristmill fight—a story that, like so much of the Baker legend, may be apocryphal—Baker observers detect a significant change in his personality. Breihan says that Baker became a braggart and sought prowess, not with his fists, but with a handgun. He experienced "great disappointment" without "an opportunity for personal heroism." Because of his alleged skill with a rifle and revolver, "every boy who knew him made a point of keeping out of his way." This convinced Baker "he really was dangerous." His weakness for whiskey and an added inferiority complex led Baker to challenge "any bystander to meet him in mortal combat." Everyone supposedly knew he was a "crack shot," and they were careful not to give him any reason to draw his gun. [25]

Although Baker's early life demonstrates a propensity for strangeness and aloofness, there is simply no contemporary or documentary record to suggest what kind of character he really exhibited. He may have been deeply disturbed at his mother's death and resented his stepmother, but nothing in the literature indicates this. Moreover, the idea that he became proficient with a rifle and a revolver cannot be substantiated. Surely, he wandered the woods and learned how to use a rifle, normal activities for a frontier boy. But that he practiced to become a quick-draw artist cannot be demonstrated. Thus, it is probable but not proven that at eighteen, Baker had few personal traits that would endear him to anyone.

24. Taylor, "Swamp Fox of the Sulphur," 3–4; Triplett, "Cullen Montgomery Baker," 437; Eason, "Cullen Baker," 6; Bartholomew, *Cullen Baker,* 24–25; Orr, *Life of the Notorious Desperado,* 6; Breihan, "Cullen Baker," 67; "First of the Gunfighters," 16; Vestal, *The Borderlands,* 13.

25. Breihan, "Cullen Baker," 67. Bartholomew, *Cullen Baker,* 14, contends that Baker "had been the acknowledged bully of his home neighborhood for some years and his nature changed for the worse as he traveled the frontiers." In *Life of the Notorious Desperado,* 6, Orr states, "Cullen was known among the boys of the neighborhood as the master spirit of his age, always remembering and repaying homages done him by his companions, and never forgetting to retaliate for injuries received from his associates; always ready with both purse and hands, if perchance he should have a few pence, to extend assistance to a distressed friend, and with an arm forever raised against those who had the misfortune of doing him an imaginary wrong."

We only have secondary hints and suggestions of what Cullen Montgomery Baker was like as a young boy and how he interacted with his family. There are few if any references made to his environment or family situation. Nonetheless, Baker's attraction to alcohol has intrigued almost every investigator of his life. Early writers, beginning with Orr, frequently mention Baker's weakness for whiskey and often emphasize that fact. Modern writers have suggested alcohol fueled Baker's violent activities.

The view of two Baker chroniclers on this topic is worth consideration. Traylor and Robert Russell wrote that "at an early age Cullen learned to imbibe too freely of whiskey. Never in his life did he let himself become so busily engaged that he could not lay aside his business," no matter how important or how long neglected, "for a few hours of drinking." By the time he was eighteen years old, Baker had become "exceedingly quarrelsome and disagreeable, even with his old associates." Part of his irascible nature the Russells attribute to liquor. Smallwood likewise asserts that "by the time he was fully matured, Baker was probably an alcoholic." In fact, he contends that "during most of his nefarious exploits" Baker "was under the influence of alcohol."[26]

Baker's drinking was excessive even by the standards of his own day. The temperance movement was never strong in the South, especially in backwoods areas, but even in those areas alcohol consumption had drastically declined by the 1850s and 1860s, the period of Baker's prominence. How Baker's drinking habits compared with those of other young men in the antebellum South or in east Texas in particular cannot be fully ascertained, but if we believe the comments by his contemporaries, then Baker was certainly a hard drinker and exceeded the bounds of propriety among those of his class.[27]

Perhaps unsurprisingly, Baker developed a mean-spirited temper as he began to drink heavily. At sixteen, Baker was "an underweight, whiskey-drinking gun bully of near-zero literacy," according to Denis McLoughlin's

26. Russell and Russell, *Some Die Twice*, 4; Smallwood, "Swamp Fox," Pt. 1, p. 21.

27. We could find nothing explicit on east Texas drinking patterns during the antebellum years, but the following studies aided us in contextualizing Baker's relationship to alcohol: Ian R. Tyrrell, "Drink and Temperance in the Antebellum South: An Overview and Interpretation," *JSH*, XLVIII (November, 1982), 485–510; Tyrrell, *Sobering Up: From Temperance to Prohibition in Antebellum America, 1800–1860* (Westport, Conn., 1979); W. J. Rorabaugh, *The Alcoholic Republic: An American Tradition* (New York, 1979); Bill Cecil-Fronsman, *Common Whites: Class and Culture in Antebellum North Carolina* (Lexington, 1992), 176–78.

unflattering portrait of him. He guzzled "hard whiskey from a fruit jar and with the independent attitude that was ingrained in his nature, [and] he could become downright mean as hell." Baker began to abuse helpless and defenseless individuals whom he knew would not retaliate. While using a heavy stick to beat an old man, Baker simultaneously forced the man to run. Another version of this story has it that, in front of a crowd held at gun point, Baker compelled the old man to trot. The old man's fear "inspired" Baker to continue this harassment and drive him out of town.[28]

The eighteen-year-old Baker frequented the small settlements of Forest Home and Courtland, visiting saloons, drinking, and fighting. These "groggeries," in the nineteenth-century prose of Triplett, "exerted a fatal fascination upon the base, sensual nature" of Baker, and he quickly joined a "group of idle loungers" who "infested both of these hamlets." He "soon became a confirmed drunkard, and the ferocity of his nature was also intensified." Triplett characterized Baker's behavior as "fiendishness." Henceforth out of control, Baker followed his selfish proclivities. Whether he still lived at home or found his own domicile is not known. Ultimately, he chose a life outside his family and outside the law.[29]

Baker's drinking and cock-of-the-walk attitude would eventually lead him into serious difficulties. Apparently he exulted in this perception of himself and attempted to prove it, particularly when drinking. On one occasion in 1853, Cullen's brother-in-law Matthew Powell joined him in a barroom brawl. Powell, who was thirty-nine years old, had been born in Virginia, and his second wife, Mahala, was Baker's sister. A farmer who doubled the size of his real and personal estate during the 1850s, Powell did not appear to be a man who would engage in the type of dissipated activities that attracted Baker.[30]

Nevertheless, Baker and Powell visited one of the local saloons in Forest Home (near present-day Queen City). Men and boys were drinking freely,

28. Denis McLoughlin, *Wild and Woolly: An Encyclopedia of the Old West* (Garden City, New York, 1975), 27; Triplett, "Cullen Montgomery Baker," 439–40; Breihan, "Cullen Baker," 67–68; Breihan "First of the Gunfighters," 17; Bartholomew, *Cullen Baker,* 24–25; Russell and Russell, *Some Die Twice,* 3.

29. Triplett, "Cullen Montgomery Baker," 438–40.

30. MCR, Seventh Census (1850), Cass County, Texas, p. 785; Eighth Census (1860), p. 105, both in RG 29, NA; Taylor, "Swamp Fox of the Sulphur," 5. Powell and his first wife apparently had three children (three boys); and he and Mahala, married on June 14, 1849 (Teel to Brice, August, 1993), were the parents of four children (three boys and a girl). The census suggests that Powell farmed diligently and accumulated a small estate.

asserts Taylor, and the "inevitable row broke forth." Some bystanders decided to assist a man who had antagonized Baker, and a general melee ensued. While being pelted, Cullen drew a knife to stab his opponent when one of his adversaries, Morgan Culp, seized a hatchet or tomahawk and smashed Baker across the head. This blow, Orr explains, "brought him almost lifeless to the ground, where he remained bleeding freely until the fight was over, when his friends removed him to a neighbor's home." It took several months for Baker to recuperate. Powell was stabbed in the calf of the leg.[31]

It is impossible to know the severity of Baker's head injury from this episode. Bartholomew claims that "this near decapitation would point to a partial reason for the rampaging and violent years that followed, until he was struck down in the year 1869." Baker had exhibited undesirable character traits before he suffered this blow, but it possibly exacerbated them. Another Baker biographer, Johnson, summarized the consensus of Baker writers when he wrote that "some think the blow on the head permanently injured Baker's brain, and they attribute [many] of his future escapades to the injury."[32] It may have further disturbed a mind that already leaned toward instability.

Baker's life took a dramatic turn after this incident. He married a young woman and nine months later killed his first man. How Baker met Mary Jane Petty or how long the courtship lasted has escaped the historical record, but on January 11, 1854, they were wed. The bride's parents, Hubbard and Nancy Petty of Lafayette County, Arkansas, had been born in Tennessee. It is unknown when they migrated to Arkansas, but Mary Jane's father was a farmer who had accumulated nothing the 1850 census taker found of value. Born in Arkansas, Mary Jane was the family's oldest

31. Taylor, "Swamp Fox of the Sulphur," 5–6; Orr, *Life of the Notorious Desperado,* 9. These kinds of brawls are examined in Elliott J. Gorn, " 'Gouge and Bite, Pull Hair and Scratch': The Social Significance of Fighting in the Southern Backcountry," *American Historical Review,* XC (February, 1985), 18–43.

32. Johnson, "Cullen Montgomery Baker," 230; Bartholomew, *Cullen Baker,* 25–26; Orr, *Life of the Notorious Desperado,* 9–11; Breihan, "Cullen Baker," 67–68; Breihan, "First of the Gunfighters," 17; Vestal, *The Borderlands,* 13–14; Smallwood, "Swamp Fox," Pt. 1, 21. Baker's encounter with the tomahawk is highlighted in Jerry Arnold, "Cullen Montgomery Baker," *Marshall News Messenger,* October 28, 1973, p. 8. Taylor, "Swamp Fox of the Sulphur," 5–6, states that Powell carried the scar in his leg until his death. His son, Cullen Powell (obviously named for Baker), informed Taylor that the "hole" in his father's leg "showed distinctly when he died."

daughter and had four siblings, two sisters and two brothers. The Pettys eventually did Baker the invaluable service of raising Louisa, Baker's only child.[33]

Triplett takes a nineteenth-century view of Cullen's marriage and remarks that "like all of her sex, Miss Petty fancied that she had a mission, and did not doubt her ability to entirely reform young Baker." Although his chronology is somewhat askew, Breihan claims that the community forgave Baker his past transgressions because he married a local girl. For "nearly a year he [Baker] lived like a respectable citizen," he postulates, "and people were inclined to think of his past mistakes as the wild oats of youth."[34] Unfortunately, no contemporary record exists describing how the local denizens viewed Baker's nuptials. It is possible they hoped that such an event would rid Baker of his tendency to harass less fortunate community members.

One of the rather odd facts that surround Baker's quick decision to marry—one that seems to bother none of the previous writers—is Baker's labor status. In that era, it was generally accepted by most classes that a man would be gainfully employed at the time he established a household. In none of the Baker literature (including manuscript records) is it recorded how Baker made a living or how he planned on supporting Mary Jane. Surely this much would have been expected of him by the Pettys. He may have assisted Hubbard Petty with the latter's farm, or done the same with his father, but this remains unknown.

The tomahawk fight and marriage seemed to sober Cullen; he briefly altered his life style and experienced a transient reformation. For nine months he avoided trouble, but then he became "quarrelsome and dissipated" and reverted to his previous habits. His deeds were even more mean-spirited and hateful than before. The situation that led to his first killing involved a perceived personal slight from an orphan boy named Stallcup on the street of Forest Home. Baker accused Stallcup of "carrying arms for him," or threatening to kill him. The boy owned a rifle but told Baker that he did not intend to use it to shoot anyone. Baker had "no inclination to

33. Marriage License, Recorded April 14, 1854, Marriage Records, Cass County Courthouse; MCR, Seventh Census (1850), Lafayette County, Arkansas, p. 168; Ninth Census (1870), Titus County, Texas, p. 125, both in RG 29, NA. By 1870, neither Nancy nor any of the children listed in the 1850 census, with the possible exception of Margaret, were living with Hubbard Petty.

34. Triplett, "Cullen Montgomery Baker," 441; Breihan, "First of the Gunfighters," 17.

believe it," reported one newspaper, and acquaintances could not convince him otherwise.[35]

Whatever originally occurred between Baker and Stallcup to provoke Baker into publicly chastising the orphan has been lost. Nevertheless, Baker fetched a long black-snake whip from David Moore's store and proceeded, in front of several witnesses, to flog Stallcup almost to death. His "resort to harsh means," suggested the same newspaper, "far surpassed all the pleading that the boy was able to offer at that time." Afterwards, Stallcup had a writ sworn out, perhaps solicited by some other citizen. Indicted and tried, Baker was convicted of assault. One of the observers, a man named Wesley Baily, who was apparently an important member of the community, served as chief witness against Baker and may have been responsible for inducing Stallcup to pursue the case.[36]

To Baker, it apparently made no difference what the witness' status was in the community. Baily, a farmer, had been born in Tennessee, owned $640 worth of real estate (probably a headright like John Baker), and had moved to Texas after originally settling in Alabama. Unquestionably a family man, Baily and his wife, Louissa, were the parents of seven children, four girls and three boys. As he was fifty-two years old at the time of his altercation with Baker, Baily posed no physical threat. Obviously he had performed what he considered to be a civic duty after observing Baker's uncontrolled behavior in the Stallcup whipping. Whether any previous animosity existed between the two families cannot be ascertained, but it is doubtful.[37]

Incensed at Baily's testimony, Baker determined to seek revenge. On October 8, 1854, about one hour after the conclusion of the trial, Baker ap-

35. *Weekly Harrison Flag* (Marshall), January 28, 1869, p. 2; Johnson, "Cullen Montgomery Baker," 230; Bartholomew, *Cullen Baker*, 26–27; Orr, *Life of the Notorious Desperado*, 6–12; Triplett, "Cullen Montgomery Baker," 441–44; Eason, "Cullen Baker," 7; Taylor, "Swamp Fox of the Sulphur," 6–9; Smallwood, "Swamp Fox," Pt. 1, 21; Breihan, "Cullen Baker," 67–68; Breihan, "First of the Gunfighters," 17.

36. *Weekly Harrison Flag* (Marshall), January 28, 1869, p. 2; Taylor, "Swamp Fox of the Sulphur," 8–9; Johnson, "Cullen Montgomery Baker," 230; Eason, "Cullen Baker," 7; Breihan, "Cullen Baker," 68; Breihan, "The First of the Gunfighters," 17; Orr, *Life of the Notorious Desperado*, 10–12; Triplett, "Cullen Montgomery Baker," 442–44; Bartholomew, *Cullen Baker*, 26–27; Vestal, *The Borderlands*, 14; Smallwood, "Swamp Fox," Pt. 1, p. 21.

37. MCR, Seventh Census (1850), Cass County, Texas, p. 779, RG 29, NA. We have adopted the census takers' spelling "Baily." All other Baker writers, with the exceptions of Orr and Breihan, spell it "Bailey."

peared at Baily's home. Riding up to the barn, Baker summoned Baily, who was feeding his horses. Baker accused Baily of turning Stallcup against him, and questioned Baily about the issuance of the writ. Baily "positively denied" these accusations and stated he had no connection with bringing Baker to trial. His declarations, noted an 1869 newspaper article, "were not sufficient to save him from being butchered by one whose enemies have now surpassed his years in number." Baker vehemently stated he had planned all along to shoot Baily for speaking against him at the Stallcup trial.[38]

Raising a large-bore double-barreled shotgun, Baker supposedly exclaimed, "I'll teach you or any other man to go into court and swear against [me]. Stand out, damn you." Baily pled for his life. Baker replied that he would only shoot him in the legs. When the old man stepped out, Baker opened fire, blasting him in the hips and legs. Baker rode away, and Baily suffered for three or four days, then died. Baker admitted he intended to shoot but not kill Baily. The Democratic *Weekly Harrison Flag* years later wrote that it did not "consider him any less guilty, for he committed murder in the first degree." If justice had triumphed, "great troubles as well as many deaths might have been avoided."[39]

Orr related the incident in the following manner. About one hour after Baily arrived home, Cullen rode up and "accosted the old gentleman, telling him that he was going to shoot him." Baily, who had "no chance to get away, placed himself behind a small post for protection, and begged Cullen not to

38. *Weekly Harrison Flag* (Marshall), January 28, 1869, p. 2; Taylor, "Swamp Fox of the Sulphur," 8–9; Johnson, "Cullen Montgomery Baker," 230; Eason, "Cullen Baker," 7; Breihan, "Cullen Baker," 68; Breihan, "First of the Gunfighters," 17; Orr, *Life of the Notorious Desperado,* 10–12; Triplett, "Cullen Montgomery Baker," 442–44; Bartholomew, *Cullen Baker,* 26–27; Smallwood, "Swamp Fox," Pt. 1, p. 21; Vestal, *The Borderlands,* 14.

39. *Weekly Harrison Flag* (Marshall), January 28, 1869, p. 2; Taylor, "Swamp Fox of the Sulphur," 8–9; Johnson, "Cullen Montgomery Baker," 230; Eason, "Cullen Baker," 7; Orr, *Life of the Notorious Desperado,* 10–12; Triplett, "Cullen Montgomery Baker," 442–44; Bartholomew, *Cullen Baker,* 26–27; Breihan, "Cullen Baker," 68; Breihan, "First of the Gunfighters," 17–18; Bill O'Neal, "Cullen Montgomery Baker," in *Encyclopedia of Western Gunfighters* (Norman, 1969), 31. The *Flag*'s story, it must be remembered, appeared fifteen years after the actual event (Baker had been dead three weeks), and it could righteously stress the need to enforce the law and punish Baker. Into the twentieth century, writers have continued to make much of Baker's "cowardly" murder of Baily. See "Cullen Baker," *Marshall News Messenger,* March 30, 1930, reprinted in *Texarkana USA Genealogist's Quarterly,* XIII (Spring, 1986), 15; "The Story of Cullen Montgomery Baker," Jefferson *Jimplecute,* May 20, 1971, p. 9; Arnold, "Cullen Montgomery Baker," Marshall *News Messenger,* October 28, 1973, p. 8.

shoot him." Baker replied that he did not intend to kill Baily; "he only wanted to shoot him in the legs to see him jump." When Baily refused to come out from behind the post and "submit to the sentence which had been passed against him," Cullen threatened to "shoot him through the head." Baily came out, Baker "raised his fowling-piece with as much solicitude as if he had been going to shoot a beef," and "discharged a double-load of shot and ball."[40]

Triplett paints the Baily episode so as to exaggerate Baker's weaknesses. A wife and daughter run to Baily's assistance and beg for his life. Baker, "howling" like a "ruffian," told them that if Baily came out from behind the shed he would not kill him, only shoot him in the legs "to punish him." But Baker declared that if he had to get down from his mule, he would "blow his infernal head off." Once Baily's wife and daughter moved aside, the "fiendish Baker, aiming at the old man's knees, emptied both barrels of his gun." A "faithful negro" had summoned Baily's son, and now "an avenger was on the track." When the "cowardly murderer" saw the approaching son, he fled.[41]

Eason wrote that nineteen-year-old Baker had killed his first man and embarked on the "trail of no return." Twentieth-century Baker essayists have made much of Baker's "cowardly" murder of Baily. Yet, while every pro-Baker writer accepts the basic facts surrounding this killing, they later promote the idea that blacks were responsible for leading Baker astray and compelling him to become a desperado. Never explored is the fact that murdering someone for testifying against you in a court of law suggests deep behavioral problems. From the Baily incident until his death in 1869, Baker was an unwanted presence, at least among many of the respectable families of the area.[42]

One of the central contradictions in this matter is Baily's denial of involvement when almost all clues point to his role in this significant event in Baker's early manhood. Baily may have lied when approached by Baker in order to try to save his own life, notwithstanding Baker's declared intent only to maim him. Writers sympathetic to Baker do not question his culpability, but they represent his action as self-defense. Considering what we know about Baily's background, there is absolutely no reason to believe that he would have openly challenged Baker. In any event, Baker's manner of

40. Orr, *Life of the Notorious Desperado*, 11–12.

41. Triplett, "Cullen Montgomery Baker," 443–44.

42. Eason, "Cullen Baker," 7. Apart from Orr, Triplett, and Johnson, most Baker writers confirm the perception that his presence was unwanted.

killing Baily became a blueprint for his future: the murder in cold blood of an individual who least suspected such drastic action.

Although no court records or newspaper accounts seem to exist of the case that precipitated Baker's killing of Baily, every Baker chronicler has included this episode in his writings. That he murdered the "old man" Baily cannot be doubted, but where the story originated with all its attendant background, and by whom, is unclear. All chroniclers do agree, however, that this killing dramatically changed Baker's life. Before the Baily matter, he had simply been a troublesome presence in the neighborhood with a reputation for nastiness and meanness. Baker's neighbors tolerated his unsettling activities up to a point. Even Baker seems to have realized that fact. But by shooting Baily, he had crossed the line dividing mean from criminal.

Baker fled the Sulphur River country to avoid revenge from Baily's son, and the events in his life during the next six years (from October, 1854, to 1860) are hazy. For example, Baker's activities for the first two of these years are disputed by his biographers. There are claims that he crossed the state line and lived in Perry County, Arkansas, with his uncle Thomas Young. Some believe he remained somewhere in northwest Texas. In 1856, Breihan surmises, he returned home and "all members of his family, including his wife, had been without any news of him."[43]

One suspects that Baker may never have gone too far from Cass County. He seems to have often escaped to Thomas Young's farm in Perry County, Arkansas. Young, Baker's mother's brother, was about the same age as Baker's father, and like many other Baker acquaintances and enemies, Tennessee born. By 1860, his wife was dead and his four sons and daughter, (ranging in age from one year to fifteen years) all born in Arkansas, still resided at home. The evidence suggests that Young managed family and farm respectably. With land valued at $1,800 and a personal estate worth $2,313, Young had property that, sources often suggest, became a place of refuge for the trouble-plagued Baker.[44]

Those who report unsubstantiated escapades for Baker for the years 1854–1858 have lifted their material from Triplett and from an 1884 account of the life of another Texas desperado, Wild Bill Longley. Triplett has Baker associating with "Tonkaway Indians," killing two men, and murdering

43. Breihan, "Cullen Baker," 68; Breihan, "First of the Gunfighters," 18; Taylor, "Swamp Fox of the Sulphur," 9; Orr, *Life of the Notorious Desperado*, 12–13; Bartholomew, *Cullen Baker*, 27.

44. MCR, Seventh Census (1850), Perry County, Arkansas, p. 273, RG 29, NA.

an Indian named "Herfleet." Ed Bartholomew says Baker killed a ferryman, murdered an Indian scout, and savagely pistol-whipped three men while drunk. All these who are comprised in the Baker "gun-fighter school" say he became an expert with a six-gun and pioneered the "art of shooting from the hip." He became "Dean of 'Baker's College of Six-Shooterology,'" as his special handiwork with the six-gun became known over the southwest."[45]

A "Texas hard-case had been born, the artist surpreme [*sic*] with the six-shooter, the wizard of the short arms was in the making," enthuses Bartholomew. He has Baker fighting with William Quantrill at Lawrence, Kansas, in 1856 (Quantrill's raid was in 1863) and later joining a band of "Destroying Angels" in Utah territory who wanted to eliminate Gentiles from the area under Mormon control. Smallwood simply contends that Baker probably "remained in Perry County." Johnson agrees that the "entire tale of his plains and Mormon life [were] but figments of his florid imagination." Taylor, Eason, Orr, and Breihan have no information on Baker during these years. There is much speculation but no concrete evidence of his whereabouts.[46]

45. Eason, "Cullen Baker," 7; "Cullen Baker," Marshall *News Messenger,* March 30, 1930, reprinted in *Texarkana USA Genealogist's Quarterly,* XIII (Spring, 1986), 15; "The Story of Cullen Montgomery Baker," Jefferson *Jimplecute,* May 20, 1971, p. 9; Arnold, "Cullen Montgomery Baker," Marshall *News Messenger,* October 28, 1973, p. 8; Triplett, "Cullen Montgomery Baker," 445–46; Bartholomew, *Cullen Baker,* 13–16, 17, 19–21. Breihan, "First of the Gunfighters," 18, has a picture of the type of gun Baker used. Carroll C. Holloway, *Texas Gun Lore* (San Antonio, 1951), 184, describes Baker as "chieftain of a band of outlaws and killers in east Texas during the reconstruction era. He is credited with being the first to perfect the quick-draw technique"; see also chapter 13. For background on the weapons used during this era, see Louis A. Garavaglia and Charles G. Worman, *Firearms of the American West, 1803–1865* (Albuquerque, 1984), 153–340, and the magnificent R. L. Wilson, *The Peacemakers: Arms and Adventure in the American West* (New York, 1992), 147–83. For an explanation of "leather slapping," see Eugene Cunningham, *Triggernometry: A Gallery of Gunfighters, With Technical Notes on Leather Slapping as a Fine Art, Gathered From Many a Loose Holstered Expert Over the Years* (New York, 1934); Philip D. Jordan, "The Wearing of Weapons in the Western Country," in Jordan, *Frontier Law and Order: Ten Essays* (Lincoln, 1970), 1–22.

46. Johnson, "Cullen Montgomery Baker," 230–31; Bartholomew, *Cullen Baker,* 21, 27–33, 38; Triplett, "Cullen Montgomery Baker," 445–47; Breihan, "First of the Gunfighters," 17–18. As for Kansas, Baker is not mentioned or listed in John N. Edwards, *Noted Guerrillas, or the Warfare of the Border* . . . (St. Louis, 1877); Captain Kit Dalton, *Under the Black Flag* (Memphis, 1910); Breihan, *Quantrill and His Civil War Guerrillas* (New York, 1959); Albert Castel, *William Clarke Quantrill: His Life* (New York, 1962). Perhaps the most succinct account of Quantrill and his activities is O. S. Barton, *Three Years with Quantrill: A True Story Told by*

Baker may have appeared briefly in Texas in 1858, but one suspects that, as one writer suggests, he may have worked at a ferry on the Red River that allowed him to occasionally visit his wife and daughter. A girl, Louise Jane (her name is also given as Loula and other variations), was born on May 24, 1857. Her birth suggests that Baker was in the vicinity in the fall of 1856. He may have led a desultory life, doing some farming and ferrying, but Baker could never entirely avoid trouble. One account has him receiving a bullet wound in an altercation with a gambler and later retaliating by assaulting the man. In 1858, Baker very likely moved his wife, baby girl, and two sisters to Perry County, Arkansas.[47]

Although it cannot be definitively proved, Baker probably lived in the McCool Township, where the post office had the exotic name of Onyx Tyler's Bluff, between 1858 and 1860. H. W. Burrows, the assistant marshal for the 1860 census in this particular Arkansas region, found Baker in residence. Cullen is listed as "Montg'ry Baker," twenty-three years of age (which would make his birth date 1837, not 1835), born in Tennessee, and a farmer. Baker must have disciplined himself to farm work as he had accumulated real estate valued at $500 and personal property worth $275. Listed in the household with him were his wife, their daughter "Louesa," Baker's sister Eliza, and probably another sister, named Hila J.[48]

There can be little doubt that this was Cullen Montgomery Baker. Perhaps the idea originated from this period that Baker farmed and owned property. Earlier writers did not check Arkansas to confirm this idea, however. The only trace of evidence on which to base it is this brief listing in the 1860 census. How long Baker resided at this location, or even how he was able to acquire the land that he farmed, is unknown. The strongest possibil-

His Scout, John McCorkle by (Norman, Okla., 1992). See also Thomas Goodrich, *Bloody Dawn: The Story of the Lawrence Massacre* (Kent, Ohio, 1991), and *Black Flag: Guerrilla Warfare on the Western Border, 1861–1865* (Bloomington, 1995). For a comparison of how guerrilla war affected various regions in the South and the different tactics used, see Richard P. Gildrie, "Guerrilla Warfare in the Lower Cumberland River Valley, 1862–1865, *Tennessee Historical Quarterly,* XLI (Fall, 1990), 161–76; Archer Jones, *Civil War Command and Strategy: The Process of Victory and Defeat* (New York, 1992), 86–88, 144–45.

47. Vestal, in *The Borderlands,* 14, 16, states they named her "Loula." Orr, *Life of the Notorious Desperado,* 13; Johnson, "Cullen Montgomery Baker," 231; Triplett, "Cullen Montgomery Baker," 447; Smallwood, "Swamp Fox," Pt. 1, 21; Bartholomew, *Cullen Baker,* 33; Eason, "Cullen Baker," 7; Breihan, "Cullen Baker," 68–69.

48. MCR, Eighth Census (1860), Perry County, Arkansas, p. 53, RG 29, NA.

ity is that his uncle Thomas Young, who resided in the same township and was a neighbor, may have assisted him financially. Baker did not have the wherewithal to purchase such property, and his record for staying in one place for any length of time would not have recommended him to a seller.

Mary Jane Baker died on July 2, 1860, shortly after the census taker visited the household. According to family tradition, she is buried at the Nooner Cemetery in Perry County, Arkansas, where Thomas Young's first wife was also interred. Baker returned to Line Ferry, Arkansas, where he left his daughter—who rarely saw him again—with Hubbard Petty, her grandfather. Breihan writes that Baker, by entrusting the baby's care to his father-in-law, "released him[self] of all his responsibilities, and he made no further effort to discipline himself in any way." What happened to the two sisters in his household is unknown, but Baker may have requested that Young watch over them.[49]

After Mary Jane's death, there are suggestions Baker became deeply depressed. But he mourned only briefly, quickly returning to his former dissipated ways, but now among his neighbors. Apparently, he did not tarry in Texas and returned either to his own place or to Young's farm. Although he may have farmed haphazardly, Baker seems to have spent much of his time hunting and living in the woods and swamps. On one occasion, a writer relates, after an absence of several months, Baker returned home with hair down to his shoulders, clad in deerskins, claiming he had subsisted on wild game, wood greens, and an alcoholic brew of wild grapes and berries. Now released from the need to make his own farm succeed, he would soon murder another man in defense of personal honor.[50]

Baker became embroiled in a controversy over his name and character with two of Young's neighbors, John F. and Mary E. Warthan. No evidence of this particular deed has been discovered in any manuscripts or newspapers, but almost all Baker biographers mention Warthan's murder. Thirty-seven years old and Tennessee born, Warthan was not an imposing adversary; his family consisted of seven children (who ranged in age from three to

49. Teel to Brice, August, 1993; Breihan, "First of the Gunfighters," 18; Breihan, "Cullen Baker," 68–69; Orr, *Life of the Notorious Desperado*, 13; Johnson, "Cullen Montgomery Baker," 231; Triplett, "Cullen Montgomery Baker," 447; Smallwood, "Swamp Fox," Pt. 1, 21; Bartholomew, *Cullen Baker*, 33; Eason, "Cullen Baker," 7.

50. Breihan, "Cullen Baker," 67–69; Bartholomew, *Cullen Baker*, 33; Triplett, "Cullen Montgomery Baker," 447.

fourteen years), four born in Alabama, three in Arkansas. A simple farmer with a personal estate valued at but $205, Warthan harks back to Baker's earlier victim, Wesley Baily.[51]

Mary E. Warthan, explains Eason, "seemed to be quite outspoken and severe in her condemnation of Baker and his actions in the community." Never one who could accept criticism, Baker cut hickory switches, became intoxicated, and confronted Mrs. Warthan, whom he intended to thrash. They "scuffled," and when her husband John attempted to stop the attack, Baker pulled a knife and stabbed him in the heart. Triplett claims that Baker gloated "with the delight of a fiend" over Warthan's suffering and left when "he saw that life had fled." A warrant was supposedly issued, but Baker, according to Eason, rode away to the Red River country with the "screams of Mrs. Warthan ringing in his ears."[52]

In Triplett's account, Baker returned to Cass County, where "he played the part of the repentant prodigal" though still a "black-hearted murderer." Even though it had been six years since he killed Baily, Baker remained wary of the local constabulary and "made it clear," in Breihan's view, "that he wanted to become a new man." Orr avers that he "lived a very quiet, peaceable and industrious life"; Baker "frequently spoke of his past career, which he called his misfortunes, in a light that would have caused the most obstinate hearts to sympathize with him." Orr refers to this period as the "civil portion of [Baker's] life," where he "associated with the better class of people, and had to some extent gained their confidence and esteem."[53]

Two years after the death of his first wife, on July 1, 1862, Baker wed Martha Foster, the fifteen-year-old daughter of William and Elizabeth Fos-

51. MCR, Eighth Census (1860), Perry County, Arkansas, p. 273, RG 29, NA; Eason, "Cullen Baker," 7. Mary was John's second wife. Baker writers spell the name "Warthan" variously; this is the 1860 census spelling.

52. Eason, "Cullen Baker," 7; Triplett, "Cullen Montgomery Baker," 447 (Triplett also snidely refers to Baker as a "chivalric gentleman"); Taylor, "Swamp Fox of the Sulphur," 10; Orr, *Life of the Notorious Desperado*, 13–14, for an extended account; Bartholomew, *Cullen Baker*, 34–36; Breihan, "Cullen Baker," 69; "First of the Gunfighters," 18; Johnson, "Cullen Montgomery Baker," 231; Vestal, *The Borderlands*, 16; Smallwood, "Swamp Fox," Pt. 1, 21; Eason, "Cullen Baker," 7. More recent writers also underscore the Warthan murder; *e.g.*, Arnold, "Cullen Montgomery Baker" Marshall *News Messenger*, October 28, 1973, p. 9.

53. Breihan, "Cullen Baker," 69; Breihan "First of the Gunfighters," 18; Triplett, "Cullen Montgomery Baker," 447–48; Orr, *Life of the Notorious Desperado*, 13–14; Johnson, "Cullen Montgomery Baker," 231; Bartholomew, *Cullen Baker*, 37; McLoughlin, *Wild and Woolly*, 27; Eason, "Cullen Baker," 8.

ter of Bright Star, Arkansas, a town located four miles east of the Texas line. William Foster, a Kentucky native, prospered in Arkansas and had accumulated $2,000 worth of real estate and personal property valued at $1,319 in 1860. With his wife, an Arkansas native, he had previously lived in Missouri. The Fosters settled close to the Bakers and became intertwined with Cullen for the remainder of his life. Perhaps Cullen's proposal devolved from the Fosters' acquaintance with the Powells, Baker's sister and brother-in-law. Baker may have met Martha through this couple.[54]

Before Baker married Martha, he joined the Confederate army twice. Although his later exploits against the Federal army have been widely extolled, his Civil War career is shrouded in confusion, mystery, and dishonor. Orr alleges that he was conscripted into the army "as a private soldier, and it is from this period that the second great era of his life was commenced." Baker admirers allude to his "true patriotic devotion": he forsook the "pursuits of civil life" and "promptly" shouldered his rifle "side by side with the young men" who grew to "manhood with him." However, Orr finds no patriotic motive in him and claims instead that Baker had "no love for his bleeding and bed-ridden country that forced him into [its] ranks."[55]

Baker supposedly joined a brigade raised and commanded by Colonel R. P. Crump of Red River County, which fought at Oak Hills and Elk Horn Tavern. According to this version of Baker's Civil War venture, he ignored orders, "returned home as the mood struck him," and "left the army." Smallwood depicts him as riding away "often in full view of officers whom he threatened to kill if they 'bothered' him." He began to "play out," charges Johnson; he refused details, would not work within the ranks, and paid no "attention to rules and regulations." Demonstrating "no deep-seated feelings of loyalty" to the army, in Breihan's view, Baker frequently visited his wife. The "seriousness of the war situation," Breihan theorizes, "led his officers to overlook these lapses."[56]

54. Marriage License, Cullen Baker to Martha L. Foster, July 7, 1862, Marriage Book B, p. 97, Lafayette County Courthouse, Lewisville, Arkansas; MCR, Eighth Census (1860), Lafayette County, Arkansas, p. 59 and p. 785, RG 29, NA; Orr, *Life of the Notorious Desperado,* 14. The marriage license lists Baker as twenty-six years old and a resident of Jefferson County, Texas (this confirms his birth year as 1835). Foster was from Lafayette County.

55. Orr, *Life of the Notorious Desperado,* 14–15. Orr quotes (14) patriotic lines from *Days Doings.*

56. Breihan, "First of the Gunfighters," 18; Breihan, "Cullen Baker," 69; Vestal, *The Borderlands,* 22; Smallwood, "Swamp Fox," Pt. 1, p. 22; J. K. Bivins, *Memoirs* (N.p.: privately printed, [1945]), 22; Johnson, "Cullen Montgomery Baker," 231; Orr, *Life of the Notorious Desperado,*

Whether Baker volunteered for Confederate service or was conscripted into the army only later to desert it is widely disputed among Baker biographers. Their stories do not agree, although most are partially predicated on the recollection of one of Baker's messmates. Taylor, Eason, Vestal, and Russell and Russell believe Baker voluntarily joined the army; Bartholomew wavers on Baker's status; and Orr, Johnson, Breihan, Triplett, and Smallwood follow the conscription theory. Two questions about Baker's Civil War military participation are interrelated. First, if and when Baker actually served in the Confederate army, where was he a soldier? Second, if Baker did enlist and then desert, why did he do so?

A contemporary account suggests that in 1861 or 1862 Baker went to John H. Salmon's house and requested that Salmon accompany him to the widow Wilkins' place and assist him in purchasing a horse to ride into the service of the Confederate cavalry. He told Salmon that he had tried to procure an animal but had failed in every attempt and was worn out. If he did not get one, Baker informed Salmon, he would not go into the service, and if he did, he would go and kill his share of Yankees and faithfully discharge his duties as a soldier. When Wilkins and Baker had negotiated a deal, Baker agreed to pay $150 for the horse out of his army pay. Salmon later surmised that he rode the horse into the service in Captain Rhea's company.[57]

Baker is listed in two different units. Declared a deserter from the first, he received a "disability discharge" from the second. First, Baker joined Company G, Morgan's regimental cavalry, on November 4, 1861, at Jefferson, Texas. His name is on the muster roll for Company G for September/October, 1862, and he received pay through August 31. He was desig-

---

14–15; Triplett, "Cullen Montgomery Baker," 448; Bartholomew, *Cullen Baker,* 37; Taylor, "Swamp Fox of the Sulphur," 13–14; Eason, "Cullen Baker," 8. Russell and Russell, in *Some Die Twice,* 5, quote an officer's report which they believe may have been written later, that declares Baker to be "insubordinate by nature and a coward at heart[;] there was no poorer soldier in the ranks on either side than this shirking ruffian, and his desertion in a few weeks was not looked upon as a loss by either men or officers." For background on conscription and the violent world of the southern soldier, see Emory M. Thomas, *The Confederate Nation, 1861–1865* (New York, 1979), 152–55; Albert B. Moore, *Conscription and Conflict in the Confederacy* (New York, 1924); William G. Doerner, "The Deadly World of Johnny Reb: Fact, Foible, or Fantasy?" in *Violent Crime: Historical and Contemporary Issues,* ed. James A. Inciardi and Anne E. Pottieger (Beverly Hills, 1978), 91–98.

57. John W. Salmon (Jefferson) to Col. R. P. Crump, November 7, 1868, LR, Box 2, Post of Jefferson, USACC, RG 393, NA. We found no mention of a Captain Rhea's company in the Confederate records.

nated a deserter on January 10, 1863. On February 22, 1862, Baker joined Company I of the 15th Texas Cavalry (also the 32nd Texas Cavalry and Crump's Battalion) at Linden, Texas. He is also listed on Company I's muster roll from February, 1862, to February, 1863. After August, 1862, beside Baker's name is written, "left sick on the Arkansas River." He was paid $252.80.[58]

The problem in attempting to sort out whether Baker actually served (as opposed to simply enlisting) in the Confederate army is that the records for both individuals and military units are incomplete and in some disarray. The evidence suggests that Baker did join two units, but never served for an extended period. As long as his unit remained in Arkansas, he may have seen sporadic service; but once his company moved east into Tennessee, Baker became ill and did not rejoin his unit. It is not known how much time he actually served or how much he participated in the fighting. The military papers declare that he deserted one unit and received a "disability discharge" from the other.

Why might Baker have deserted once and then sought a disability discharge? Past Baker biographers have supplied two reasons, neither of which is satisfactory or documented. Breihan speculates that Baker saw so much "cruelty and death" in the army that "his old longing to become a gunfighter was revived." Yet no documentary evidence proves that Baker ever participated in a battle. Baker's most compelling reason for avoiding further military service, according to other Baker chroniclers, was to protect his sisters from blacks. Vestal claims that he found "during his absence in the Army, negroes had been robbing his family." It took him so long to "clean" them up, Vestal adds, that Baker saw no need to return to the army.[59]

Did Baker desert the army to protect his sisters and the community? At the outbreak of the Civil War, the slave population of Cass County stood at

58. Muster Roll, 15th Texas Cavalry Regiment, Company I, August 1862–February 1863, Box 497, Muster and Pay Rolls, War Department Collection of Confederate Records, RG 109, NA; Cullen M. Baker, Compiled Military Service Record, *ibid.* We were unable to locate the muster and pay rolls for Morgan's Regimental Cavalry, Company G, which Baker seems to have first joined. For the campaigns in which these regiments participated, and with which Baker was possibly involved in battle, see Alvin M. Josephy, Jr., *The Civil War in the American West* (New York, 1991), 157–224; Anne J. Bailey, *Between the Enemy and Texas: Parson's Texas Cavalry in the Civil War* (Fort Worth, 1989); William L. Shea and Earl J. Hess, *Pea Ridge: Civil War Campaign in the West* (Chapel Hill, 1992).

59. Breihan, "Cullen Baker," 69; Vestal, *The Borderlands,* 22; Arnold, "Cullen Montgomery Baker," Marshall *News Messenger,* October 28, 1973, p. 9.

3,515, ballooning to 5,189 by 1864, an increase of 68 percent. In Bowie County, the number of slaves rose from 2,474 to 4,138, a 60 percent addition. Refugee slaveholders from other states accounted for this rise in the number of slaves, yet no evidence of slave unrest exists. And no free blacks are listed in Bowie and Cass Counties in 1850 and 1860. But the significant addition to the black presence must have stirred white fears of revolt. Baker and his relatives may have become frightened, but no extant material indicates slaves bothered the family.[60]

Another plausible reason for Baker's decision to leave the army may have been his local ties, no matter how tenuous, and his provincialism. Five months after he had enlisted for the second time, now in the 15th Texas Cavalry, Baker married Martha Foster. It was only about two months later that he received his disability discharge. Baker never ranged very far from Cass County, Texas, Perry County, Arkansas, and their environs. Moreover, Baker's father may have died about this time, and as unlikely as it may seem, the son may have desired to make certain that his father's legacy would survive intact and be perpetuated. Time and time again, throughout his life, no matter what kind of trouble followed him, Baker invariably returned to Cass County.

Whatever Baker's reason for leaving the Confederate army, it was about mid-1863 that his abiding and pathological hatred of blacks began to emerge. Many writers have commented upon his viciousness, but no one has satisfactorily explained why Baker became this way. There is no evidence of any altercation or event in the prewar years that would have shaped Baker's thinking about black people. Yet many writers find his anti-black attitude first manifesting itself during the Civil War. Unfortunately, no contemporary material sheds light on Baker's racist actions.

One often-mentioned incident involved one of Baker's trips home, while he was riding through Sevier County, Arkansas. Western Arkansas was in a chaotic state during this period; armies from both sides and guerrillas were devastating its countryside in clashes with each other. In this environment, Baker encountered a wagonload of people fleeing to Texas, which had been relatively untouched by the ravages of war. In fact, a master may have been taking his slaves to the Lone Star State for safekeeping, or "refugeeing," as it was often called: to protect his investment and the institution itself. Seeing a black woman "whose looks he did not much admire," Baker without

60. Campbell, *An Empire for Slavery,* 264.

warning or apparent hesitation drew his pistol and cold-bloodedly murdered her.[61]

Perhaps the most frequently repeated undocumented tale of Baker's animosity toward blacks involves his vicious killing of a black boy. For whatever reason—and with Baker it could have been the smallest pretext—he became extremely annoyed with a black youngster who belonged to the estate of Ira Pugh. Initially, Baker caught the lad, tied him up, and began to search for some hickory branches with which to whip him. While Baker searched for an appropriate switch, the boy managed to escape. Baker fired at the lad but missed. The boy's employer took him to another farm, but Baker sought him out. When the boy fled into the woods, Baker followed and "shot six balls into his body, leaving him upon the ground a mangled corpse."[62]

Breihan relates perhaps the most exaggerated story about Baker's murder of blacks. According to this story, black troops in Spanish Bluffs, Texas (there were none in the area), searched for federal deserters in 1864. Four soldiers visited a local saloon and encountered Baker, sporting a battered gray hat. A sergeant asked Baker his name and where he hailed from; and "Baker's hand darted down and came up filled with a blazing six-gun." The sergeant fell dead before he could raise a hand. Baker's second bullet felled another soldier. Breihan concludes, "the remaining pair died where they stood, their mouths gaping."[63]

We have been unable to discover any contemporary evidence that would explain why Baker became such a hater of blacks or confirm any of the alleged murders related above. There is abundant documentation for his assassinations and economic terrorization of freedmen and freedwomen once

61. Orr, *Life of the Notorious Desperado,* 15; Johnson, "Cullen Montgomery Baker," 232; Triplett, "Cullen Montgomery Baker," 448–49; Bartholomew, *Cullen Baker,* 38. Bivins, *Memoirs,* 22, states that "about this time he was becoming notorious for killing negroes and committing other atrocious cruelties."

62. Orr, *Life of the Notorious Desperado,* 15–16; Triplett, "Cullen Montgomery Baker," 449; Bartholomew, *Cullen Baker,* 38; Smallwood, "Swamp Fox," Pt. 1, p. 22. Listed as a farmer in the 1860 Lafayette County, Arkansas, MCR, and born in Alabama, thirty-six-year-old illiterate Elizabeth Pugh may have been the widow of Ira Pugh; one son was named Ira F. She had a personal estate of only $123 according to the Eighth Census (1860), p. 59, RG 29, NA. Nobody ever bothered to explain why the slaveholder did not prosecute Baker for the murder as the boy was valuable property. Perhaps the master was afraid to confront Baker.

63. Breihan, "Cullen Baker," 69–70; "First of the Gunfighters," 18–19. This story is highly suspect because Federal troops did not occupy Texas until 1865 and never successfully invaded the state during the war.

the war ended, but all of the tales in past writings about Baker killing blacks during the course of the war lack support. In fact, the information is so sparse that it is difficult to ascertain Baker's movements and actions after he severed his tenuous ties with the Confederate army. Those sympathetic to Baker have connected his racism with guerrilla activities in Arkansas to suggest that in his own way he was "loyal" to the southern cause.

Baker's subsequent wartime activities are shrouded, like much of his life, in mystery, and opinions about them vary. As a deserter, Baker had to be wary. As the military situation became more desperate, the Confederacy began effectively to organize its enrolling officers to search Arkansas and Texas for defectors. Baker must have realized he would be apprehended and decided to hide out in the junglelike thickets of the Sulphur River bottom to avoid being either captured and forced back into military service or sent to the stockade. He "learned all the trails and hideouts from Hyett's Bend in Arkansas to Petty's Ferry—knowledge which would save his life in the coming years," according to Eason.[64]

To avoid capture, Baker went on another and more daring escapade. This story reflects his reputation for deviousness and hostility to blacks. He reportedly rode to Little Rock, through enemy lines, and joined the northern army. Unbelievably, the Federal authorities employed Baker as a freedmen's overseer. He quickly became dissatisfied with one of the black men under his supervision, drew his revolver, and killed him. Realizing the Federal authorities would not look favorably upon his action, Baker did what he did best: he fled to Young's place in Perry County.

During the last year or two of the war, Baker may have consorted with a guerrilla group in that region, an alliance more suited to his demeanor.[65] But stories about Baker's Arkansas Civil War guerrilla activities, though rife in the Baker literature, are not documented. His name has not been found in contemporary accounts; however, the army archival material for this region is vast and his name might be buried within it. Given Baker's previous behavior and characteristics, it would seem that joining or even leading an outlaw group was not his style. The most repeated description of Baker's

64. Orr, *Life of the Notorious Desperado,* 16; Bartholomew, *Cullen Baker,* 37–38; Eason, "Cullen Baker," 8.

65. Eason, "Cullen Baker," 8; Triplett, "Cullen Montgomery Baker," 449; Johnson, "Cullen Montgomery Baker," 232; Orr, *Life of the Notorious Desperado,* 16; Taylor, "Swamp Fox of the Sulphur," 16; Vestal, *The Borderlands,* 23; Smallwood, "Swamp Fox," Pt. 1, p. 22.

personality is that he was a loner, but he is often depicted in his later years as being the leader of some gang. Gang violence would become his modus operandi after the war, but writers pinpoint no reason for this change.

Arkansas was indeed devastated by partisan warfare, and at least two guerrilla organizations did exist in western Arkansas. However, there is no evidence that Baker participated in or led a group of guerrillas between 1863 and 1865. Still the stories persist. One group, the "Mountain Boomers," considered themselves Union sympathizers. The second, the "Frontier Rangers" or "Independent Rangers," consisted of irregular Confederates, deserters, and outcasts who "engaged in the raiding and looting" of the countryside. One day, legend has it, the Independent Rangers overtook Baker and his uncle, believing they might be affiliated with the Union. With much pleading, Baker and his uncle escaped being shot. Baker soon cast his lot with the Rangers.[66]

Although he had never demonstrated any leadership qualities, Baker became the leader of the Rangers in many accounts of his life. In accord with Baker's nature, this gang impulsively raided, plundered, and murdered. In Eason's view, the Rangers were simply "outlaws who preyed on the defenseless settlers while the able-bodied men were at war," with "no one to bring them to justice for their depredations." After driving the Mountain Boomers from western Arkansas, Baker and his Rangers reportedly focused their wrath upon unionists leaving the state. In what became known in some writers' tales as the "Massacre of the Saline," Baker and his gang encoun-

66. Orr, *Life of the Notorious Desperado,* 16; Johnson, "Cullen Montgomery Baker," 232; Triplett, "Cullen Montgomery Baker," 449; Bartholomew, *Cullen Baker,* 38. Smallwood, "Swamp Fox," Pt. 1, p. 22, states that this is when Baker went to Little Rock and presented himself to the Union commander as "a persecuted Unionist." See the important recent work, Carl H. Moneyhon, *The Impact of the Civil War and Reconstruction on Arkansas: Persistence in the Face of Ruin* (Baton Rouge, 1994), 101–171, and William L. Shea, "A Semi-Savage State: The Image of Arkansas in the Civil War," *AHQ,* XLVIII (Winter, 1989), 309–28; Leo E. Huff, "Guerrillas, Jayhawkers and Bushwhackers in Northern Arkansas During the Civil War," *AHQ,* XXIV (Summer, 1965), 127–48; Diane Neal and Thomas W. Kremm, *Lion of the South: General Thomas C. Hindman* (Macon, 1993). The best surveys of what occurred in Arkansas during the Civil War, which do not mention Baker or the events in which he was supposedly involved, are Daniel E. Sutherland, "Guerrillas: The Real War in Arkansas," *AHQ,* LII (Autumn, 1993), 257–85; and Jayme Lynne Stone, "Brother Against Brother: The Winter Skirmishes Along the Arkansas River, 1864–1865," *Military History of the West,* XXV (Spring, 1995), 23–49. Perry County, where Baker often sought refuge, was part of the Arkansas River valley.

tered nine unionists leaving the state. When they collectively refused to surrender, Baker shot the leader. The remaining eight were taken to the woods and executed.[67]

After this, Baker's brigands burned six homes and murdered six more men in Saline County. Forming a wagon train loaded with their contraband, they turned toward Texas. Although they mostly focused their wrath upon unionist partisans, they occasionally levied tribute upon Confederate supporters of the Perry County region. A motley organization, Baker's group had little discipline; they could not withstand a general engagement against organized forces. As the gang's exploits and cruelty gained increasing attention, the local inhabitants became disgusted at the state of their region and determined to prevent further disruption of their lives.[68]

By December, 1864, Baker allegedly was the leader of a reorganized band of outlaws. He began to raid Union army scouting parties, attack army outposts, and plunder the countryside. This small group, with the addition of Benjamin F. Bickerstaff, reportedly conducted raids into Louisiana and harassed Federal headquarters at Natchitoches. Vestal states that during the winter of 1864–1865, Baker "rode under the black flag," pretended to be a Confederate officer on special service, "fought in several brilliant skirmishes," and attacked two bands of Mountain Boomers, "defeating them with terrible slaughter and butchering all of the prisoners taken." In

67. Eason, "Cullen Baker," 8; Bartholomew, *Cullen Baker,* 38; Breihan, "Cullen Baker," 70; Breihan, "First of the Gunfighters," 19; Triplett, "Cullen Montgomery Baker," 449–50; Johnson, "Cullen Montgomery Baker," 232–33; Orr, *Life of the Notorious Desperado,* 16–17; Triplett, "Cullen Montgomery Baker," 449–50; Smallwood, "Swamp Fox," Pt. 1, pp. 22–23; Vestal, *The Borderlands,* 23–24.

68. Johnson, "Cullen Montgomery Baker," 232–33; Orr, *Life of the Notorious Desperado,* 17–18; Bartholomew, *Cullen Baker,* 38–39; Breihan, "Cullen Baker," 70–71; Breihan, "First of the Gunfighters," 19–20; Triplett, "Cullen Montgomery Baker," 450; Taylor, "Swamp Fox of the Sulphur," 17. As noted in the Introduction, guerrillas generally did not prey upon women, but Baker and this group were qualitatively different from those Missourians about whom Fellman writes. Johnson states (233) that "men were tortured and killed and women outraged and murdered by these cutthroats." We have located no concrete evidence, however, that Baker ever ravaged a woman. Moreover, there is no suggestion in the source material that his gang engaged in sexual assault. For the story of a Texan who followed the opposite course, see William E. Sawyer, "Martin Hart, Civil War Guerrilla," *Texas Military History,* III (Fall, 1963), 146–53. In a related vein, Phillip Shaw Paludan's *Victims: A True Story of the Civil War* (Knoxville, 1981) tells a compelling story of the killing of thirteen suspected unionist guerrillas by Confederate soldiers in North Carolina.

descriptions of these engagements, Baker was "under the influence of whiskey."[69]

Southerners in this region became disillusioned, and outrages and depredations increased in frequency, as jayhawkers and brigands brought upheaval to several counties. "Absentees and deserters" infested the area, complained the inhabitants to the governor; these outlaws robbed, stole, murdered, and perpetrated "other dark crimes." One petition spoke of lawless men who "prowled over our farms and prairies and held our country terror-stricken." No one was spared as "decrepit age and helpless innocence were alike the subjects of the most brutal indignities. Life and property were alike insecure." Powerless to protect themselves, the citizens pleaded for assistance from the state and the Confederate army.[70]

Tradition has it that by early 1865, the citizens of Perry and surrounding counties prepared to eliminate Baker and his gang. When the desperadoes learned they had been targeted for destruction, in one last burst of violence they killed several individuals, burned homes, and drove women and children into the woods. Pursued by a militant group of outraged inhabitants and some Arkansas militia seeking to avenge past wrongs, Baker and his cohorts took several wagons loaded with booty and headed for Texas. Forced to abandon their spoils, the group dispersed. Baker fled to the Sulphur River bottom.[71]

Baker biographers ambivalently represent Baker's wartime guerrilla activities. His sympathizers defend Baker's actions on the grounds that he might have been officially affiliated with the southern government. "Whether Baker's band of rangers were acting as spies and agents for the Confederacy," admits Vestal, "or as an outlaw band involved in random

69. Vestal, *The Borderlands,* 25; and the sources in n. 68 above.

70. G. A. Dickerman and Six Others (Sherman) to Governor Pendleton Murrah, November 9, 1864; J. W. Throckmorton to Murrah, December 9, 1864; Petition from Twenty-Three Citizens, Collin County, to Murrah, [1864]; all in GC (Murrah), TSL; James Marten, *Texas Divided: Loyalty and Dissent in the Lone Star State, 1856–1874* (Lexington, 1990), 103–105.

71. Johnson, "Cullen Montgomery Baker," 233; Triplett, "Cullen Montgomery Baker," 451; Orr, *Life of the Notorious Desperado,* 17–18; Bartholomew, *Cullen Baker,* 38–39, 41; Breihan, "Cullen Baker," 70–71; Breihan, "First of the Gunfighters," 19, 41–42. Baker's three comrades were allegedly Seth Rames, Preacher Jones, and Olny Daggs. Benjamin F. Bickerstaff, another infamous Reconstruction desperado in Texas, may have joined the four on the Sulphur River.

murder, arson, robbery, rape and pillaging is not known."[72] There is no evidence that the Confederate government ever sanctioned such wanton violence although they approved of "partisan rangers." By preying on everyone, no matter their allegiance, Baker indicated that he had only one allegiance: himself. After all, he had deserted the southern cause (and if folklore is true, the northern cause also).

One of the legends that contributes to the Civil War Baker saga involves his second wife. During Baker's guerrilla phase, Martha lived with her father near Line Ferry. She heard that her husband had been captured by the Federals. Barely nineteen years old, on February 5, 1865, she secretly set out on a two-hundred-mile journey for Perry County, where Baker's uncle resided. Local folklore relates that she traversed swamps and rivers, riding at one stretch for thirty-six hours without food or sleep for herself or her horse. She found Baker safe. Eason rhapsodizes about Martha that this "jewel among women" was "probably the only living being Baker ever really loved other than his mother."[73]

72. Vestal, *The Borderlands*, 25. On northern and northeast Texas and guerrillas, see C. B. Breedlove (McKinney) to Murrah, November 19, 1864, GC (Murrah), TSL; Richard B. McCaslin, "Wheat Growers in the Cotton Confederacy: The Suppression of Dissent in Collin County, Texas, During the Civil War," *SwHQ*, XCVI (April, 1993), 527–46; McCaslin, *Tainted Breeze: The Great Hanging at Gainesville, Texas, 1862* (Baton Rouge, 1994); Marten, *Texas Divided*, 103–105. On guerrillas, see Albert Castel, *General Sterling Price and the Civil War in the West* (1968; rpr. Baton Rouge, 1993); John N. Edwards, *Shelby and His Men; or, The War in the West* (Cincinnati, 1867), an important contemporary account; Castel, "The Guerrilla War, 1861–1865," *Civil War Times Illustrated*, XIII (October, 1974), 4–50, estimates there were between 18,900 and 26,550 southern guerrillas. Richard S. Brownlee, *Gray Ghosts of the Confederacy: Guerrilla Warfare in the West, 1861–1865* (1958; Baton Rouge, 1984), offers the standard account. For a valuable addition to the literature, see David Paul Smith, *Frontier Defense in the Civil War: Texas' Rangers and Rebels* (College Station, Tex., 1992); Fellman, *Inside War;* Castel, "The Jayhawkers and Copperheads of Kansas," *Civil War History*, V (September, 1959), 283–93; Thomas D. Isern and Mark D. Weeks, " 'Quantrill's Raid on Lawrence': From Disaster Song to Outlaw Ballad," *Mid-American Folklore*, XIV (Fall, 1986), 1–14. Gary L. Cheatham, " 'Desperate Characters': The Development and Impact of the Confederate Guerrillas in Kansas," *Kansas History*, XIV (Autumn, 1991), 144–61; and, most recently, Goodrich, *Bloody Dawn* and *Black Flag*.

73. Eason, "Cullen Baker," 9; Orr, *Life of the Notorious Desperado*, 19–21; Taylor, "Swamp Fox of the Sulphur," 19–20; Breihan, "Cullen Baker," 71; Breihan, "First of the Gunfighters," 42; Bartholomew, *Cullen Baker*, 41; Vestal, *The Borderlands*, 24–25; Smallwood, "Swamp Fox," Pt. 1, p. 23.

Confusion also exists about Baker's location in the final months of the war. Taylor has Baker returning to Cass County with some of his men in the spring of 1865. In July, Taylor posits, he began to raid in Cass, Marion and Bowie Counties. Johnson agrees but observes, "There his reputation had preceded him . . . and the people let him know he was not welcome. After a few weeks Baker returned to Perry County." In contrast, Bartholomew claims that east Texans welcomed Baker back home. He had made "quite a name for himself as a guerrilla captain" and his "campaigns in the last days of the war, even after the surrender, had gained him a respect by his friends and every southerner who heard of it."[74]

Whether Texas citizens were as hostile to Baker as Johnson maintains is unknown. Surely there were those who opposed his presence, but others felt an affinity with him and would support his later actions, as Bartholomew suggests. Undoubtedly, Baker had a checkered reputation, especially in his own neighborhood. He had married two local women and knew their families. But he was also known as a drinker, a fighter, and a killer; he was, in short, unstable. He had cold-bloodedly murdered innocent people and then fled to escape punishment. When he returned, as he frequently did, local authorities seem to have made no effort to apprehend him for past transgressions. No one bothered him, probably because they were afraid of the consequences.

Immediately after the war, Baker briefly established a reputation as a Robin Hood, according to Eason and others. In July, 1865, Baker met a group of men driving several head of horses and cattle. Later, he stopped at the residence of a Mrs. John Drew, a widow. Almost in tears, she complained of losing animals to Baker and some men who claimed to be his cohorts. The real Baker offered to retrieve them, and Mrs. Drew promised a reward. He subsequently returned the beasts and received the money and a "heartfelt thanks." Mrs. Drew gave Baker's deed "such wide publicity that many people began to doubt he could be the unscrupulous individual they had heard about."[75]

74. Taylor, "Swamp Fox of the Sulphur," 22; Johnson, "Cullen Montgomery Baker," 233–34; Bartholomew, *Cullen Baker*, 42.

75. Bartholomew, *Cullen Baker*, 42; Eason, "Cullen Baker," 9; Orr, *Life of the Notorious Desperado*, 21; Triplett, "Cullen Montgomery Baker," 452; Breihan, "Cullen Baker," 71–72; "First of the Gunfighters," 42; Taylor, "Swamp Fox of the Sulphur," 22; Vestal, *The Borderlands*, 34; Smallwood, "Swamp Fox," Pt. 1, p. 23.

As the war drew to a close and the southern armies capitulated, Baker did not immediately manifest any inclination to resist the Federal occupation of the area. Whatever the extent of his wartime activities (even if only one of the tales is true), he was educated along with many other dissatisfied and disillusioned compatriots on how best to conduct a guerrilla war against the Union army and other intruders. From his base in the Sulphur River country, Baker and his gang of desperadoes would become national news two years later. More generally, Baker's kind would eventually come to symbolize southern intransigence and exemplify the idea that the South might have been beaten but never conquered.

According to an 1872 Arkansas newspaper, when the South surrendered, Baker "declined to accept the terms or abide the conditions." Riding away on his "fiery horse" to the east Texas wilds, he proclaimed himself "the last survivor of the Lost Cause, who would never surrender until the Confederacy was fully established and its authority recognized by all the powers of the earth."[76] Whether Baker ever felt this strongly about the cause of the South is doubtful, but he did resent the presence of the military and of the Freedmen's Bureau in the South. He did not become an immediate menace to Federal forces, although freedmen tended to avoid any contact with him. It took Baker two years to become a scourge to Reconstruction in his home region.

76. Van Buren (Arkansas) *Gazette,* July 16, 1872, p. 1.

TWO

The Emergence of a Desperado

———————•———————

THE SOUTH'S DEFEAT in the War between the States elicited both immediate and delayed responses from newspapers and the citizenry. In Cullen Baker's case, for two years he ignored the question of how his defeated section should be treated by the victors. Other Texans reacted quickly. The situation in Texas was quite different from that of other Confederate states at the close of the war. In fact, among all the Confederacy it had remained relatively untouched by outside forces. Although north Texas was racked by civil conflict during the fighting, Union forces never successfully invaded the area. Once the war ended, violence gripped the region. This trend continued throughout the Reconstruction years.

With the surrender of the southern armies, Texas newspapers began to discuss "peace" terms. In Baker country—*i.e.,* the area where Texas, Arkansas, and Louisiana conjoin—Robert W. Loughery's *Texas Republican* (Marshall) may have been the most strident. It suggested only two options. On the one hand, feelings of "kindness and conciliation" could be exhibited on the part of the North. On the other hand, "oppression and tyranny," confiscation and/or disenfranchisement, and an "armed soldiery" could be instituted. If the first approach were adopted, prosperity would reign. If the second one were, the unbroken "spirits of the people," "not yet fit for slaves," would react against the government imposing a stringent Reconstruction. The "commencement of a guerrilla system of warfare of which no man can see the end" would transpire.[1]

1. *Texas Republican* (Marshall), May 26, 1865, p. 2; James Curtis Armstrong, "The History of Harrison County, Texas, 1839 to 1880" (M.A. thesis, University of Colorado, Boulder, 1930),

In northeast Texas, opposition to the occupation army and governmental policy quickly appeared. Whether many in the North realized it or not, a second civil war with a different cast of characters was beginning. Writing from Linden, the county seat of Cass County, in August, 1865, J. M. McAlpine sustained the provisional governor Andrew J. Hamilton's program, believing conciliation a good thing. But attempting to promote such a goal among the people of Texas was " like throwing pearls before swine." Texans had "lost all sense of duty" and were determined to rule themselves or go down in ruin. Claiming themselves to be in the right, they vowed they "would inaugurate the same struggle again if they could," rather than live under the national government.[2]

D. J. Baldwin, later a judge of the United States District Court at Galveston, told the provisional governor that most of the Texas citizenry remained hostile to emancipation and occupation; he often heard expressions such as "god damned Yankee soldiers" or the "god damned Yankee radicals." Southerners were saying they had been "whipped but not conquered." When it was suggested that the former slaves be educated, one woman remarked: "Educate niggers! Why I would put a bullet through their heads before I would allow them to learn to read!" The former slaveholders and a majority of other whites were determined that emancipation should fail. The rebel-

---

181. On Loughery, see Max S. Lale, "Robert W. Loughery: Rebel Editor," *East Texas Historical Journal,* XXI (1983), 3–15. For background, see Randolph B. Campbell, *A Southern Community in Crisis: Harrison County, Texas, 1850–1880* (Austin, 1983). For the surrender, see Robert L. Kerby, *Kirby Smith's Confederacy: The Trans-Mississippi South, 1863–1865* (New York, 1972), 377–434.

2. J. M. McAlpine (Linden) to A. J. Hamilton, [August (?), 1865], GP (Hamilton), RG 301, Folder 18, Box 49, TSL. Others confirmed this viewpoint, F. B. Sturgis to Hamilton, March 19, 1866, GP (Hamilton), RG 301, Box 52, Folder 48, TSL. On Hamilton and his policy, see the older work by Charles William Ramsdell, "Texas from the Fall of the Confederacy to the Beginning of Reconstruction," *Quarterly of the Texas State Historical Association,* XI (January, 1908), 199–219; Ramsdell, *Reconstruction in Texas* (New York, 1910), 55–84; John L. Waller, *Colossal Hamilton of Texas: A Biography of Andrew Jackson Hamilton, Militant Unionist and Reconstruction Governor* (El Paso, 1968), 59–77; Allan C. Ashcraft, "Texas: 1860–1866, The Lone Star State in the Civil War" (Ph.D. dissertation, Columbia University, 1960); Ashcraft, "Texas in Defeat: The Early Phase of A. J. Hamilton's Provisional Governorship of Texas, June 17, 1865 to February 7, 1866," *Texas Military History,* VIII (1970), 199–219; Nora Estelle Owens, "Presidential Reconstruction in Texas: A Case Study" (Ph.D. dissertation, Auburn University, 1983). See also William A. Russ, Jr., "Was There Danger of a Second Civil War During Reconstruction?" *Mississippi Valley Historical Review,* XXV (June, 1938), 39–58.

lion was "more of a sentiment with them than ever it was."[3] Baker would later be engrossed with such feelings, but his immediate goal was to seek respectability.

Baker seemed intent on leading a "normal" life. Back in Cass County, he and his wife settled down for a very brief period, living quietly in the complete antithesis of the preceding three years' lifestyle. According to Thomas Orr, from July, 1865, until January or February, 1866, Baker desired to become engaged in the ferry business. He seems to have first sought financing in Jefferson for a crossing on the Sulphur River, but when this plan failed, he and his wife, in the fall of 1865, moved to Mush Island, again on the Sulphur River, hoping to establish a ferry in that section. It was a bad location to choose because there were two other ferries close by, Line and Petty's, which quite adequately serviced this sporadically traveled area.[4]

After Baker became sick (nobody specifies the illness), he temporarily abandoned the project. His malady apparently incapacitated him. He and Martha moved in with her parents, the Fosters, and stayed with them until January, 1866. In mid-January, with Baker recovered, the couple went to Line Ferry where they again attempted to earn a livelihood in the ferry

3. D. J. Baldwin to A. J. Hamilton, November 7, 1865, GP (Hamilton), Box 51, Folder 33, RG 301, TSL; Carl H. Moneyhon, *Republicanism in Reconstruction Texas* (Austin, 1980), 64–65.

4. T. U. Taylor, "Swamp Fox of the Sulphur or Life and Times of Cullen Montgomery Baker," *ca.* 1936 (Typescript in ECBTHC), 22, 26; Al Eason, "Cullen Baker—Purveyor of Death," *Frontier Times*, XL (August–September, 1966), 9; Boyd W. Johnson, "Cullen Montgomery Baker: The Arkansas-Texas Desperado," *AHQ*, XXV (Autumn, 1966), 234; Carl W. Breihan, "Cullen Baker," in his *Great Gunfighters of the West* (San Antonio, 1962), 72; Breihan, "Cullen Baker—First of the Gunfighters," *The West*, VII (July, 1967), 42; Frank Triplett, "Cullen Montgomery Baker," in his *Romance and Philosophy of Great American Crimes and Criminals* . . . (New York and St. Louis, 1884), 452; Thomas Orr, *Life of the Notorious Desperado Cullen Baker, from His Childhood to His Death, with a Full Account of All the Murders He Committed* (Little Rock, 1870), 21–22; Yvonne Vestal, *The Borderlands and Cullen Baker* (Atlanta, Tex., 1978), 34; James Smallwood, "Swamp Fox of the Sulphur," Pt. 2, *True West*, XXXVIII (November, 1991), p. 38. Myreline Bowman, *The People of Cass County: Atlanta, Queen City, Texas* (Atlanta, Tex., 1973), has an account that contends that Lee Rames was Baker's partner. After Baker's wife died, he "either sold or gave the Ferry" to William Foster (225). As no railroad existed in this region, much of the commerce centered on the town of Jefferson. One of the major roads led from Jefferson to Little Rock. To escape the headwaters of the bayous, the road went about thirty miles north of Jefferson then turned east to cross the Sulphur River, almost following the boundary between Texas and Arkansas: hence the name Line Ferry.

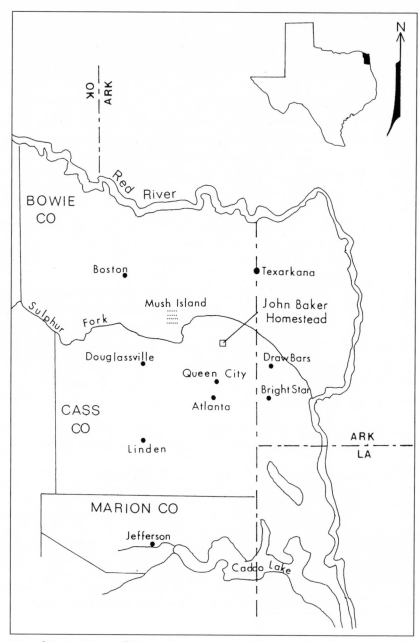

Map of Bowie, Cass, and Marion Counties, Texas, showing Baker's homestead and the larger Baker territory

Map by Keith Cheshire

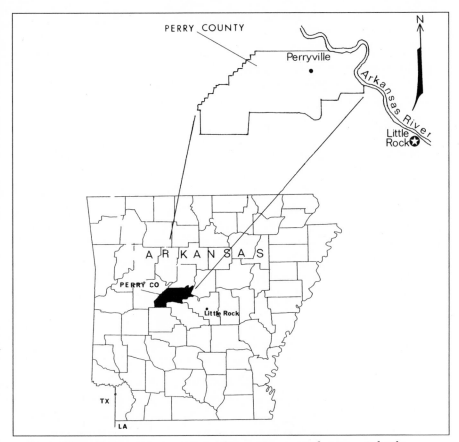

Map of Perry County, Arkansas, where Thomas Young—and at times Baker himself—lived

Map by Keith Cheshire

business. This time may have been more successful than Baker's previous efforts as he seems to have been intermittently employed for perhaps a year or so at Line Ferry. However, a personal disaster brought this period of quietude to an end. Martha became seriously ill. She may still have been suffering from the exhausting and debilitating effects of her February ride.[5]

Martha Foster Baker died on March 1, 1866. "In that grave," Orr writes, Baker "appeared to bury his senses, his reason, and his remaining respect for the human race." Al Eason asserts that Baker "went into a state of shock approaching sheer madness," an echo of Ed Bartholomew's claim that he became a "madman." According to Frank Triplett, Baker "appeared at all times to have been partially insane," but Martha's death "completely unhinged" his intellect. Baker constructed an effigy ("so natural as to startle the beholder"), dressed the likeness in her clothes and trinkets, and talked to it for hours. But this display of grief notwithstanding, two months after Martha's death, Baker proposed marriage to her sixteen-year-old sister, Belle Foster.[6]

From mid-1866 until mid-1867, before Baker went on a rampage against Federal forces, he became part of a seriocomic controversy with Orr, a schoolteacher who became Baker's enemy and rival for Belle Foster's hand and who assisted in killing him. It is not surprising that the Fosters, and Belle herself, rejected Baker's marriage proposal. He had not previously been an ideal husband to Martha. Baker became very embittered over the rejection. Belle's romantic involvement with Orr further angered him, because Orr's deformed right hand and crippling rheumatism made him less than a man in Baker's eyes. The animosity between the two men continued until Baker's death in 1869.[7]

5. Same sources as in note 4.

6. Orr, *Life of the Notorious Desperado*, 22; Eason, "Cullen Baker," 9; Taylor, "Swamp Fox of the Sulphur," 27, 30–31; Ed Bartholomew, *Cullen Baker: Premier Texas Gunfighter* (Houston, 1954), 51–52; Triplett, "Cullen Montgomery Baker," 452–53; Breihan, "Cullen Baker," 72; Breihan, "First of the Gunfighters," 42, who writes that after his rejection by Belle, Baker "left with a new bitterness in his heart"; Johnson, "Cullen Montgomery Baker," 234; Vestal, *The Borderlands,* 34–35; Smallwood, "Swamp Fox," Pt. 2, p. 38. The testifier in Bowman, *The People of Cass County,* claims Baker "did not go wild until after Martha's death" (225).

7. Johnson, "Cullen Montgomery Baker," 234; Orr, *Life of the Notorious Desperado,* 21–22; Breihan, "Cullen Baker," 72; "First of the Gunfighters," 42; Triplett, "Cullen Montgomery Baker," 453; Bartholomew, *Cullen Baker,* 51–52; Smallwood, "Swamp Fox," Pt. 2, p. 38; Vestal, *The Borderlands,* 37. Eason, "Cullen Baker," 10, states that Belle's romantic interest in Orr,

Born in 1844 in Henry County, Georgia, Thomas Orr was the oldest child of his father William Orr's first wife, Lucy D. Stewart. This family of Irish lineage had established its American roots in South Carolina and later migrated to Georgia. There William Orr was a moderately prosperous farmer. When he died in 1864 (a son was born three weeks after his death), his survivors included his second wife, Margaret Stewart (his first wife's sister), and eight children. With the assistance of two brothers-in-law and Thomas, then twenty years old, the family managed to endure the final months of the Civil War. One genealogical history describes Thomas as a "man of sturdy character, resourceful and thrifty."[8]

Precisely what compelled Thomas Orr to migrate to Arkansas cannot be ascertained, but it may have been the possibility of a teaching position. Orr became an instructor in a small school near what is now Bloomburg, Texas. Leaving his trouble with Baker aside for a moment, we should note that Orr became a quite valuable citizen of the area. After Baker's death, he was appointed surveyor of Lafayette County, Arkansas, laying out the boundaries for Miller County and establishing the town site for Texarkana. He became its first mayor and promoted its civic and cultural life. Orr initiated the first opera house in the region and the first "street railway system." He also served as Miller County judge between 1880 and 1882.[9]

In January, 1866, Orr appeared in Cass County, Texas, and Lafayette County, Arkansas "prospecting" for a school. (Some claim that Baker convinced Orr to establish a neighborhood school; others give credit to the more likely supporter of education, Foster.) Orr boarded with the Fosters and began teaching. While Martha Foster Baker still lived, Orr met Baker on several occasions, "at various times and places." Orr claims that the two initially had amicable relations. At first, he asserts, Cullen treated him "with great kindness, for a stranger, requesting him to come and stay with him

---

coupled with his "political background, and region of origin, caused Baker to hate him above all men." Eason presumes here and elsewhere, erroneously, that Orr was a northern Republican. Smallwood, "Swamp Fox," Pt. 2, p. 38, writes that "Baker was after Orr because he had married a girl the Fox had wanted. Worse, he was a Union man and a pre-war abolitionist in Confederate territory." There is no indication that Orr was ever an abolitionist.

8. MCR, Ninth Census (1870), Lafayette County, Arkansas, p. 223, RG 29, NA; Marvin D. Evans, comp., *The Orrs of Miller County Arkansas* (Fort Worth, 1951), 29–31, 33.

9. Evans, *The Orrs of Miller County*, 34; Barbara Overton Chandler and J. Ed Howe, *History of Texarkana . . . and . . . Bowie and Miller Counties Texas–Arkansas* (Texarkana, 1939), 64. The territory that comprised Miller County remained part of Lafayette County until its reorganization in 1874.

when not otherwise employed." (It is not clear where Baker lived at this time.) After his wife died and Belle rejected him, however, Baker exhibited a hostile attitude toward Orr.[10]

During this interlude, Baker seemed intent on bidding for the ferry concession at Line Ferry. He traveled to Linden to procure a license, but nothing came of this. He lost the concession to another party and made several threats against anyone who might use the ferry. He kept informed on Orr's whereabouts and dabbled in the ferry business, choosing a spot seven miles from the Texas state line to begin an operation of his own.[11] Baker continued to drink heavily and slide further into a psychologically disturbed state. He apparently brooded about Belle spurning his proposal and about his treatment by his former in-laws. His anger would be aimed at Orr, however.

On June 2, 1866, three months after Martha's death, Orr approached the Sulphur's south bank at Line Ferry, where he intended to engage the ferry, which Cullen operated. (Baker either was employed by those holding the concession or had somehow gained the prize himself.) Baker was absent. John Herring and a freedman began to ferry Orr across. Cullen appeared on the north bank "with a jug of whiskey, minus what he had already consumed," and awaited the ferry's arrival. He asked Orr to have a drink with him, which Orr "kindly refused." Cullen persisted, but Orr "told his friend (for such he considered him) that he never used it." Orr claims that Baker well knew of his abstinence "but wanted an excuse for a difficulty." He failed to persuade Orr to drink with him.[12]

Baker became petty, accusing Orr of "talking about him" and claiming that Orr had stated that he did not like whiskey or anyone who drank it. Orr denied the charges and asked from what source Baker had garnered his information. Baker exclaimed that he had it on reliable authority, simultaneously seizing the schoolteacher by the throat and throwing him upon the ground. Orr admitted that Cullen was "getting the best" of the contest, "for

10. Orr, *Life of the Notorious Desperado*, 22.

11. *Ibid.*, 26–29; Taylor, "Swamp Fox of the Sulphur," 37, 40; Breihan, "Cullen Baker," 75–76. In "First of the Gunfighters," 43, Breihan states that Baker, unable to "outbid others for the Line Ferry concession," threatened to assume control of it anyway and defied "any man to compete with him, making sure to emphasize that his fast gun would back him up."

12. Orr, *Life of the Notorious Desperado*, 22–23; Eason, "Cullen Baker," 10; Taylor, "Swamp Fox of the Sulphur," 27, 32; Johnson, "Cullen Montgomery Baker," 234; Bartholomew, *Cullen Baker*, 52; Breihan, "Cullen Baker," 72–73; Breihan, "First of the Gunfighters," 42; Triplett, "Cullen Montgomery Baker," 453; Vestal, *The Borderlands*, 37; Smallwood, "Swamp Fox," Pt. 2, p. 38.

he was a large, stout, healthy man, while his opponent was exactly the reverse," with an almost useless right hand deformed by rheumatism. Baker hit Orr on the head with a pine limb and ran away, leaving his victim bleeding on the ground.[13]

After regaining his senses, Orr mounted the same bay mare Baker's second wife had ridden during her famous journey, and sought medical assistance. He later wrote that "his feelings concerning a difficulty so unnecessary as that was cannot easily be imagined." A stranger in the area where he had lived but a few months, Orr had "kept close at his occupation, making but few acquaintances outside of his school dominion." Previous to this time he knew nothing of Baker's reputation, "but soon the history of this noted character was opened to him, and many hidden things brought to light." He trembled at the thought of "being an enemy to a person who was but little better than the great arch-demon of the infernal regions."[14]

Orr was astonished that a civil community would allow "such an outlaw to reside among them" after he heard of Baker's "midnight assassinations and unscrupulous outrages upon innocent women and children." Indeed, Orr was not willing to leave the subject of his own assault thus unsettled, "and without even knowing why the difficulty occurred." He boldly and foolishly procured a pistol and intended to return to the ferry, but was persuaded by friends to use an alternate route.[15] Thus originated the feud between the two men, which involved physical, verbal, and printed jousts, and which resulted in Orr's near death and ultimately the killing of Baker. Previous writers have suggested that Orr did not comprehend that Baker was a formidable foe and would seek revenge, but Orr knew it.

A month after the assault, Baker, who accused Orr of "tale-bearing and slander," appeared at the schoolhouse along with Lee Barnes. Baker demanded the ferryage amount, which Orr had not paid because of the altercation and his injury. After Orr paid, Baker verbally abused him in front of the pupils, stating that the schoolteacher had told "three thousand lies"

13. Orr, *Life of the Notorious Desperado*, 23. Most Baker accounts accept Orr's version of this incident.

14. *Ibid.*

15. *Ibid.*; Triplett, "Cullen Montgomery Baker," 453; Breihan, "Cullen Baker," 73; Breihan, "First of the Gunfighters," 42. Taylor, Bartholomew, and Eason believe Orr's evidence was tainted because of his conflict with Baker and his supposed regional and political affiliation. In "Cullen Baker," 73, Breihan contends that after this incident, Orr "procured a pistol and meant to have it out with Baker on his return trip"; however, he earlier emphasized that Orr had been told of Baker's "swiftness with the revolver."

about the difficulties between the two and that if he spread any more pre-varications he should leave the country or prepare to die. In addition, Baker threatened that if he caught Orr riding his dead wife's horse again, he would "shoot his head off smooth with his shoulders." This confrontation led to the withdrawal of two students.[16]

What Baker intended to accomplish by his actions is uncertain. On July 20, 1866, he had a threatening letter delivered to Orr by one of the students who withdrew, George Couch. "If you Wish to Teach your School you had bitter Bea At It every Day," Baker had scribbled. "I here of you Beeing fishing My Lad, you Don't No that my Gizzard is Grinding on Dam Lies that you told over the River." Baker did not want to hear of Orr "Beaing Absent from that School Any more for It Is all that I Can Do to keep from giving you another & good call & if I find one thing to Bee So You May Look for me." He closed by stating, "I am Sir yours as Mad as Hell till Death" and did not "Want the friendship [of] Any one that you Can turn Against me."[17]

By this time, Cullen's conduct had become "so desperate," contends Orr, "that civil and well disposed citizens could not stand it any longer." A justice of the peace was consulted to suggest some remedy, but nothing came of this tactic as "none dared approach [Baker] upon the subject of his conduct." Orr describes how a meeting of the community citizens and school patrons "began to devise some plan to settle his conduct or his person, they did not care much which." One older gentleman named William Foster (not Baker's father-in-law) opposed the plan. He suggested sending a delegation to deal with Baker. Ironically, Baker later killed him. The community, obvi-

16. Triplett, "Cullen Montgomery Baker,"453; Orr, *Life of the Notorious Desperado,* 23–24; Taylor, "Swamp Fox of the Sulphur," 33; Eason, "Cullen Baker," 10; Breihan, "Cullen Baker," 73; Breihan, "First of the Gunfighters," 42; Vestal, *The Borderlands,* 38. The two students, Couch and John Nichols, professed friendship for Baker and went to live with him; he may have persuaded them that he would either kill Orr or drive him from the area.

17. Orr, *Life of the Notorious Desperado,* 24; Eason, "Cullen Baker," 10; Taylor, "Swamp Fox of the Sulphur," 33; Breihan, "Cullen Baker," 73; Breihan "First of the Gunfighters," 42; Vestal, *The Borderlands,* 38. Both Eason and Taylor changed the letter's wording to conform with standard English. Whenever any of Baker's writings have been quoted, we have used Orr's version when we could not locate a contemporary newspaper account. Orr commented (24) that "many persons were once very fond of boasting on Cullen's scholarship, representing him as being a man of great refinement, a good scholar, with great business qualifications"; but the letter "does not display more genius than two well-bred lawyers ought to possess." Bartholomew includes nothing about the Orr/Baker conflict in his biography.

ously fed up with Baker's aggression, desired a cessation of his constant out-bursts.[18]

According to Orr's account, a committee that parlayed with Baker at Line Ferry attempted to ascertain his intentions and intimated that the "citizens had met *en masse,* and had come to the conclusion not to submit to such conduct any longer." Baker originally made some "heavy threats" about "what he would do if anybody attempted to interfere with his freedom," but he finally relented and offered to appease the group to a limited extent. On July 27, 1866, Baker supposedly declared that "I here By sertify to the Neighbors of Hiett's Bind [Hyatt's Bend] that I will In No Manner Interrupt Nor Bother one Thos Orr further more I Consider my word as good as any Body's or as good as the word of Jesus Christ I witness my hand."[19]

On July 29, Baker also had a letter delivered to William Foster. Parts of it are difficult to understand, and some of the allusions are vague, as Baker seemed to be losing control of himself. "Mr. Foster Dear Sir Dear Father as I should say for you have Bin a father to me So has Mrs. Foster Bin a Mother," he declared in the opening. "But I Recken you Both have Resind to Bee any more therefore I think It In vain to Ever Look for Either of you here any more[.]" After mentioning in a garbled aside some pills that had been left by an "old man" some years before, Baker stated his belief that he had been cast aside in favor of Orr: "Mr. Foster It Is very hard for me to Bear and How Is It that one Can throw away an old friend for a New one[.]" Mrs. Foster had "surely here tofore held Me as a friend But she is now La-boring under a wide Mistake or Wanting me to put on that Dont fit me and wear It In Behalf of that Damd Orr." Nothing had ever made such a pro-found "impression on my Mind as that Did[.] If I had Killed Jesus Christ It would Not Raised half the Excitement this matter has[.] I hope and Pray to Live the ten months out and Keep my Same mind for I am not a Negro Neither am I bound In this Country[.] I No that I am a Liar a Drunkard and a Devil But I never tell Lies on my friends." He did not want the "friendship of any One" that Orr "Can turn against Me[.]" He commenced

18. Orr, *Life of the Notorious Desperado,* 24–25; Taylor, "Swamp Fox of the Sulphur," 35–37; Breihan, "Cullen Baker," 74; Breihan, "First of the Gunfighters," 42; Vestal, *The Borderlands,* 41.

19. Orr, *Life of the Notorious Desperado,* 25; Eason, "Cullen Baker," 10; Taylor, "Swamp Fox of the Sulphur," 35–36; Breihan, "Cullen Baker," 74; Breihan, "First of the Gunfighters," 42–43; Vestal, *The Borderlands,* 41.

in trouble and "End In the same[.]" Baker hoped to make it to the end of the school term and then act.[20]

If he did in fact pen this letter, Baker made several revealing comments about himself and his situation. Even though the Fosters had served as his surrogate parents, Baker believed he had now been replaced by Orr. In particular, Mrs. Foster had offended Baker in some manner relating to Orr and probably their daughter Belle—perhaps it was their rejection of him as a suitor to Belle, whom Orr married. Promising only to postpone his vendetta against Orr until the end of the school term, he hoped he would be alive to finish the feud. Assuming racial superiority he claimed to be neither black nor bound as a slave, but admitted he was a liar, a drunkard, and a devil. Certainly, they could have expected to have to contend with Baker in the future.

Baker did as promised and waited until school closed for the winter before taking any further action against Orr. Orr ceased instruction on November 2, 1866, and Baker arrived in the area the next day. Orr sought a warrant from a justice of the peace and protection from the county sheriff, but both officials refused to become involved. Through a series of fortuitous circumstances, Baker did not immediately locate Orr. The schoolteacher later prepared to ambush Baker in late December but finally abandoned the idea. Retaining a teaching position in the area, from that time forward Orr claimed he never ventured to school, or anywhere else for that matter, without a double-barreled shotgun and a six-shooter.[21]

According to Orr, George W. Barron informed Baker that the schoolteacher planned to ambush him on December 30, 1866. This prospect outraged Baker. Believing what Barron said to be as "true as Holy Writ," Baker lost the "last spark of kindness that had for years been nourished in his bosom," and became governed by a "more powerful rival, the desires of his passions." Allegedly, Baker swore vengeance upon those who had "called him bad" and determined to show them he had "not done anything" com-

20. Orr, *Life of the Notorious Desperado,* 25–26; Breihan, "Cullen Baker," 74–75; Breihan, "First of the Gunfighters," 43; Taylor, "Swamp Fox of the Sulphur," 34; Eason, "Cullen Baker," 10; Vestal, *The Borderlands,* 39.

21. Orr, *Life of the Notorious Desperado,* 26–29; Breihan, "Cullen Baker," 75–76; Breihan, "First of the Gunfighters," 43; Taylor, "Swamp Fox of the Sulphur," 37, 40; Vestal, *The Borderlands,* 41. Both Breihan and Vestal have extended material on how Orr planned to waylay Baker. Nothing in Orr's character suggests he would do something this brash although he seems to have briefly considered the possibility of this action. He did, however, assist in ambushing and killing Baker.

pared with what he would do. In a fit of anger he exclaimed, "If I could sink this whole country into hell by stamping upon the ground, I would stamp with all my power, and send it and every living creature, with myself, into the infernal regions."[22]

Orr made a final attempt to placate Baker and resolve their difficulties. Writing an open letter in April, 1867, which appeared in the Jefferson *Jimplecute,* Orr said he had written to Baker before but never received an answer. Assuming the note had not been delivered, Orr took the opportunity to write again. "I suppose, or at least have heard," the schoolteacher ventures, "that you say you have nothing against me. I would be glad to know that it was a fact." Orr had also been informed that Baker understood that Orr had threatened his life. As for Baker having heard it, Orr could not deny, as he was not "accountable for lies told by others." Orr asked Baker simply to produce the man who heard him make any such assertion.

The letter is conciliatory. Orr desired that the difficulty between him and Baker "could be settled, and we were, or could become, as we once were." If he had, "or could be convinced" that he had, acknowledgments to make, he "would do it with pleasure," only he did not believe that he had ever given Baker "any reason for treating me as you have, and I am not aware of giving you any cause for even being mad at me; besides, I am not apprised of what you got mad about." When Orr had found it necessary to travel in the area, he had been compelled to put himself to "much trouble and inconvenience" and been deprived of the "pleasures and comforts of life" to stay out of Baker's way. He hoped to reach some kind of accommodation.[23]

Baker refused to be appeased. To gain some revenge against the patrons of Orr's previous school and against the teacher himself, he went on a dog-killing spree in the Yatts's neighborhood around Bright Star, Arkansas, in mid-April, 1867. He visited the Fosters to obtain a horse. Two dogs charged him in the corral, and Baker killed one and crippled the other. This ruckus awakened Foster, who investigated. Baker began shooting at the roof of the Foster house. He then rode a short distance to the farm of Elizabeth Pugh

---

22. Orr, *Life of the Notorious Desperado,* 28.

23. *Ibid.,* 29–30; Taylor, "Swamp Fox of the Sulphur," 40; Breihan, "Cullen Baker," 76–77; Breihan, "First of the Gunfighters," 44; Vestal, *The Borderlands,* 42–43. It seems difficult to believe, as some writers have suggested, that Orr was so naïve that he did not understand that his problems with Baker stemmed from his relationship with Belle Foster, particularly after Baker had been rejected by her for a man who was physically deformed and considered a weakling. There are apparently no extant issues of the *Jimplecute* for this period.

and killed her dogs and a lame goose. At the Howell Smith residence he shot two more canines. He also killed Vine Barginer's dog and finished the episode by eliminating all the dogs on the William J. Hooper place.[24]

After the dog massacre, Baker, now ostracized and disgraced, lived in the Sulphur bottom away from the prying eyes of the community. Eason claims that "it was his habit to stop at a store or farm when he needed supplies, take what he needed and ride off without paying." Eason's argument, that most storekeepers "took this in good humor," is doubtful. These vendors had no choice but to acquiesce when confronted by a sociopathic killer. In one instance, Baker visited the grocery store of a Mr. Rowden near Queen City on June 1, 1867. The proprietor was absent when Baker and a companion appeared. Baker forced Rowden's wife to provide him with certain supplies, remarking that she could "charge it to the Confederacy." Rowden later complained, calling Baker a drunkard and a thief.[25]

Baker heard of the merchant's comments and decided to defend what little honor he had left. On June 10, 1867, he went to Rowden's home, called him out, verbally chastised him for his remarks, then cold-bloodedly murdered him. A young boy, Jim Clements, saw Baker pass by, hastened to the Rowden farm, and found Rowden dying with eight or nine buckshot in his chest. Baker later declared that he was not responsible for Rowden's

24. Orr, *Life of the Notorious Desperado,* 29; Taylor, "Swamp Fox of the Sulphur," 39; Eason, "Cullen Baker," 10; Vestal, *The Borderlands,* 43. The Pughs, the Bargainers, and the Hoopers all lived in the neighborhood. In 1860 Elizabeth Pugh was a thirty-six-year-old Alabama-born (as were all the children) widow who was listed as a farmer and had a personal estate of $123. Five children (three girls, two boys) lived with her. V. Bargainer was eighteen years old in 1860 and the wife of I. L. Bargainer. He had been born in Alabama, she in Mississippi. I. L.'s parents lived close by; his father, William, was a Georgian, and his mother a South Carolinian. Hooper and his wife were Tennessee natives, but all their children were born in Arkansas. For background, see MCR, Eighth Census (1860), Lafayette County, Arkansas, p. 59; Ninth Census (1870), Lafayette County, Arkansas, p. 217; Eighth Census (1860), Cass County, Texas, p. 108, all in RG 29, NA.

25. Orr, *Life of a Notorious Desperado,* 30–31; Taylor, "Swamp Fox of the Sulphur," 41–42; Eason, "Cullen Baker," 10–11; Breihan, "Cullen Baker," 77; Breihan, "First of the Gunfighters," 44; Bartholomew, *Cullen Baker,* 52; Johnson, "Cullen Montgomery Baker," 234; Triplett, "Cullen Montgomery Baker," 454–55; Vestal, *The Borderlands,* 68. Taylor defends Baker's action, contending that "instead of acting like the other merchants of the country and abiding by the levy," Rowden "became very bitter in his language and publicly denounced Baker calling him all manner of names and winding up with the statement that Baker was a drunkard and a thief." The idea that no citizen ever objected to giving Baker a meal, horsefeed, or a horse is surely exaggerated. They tolerated his behavior because they feared for their lives.

death and would "shoot down any man without mercy" who accused him of the deed, but he fled the vicinity.[26]

Baker remained in the area, but he had become the focus of community attention. He had abused and humiliated Orr, been rejected by the Fosters, and angered several other people. The civil authorities had never been able to curtail his activities, and the citizens seemed unable to agree on what to do about Baker. At this time, events on the national scene took a dramatic turn, which influenced circumstances at all levels of society. Until the middle of 1867, Baker had not run afoul of the Federal army or of the Freedmen's Bureau, which by now had made a prominent appearance in the region. His rage now turned against the government and also refocused upon blacks.

Precisely what led the Swamp Fox to harass and kill Federal officials and begin a reign of terror throughout the region is not clear. It may have been the expanded presence of the Freedmen's Bureau and of the military in the section that he inhabited. The catalyst may also have been the emancipation of enslaved blacks and the extension of civil and voting rights to them. Whatever the reason, Baker focused his animosity upon those parties tied closely to Reconstruction in the South: the army, the agents of the Freedmen's Bureau, and the freedmen and freedwomen themselves. That he did so at this time is revealed through contemporary documents rather than questionable secondary sources. The establishment of a Freedmen's Bureau office in Boston, Texas, especially drew Baker's ire.

A month before the end of the war, with Abraham Lincoln's approval, Congress established the Bureau of Refugees, Freedmen, and Abandoned Lands to assist the former slaves in their transition from bondage to freedom. It became known as the Freedmen's Bureau, and it was commissioned to exist for one year after the declaration of peace, although its duration was later extended. The first official of the Freedmen's Bureau arrived in Texas in September, 1865. The number of field officers of this governmental agency who were to serve as advisory and legal representatives to the black community remained small throughout 1866 and into early 1867. With Congress assuming control of Reconstruction policy, the duties of the head of the Texas Bureau and of the District of Texas commander were combined.

26. Orr, *Life of the Notorious Desperado*, 30–31; Eason, "Cullen Baker," 10–11; Taylor, "Swamp Fox of the Sulphur," 41–42; Bartholomew, *Cullen Baker*, 52; Triplett, "Cullen Montgomery Baker," 453–54; Breihan, "Cullen Baker," 77–78; Breihan, "First of the Gunfighters," 44; Johnson, "Cullen Montgomery Baker," 234; Vestal, *The Borderlands*, 68.

Charles Griffin considerably expanded the Texas Bureau during his brief tenure as its assistant commissioner (January–September, 1867). For the first time since the Bureau's arrival in Texas, the far northeastern area of the state received a governmental representative in the form of a Bureau agent. William G. Kirkman was this agent, head of the agency's fifty-eighth subdistrict in Texas. The drama that ensued between Kirkman and Baker depicts the opposite poles of the Reconstruction experiment to establish legal equality for the former slaves. Kirkman's "energetic operations" in behalf of Bowie and Cass Counties' black populace, wrote an admirer, led to his murder by Baker. Kirkman characterized Baker as "reckless in the extreme," a "bad man" who had escaped capture by numerous parties of soldiers.[27]

Born in Jacksonville (Morgan County), Illinois, between 1843 and 1845, Kirkman was the fourth of five sons. His early life seems to have been as strange as Baker's, but it did not lead to a career of violence and mayhem. His father, Thomas Kirkman, is listed as insane in the 1850 census; he killed his wife Catherine, and the authorities subsequently committed him to the state mental hospital in Jacksonville. As the records of this branch of the Kirkman family are sparse, how this trauma affected the children is impossible to ascertain. Whether the children were cared for by relatives or grew up in orphanages is unknown.[28]

---

27. C. S. Roberts (Agent, Clarksville) to J. P. Richardson (AAAG), November 12, 1867, AC, LR, R-58, Texas, BRFAL, RG 105, NA. For two widely divergent interpretations of the Texas Bureau, see William L. Richter, *Overreached on All Sides: The Freedmen's Bureau Administrators in Texas, 1865–1868* (College Station, Tex., 1991); Barry A. Crouch, *The Freedmen's Bureau and Black Texans* (Austin, 1992).

28. MCR, Seventh Census (1850), Morgan County, Illinois (Jacksonville), pp. 313–14, RG 29, NA. Kirkman is listed as "Gilbert" (apparently his middle name), age seven, who had attended school that year, but it was undoubtedly Kirkman. Finding reliable information on Kirkman's background is generally difficult. There is nothing about his family or associates in Charles M. Eames, comp., *Historic Morgan and Classic Jacksonville* (Jacksonville, Ill., 1885); Newton Bateman and Paul Selby, eds., *"Historical Encyclopedia of Illinois" and "History of Morgan County"* (Chicago, 1906); Charles M. Clark, *The History of the Thirty-Ninth Regiment Illinois Volunteer Veteran Infantry (Yates Phalanx) in the War of the Rebellion, 1861–1865* (Chicago, 1889), 540. Though active, the Kirkman family genealogical network has been unable to garner any significant information about Kirkman's early life; Mrs. Florence Hutchison (President, Jacksonville Area Genealogical and Historical Society) to Crouch, March 4, 1989; Robert W. Dalton (Jacksonville, Ill.) to Crouch, March 21, 1989; Terence S. Tarr to Crouch, [June, 1989]; Frances L. Woodrum (Director, Morgan County Historical Society Collection) to Crouch, September 11, 1990. The Tarr letter was the most informative and the most speculative about the Kirkman family. There are numerous suggestions that insanity and feeble-

When war broke out, Kirkman was working as a telegraph operator in Marengo, Illinois. The sixteen-year-old enlisted in Company K of the 39th Regiment Illinois Infantry on August 19, 1861, for a three-year stint. Described as an "enthusiastic and plucky" soldier, Kirkman served faithfully and conscientiously for three years. When the unit struck tents in October and formed to march to the railroad depot, he had an "extraordinarily big and heavy knapsack." A sergeant suggested he reduce its weight or he would soon "play out" and have to be transported in the ambulance. Another soldier pointed out a strapping six foot, two inch man in the company and declared that Kirkman would "hold his place longer" than the bigger man and have his knapsack, too, which he did.[29]

Serving as a telegraph operator in 1863 and 1864 in the United States Telegraph Company, Department of the South, in South Carolina, Kirkman was mustered out of the service in January, 1865. (His brother Albert, who had joined the Union Army, had been killed at Memphis in 1864.) Five feet, four and three-quarter inches tall he had a dark complexion, dark eyes, and black hair. After his war service, Kirkman was employed by the Fire Alarm telegraph service in Chicago and also performed as a telegraph operator in Rockford, Illinois. Precisely how he became a Texas Freedmen's Bureau agent is unknown; but more than likely his older brother Joel, a member of the Texas Bureau headquarters staff, encouraged him to become an agent.[30]

Kirkman, a capable, honest, and persevering individual, held the title of Subassistant Commissioner for the 58th subdistrict of Texas, which included Bowie and later Cass (renamed "Davis" between 1861 and 1871)

---

mindedness plagued the Kirkman offspring. For a superb account of the area, see Don Harrison Doyle, *The Social Order of a Frontier Community: Jacksonville, Illinois, 1825–70* (Urbana, 1978).

29. Clark, *The History of the Thirty-Ninth Regiment*, 540.

30. *Ibid.*, 540–41; WGK, Compiled Military Service Record; Regimental Descriptive Book, 39th Infantry, Companies F to K, Illinois, Records of the Adjutant General's Office, both in RG 94, NA. Also, General Orders, Special Orders, Circulars and Rosters, AC, Texas, 1865–69, June 22, 1867, Vol. 9, pp. 172–73; Charles Griffin (AC, Texas) to Oliver Otis Howard (Commissioner), June 3, 1867, Vol. 5, p. 69; JTK (AAAG) to A. H. M. Taylor (AAAG, District of Texas), June 23, 1868, Vol. 5, p. 87; WGK to Griffin, July 8, 1867, Vol. 67, p. 1; WGK to JTK, July 9, 1867, Vol. 67, p. 6; July 11, 1867, Vol. 67, p. 7; WGK to Thomas Latchford (Commander, Jefferson), August 1, 1867, Vol. 67, p. 19; Receipt, B. W. Gray (Attorney), September 26, 1868, Vol. 68, p. 134, all in Texas, BRFAL, RG 105, NA. Kirkman's brother, Joel T., was employed as acting assistant adjutant general by the Texas Bureau headquarters for approximately one year.

Counties. The area bordered the Indian Territory, Arkansas, and Louisiana. The subdistrict was comprised of 1,838 square miles and contained 13,558 people, of whom 7,930 were white (58 percent) and 5,628 black (42 percent). Cass ranked 28th and Bowie 44th among Texas counties in the number of black residents. Kirkman was headquartered at the rather small, isolated village of Boston, which had a population of three to four hundred people during the postwar years. One person described Boston as a "hard place" where shooting scrapes and fighting commonly occurred.[31]

A week after he arrived, Kirkman recounted the killing of a freedman on Saturday, June 29, 1867. One or more men had gone to the home of a black man who lived outside Douglassville with the intention of killing him, and had abused a freedwoman who could not find a light for them. The freedman was shot, and another freedwoman was ordered to get up and light a broom to see if he was dead. Baker then allegedly shot the victim four more times, five in all: once in the breast and four in the heart. The freedman had been killed for working a small farm "on his own account." Citizens testified that the black man was "peaceful, quiet and industrious."[32]

This seems to be the first recorded identification in the contemporary sources of Baker as the killer of a black person. The stories from the war notwithstanding (and they cannot be confirmed), there is no suggestion in the Bureau or army manuscripts that Baker had drawn the attention of the citizens for a previous outrage against white or black. Baker may have committed violence before mid-1867, as Kirkman suggests, but no local officials sought the army's assistance. It is indeed possible that Baker is responsible for murders of freedmen and freedwomen that are not documented. But the records for these postwar years are so extensive that his name would surely have appeared sooner if he had done something notorious.

31. WGK to C. S. Roberts, September 18, 1868, Vol. 68, p. 130; September 24, 1868, Vol. 68, p. 131; Roberts to WGK, September 22, 1868, Vol. 5, p. 414, all in Texas, BRFAL, RG 105, NA. See also Walter Prescott Webb and H. Bailey Carroll, eds., *The Handbook of Texas* (2 vols.; Austin, 1952), I, 471; S. A. Swiggert, *The Bright Side of Prison Life, Experiences, in Prison and Out, of an Involuntary Sojourner in Rebeldom* (Baltimore, 1897), 97; Louise Wimberly Hagood, "Negroes in Northeast Texas, 1850–1875" (M.A. thesis, East Texas State University, 1966), 40–64; Barbara Susan Overton Chandler, "A History of Bowie County" (M.A. thesis, University of Texas, Austin, 1937); U.S. Bureau of the Census, *Compendium to the Population Census Schedule, 1870* (Washington, D.C. 1872), 63–66.

32. WGK to Griffin, July 9, 1867, Vol. 67, p. 3, Texas, BRFAL, RG 105 NA. Webb and Carroll's *Handbook of Texas* states that "between 1860 and 1870 migration from the Southern states brought many plantation owners and their slaves to the area along Red River" (I, 516).

Kirkman, however, implies that Baker had already established a "bad reputation," alluding to rumors that "a person could hire him to shoot a freedman for a few dollars." Although certainly a menace, Baker was not the only one. In the same neighborhood, another white man had ridden up to a freedman working in a field and simply shot him. A white man had also been murdered. In the Linden vicinity, two "hard and reckless [white] men" were reported to have slain a "good many blacks" and committed other depredations. This particular area was not safe for blacks or whites, although the people, Kirkman observed, were "anxious for some kind of law, and a majority were tired of the lawless state their county [was] in." He determined the need for immediate military attention.[33]

Within three weeks of his arrival in Boston, Texas, Kirkman encountered his nemesis, Cullen Montgomery Baker. On July 24, 1867, Kirkman, DeWitt C. Brown (a future Bureau agent of the 37th subdistrict, headquartered in Paris), and three cavalrymen from the Mount Pleasant post traveled nineteen miles into Cass County (seven miles from the Sulphur River) looking to arrest Baker as well as his "first lieutenant," L. R. Rollins, and other associates. Rollins, Kirkman wrote, was reported to be the "chief man" in Baker's "clan." He had allegedly been involved in "certain robberies" and was found associating with and aiding Baker. Rollins later would twice save Baker from military arrest by supplying him with timely information.

When Cass County citizens learned that Kirkman intended to take Rollins into custody, a "large number" of them presented him with a petition in Rollins' behalf. (Nothing could be discovered about the background of Rollins.) The Boston agent attempted a compromise. If Rollins would come forward, Kirkman told the petitioners, give a $500 bond with two good sureties, and report to him every twenty days, he would refer the matter to headquarters. He thought the case "could be investigated before some civil officer." The friends of Rollins believed he would appear under this kind of arrangement. So Kirkman suggested to headquarters that the case should be investigated and tried without "too much of an opinion being formed before."[34]

Kirkman made every effort to maintain equitable relations with local whites. The agent understood that his situation was delicate in the extreme

33. WGK to Griffin, July 9, 1867, Vol. 67, pp. 4–5, Texas, BRFAL, RG 105, NA.

34. WGK to Adam C. Malloy (Agent, Marshall), September 26, 1867, Vol. 67, pp. 63–65, Texas, BRFAL, RG 105, NA.

and that he might not receive full cooperation. He hinted to a fellow Bureau agent that Rollins' neighbors were either ignorant or hiding knowledge of Baker's activities, probably the latter. After all, Kirkman reasoned, Rollins lived near Baker, he at least assisted Baker in hauling cattle, and Baker certainly had "associates" when he robbed and killed the freed slaves. Kirkman informed Adam C. Malloy, his counterpart in Marshall, that if Rollins were arrested, he would have to give bond in Marshall.[35] Interestingly, none of Baker's previous biographers mentions Rollins.

Kirkman and his group initially stopped at the Frank Crawford house seeking information. The Boston agent sent one of Crawford's sons to the Rollins residence to gather intelligence. After waiting about two hours, the Crawford boy returned and claimed that Baker was in the vicinity. Other family members verified this fact. Meanwhile, Baker had been watching the agents' horses from the woods. He had coerced the knowledge out of the wife of a Crawford son and thus knew precisely what Kirkman and his four colleagues were doing and where they were. The machinations and intelligence gathering of Baker, along with those of numerous friends and comrades in the region where he operated, made it possible for him to elude the military and remain vigilant.

No contemporary evidence other than a description of this incident has been discovered that identifies Baker with his active supporters, but Kirkman portrays Baker as leading a gang and orchestrating a form of collective violence. Baker's band seems to have emerged suddenly, and he developed a network of citizens to assist him in his fight with the Bureau and the army. The gang's origins and size cannot be ascertained. As the school incident previously demonstrated, not everyone in the region supported Baker's actions. An undercurrent of Baker sympathy may have been waiting to express itself and only became apparent when Baker attacked blacks and government officials. Older accounts of Baker emphasize that a majority assisted him. The citizens were probably divided over Baker's presence.

Kirkman believed that Frank Crawford informed Baker of Federal troop movements. Both Kirkman and DeWitt C. Brown suspected Crawford's intentions once they learned that Baker lurked nearby. When they briefly visited the household of Matthew Powell, Baker's brother-in-law, Powell confirmed their surmise. After the Federal contingent had moved on to the Crawford house, Baker appeared; subsequently, Rollins rode up and de-

35. *Ibid.* An indication of Rollins' secretiveness is that his name only appears twice in the primary sources.

clared that Crawford had informed him the "Yankees" had visited Crawford's homestead in an attempt to capture the Swamp Fox. Baker, Kirkman later claims, hid near enough to the Crawfords' place to overhear the conversation there. He supposedly told Rollins that he was "going for them."[36]

Unable to locate Baker, Kirkman and his group began the return trip to Boston on July 25, 1867. Shortly after crossing the Sulphur River at Pettit's Ferry, the detachment was ambushed by Baker and his men. This initial encounter lasted briefly. The outlaws fired "a good many shots" at the Federal contingent. (Baker told them that "his name was Johnson and that he had twenty-five men behind him in the woods.") Once the shooting began, Brown spurred his horse, leading all but Kirkman out of gunfire range. Kirkman, "utterly unimpressed" by Brown's "hasty abandonment" of him in the field and incensed at Brown's behavior, believed he had been deserted. Eventually, they all regrouped and retreated into Boston. Baker followed.[37]

Later the same morning, Baker entered Boston, walked into a store, "called for oysters and sardines," and challenged the Yankees. Kirkman and the soldiers attacked Baker in a "ten pin alley" adjoining the store. Baker had every intention of shooting Kirkman. The agent had the same idea. Baker spotted a gun sticking out of a window and jumped aside. He then fired "16 or more shots" at the Federals in another building, striking an infantry man with fifteen "large buckshot," killing him instantly. Kirkman wounded Baker in the right arm. Baker also had his hat shot off but made a successful escape, hiding at the house of a local resident. Kirkman expected his return.[38]

36. *Ibid.* A Crawford son, Frank, appears in MCR (Ninth Census), 1870, Davis (Cass) County, Texas, p. 24, RG 29, NA. He resided in Douglassville, where he kept boarders. Frank and his wife were both Georgia born.

37. WGK to Malloy, September 26, 1867, pp. 63–65; WGK to T. W. Clafflin (Commander, Mount Pleasant), July 25, 1867, pp. 13–14, both in Vol. 67, Texas, BRFAL, RG 105, NA. On Kirkman's praise for the corporal who acquitted himself well when attacked by Baker, see WGK to Ira C. Clapp, August 20, 1867, Vol. 67, pp. 30–31, Texas, BRFAL; RG 105, NA; WGK to Starr, October 17, 1867, DT, LR, S-144, Box 3, USACC, RG 393, NA; Richter, " 'The Revolver Rules the Day!': Colonel DeWitt C. Brown and the Freedmen's Bureau in Paris, Texas, 1867–1868," *SwHQ*, XCIII (January, 1990), 310.

38. Latchford to WGK, August 4, 1867, pp. 14–15; Allanson to WGK, August 5, 1867, p. 12; Adam Kramer to WGK, August 11, 1867, pp. 16–19; Adam to WGK, September 18, 1867, pp. 20–21, all in Vol. 66; WGK to Clafflin, July 25, 1867, pp. 13–14; WGK to JTK, July 25, 1867, pp. 14–16; WGK to JTK, September 4, 1867, pp. 43–44; WGK to Latchford, July 26, 1867, pp. 16–18; WGK to Latchford, August 20, 1867, pp. 32–33; WGK to Richardson, November 13, 1867, pp. 108–111; WGK to Kramer, August 1, 1867, p. 18, all in Vol. 67; WGK to Allanson,

The soldier Baker killed, Albert E. Titus, was twenty-two years old. Five foot seven and three-quarter inches tall, Titus had gray eyes, dark hair, and a fair complexion. He had been born in Waldsboro, Maine, and had been a farmer before the war. Titus enlisted for three years when he joined Company E of the 20th Maine Infantry in August, 1862. Serving throughout the conflict, he was promoted from private to sergeant, and completed his tour of duty in Washington, D.C. Disillusioned with the agricultural life, he reenlisted in January, 1867, and by the middle of the year was dead at Baker's hand. Kirkman felt deeply the loss of Titus, calling him a "good and brave soldier." Titus was buried on July 26.[39]

The Democratic newspaper of Marshall, the *Texas Republican,* emphasized that not all white conservatives shared Baker's hatred ("deep and damning as perdition itself") for the government. Reports to the contrary, the newspaper declared that the citizens "had no sympathy" for him. To aid the army, they "commenced discharging and reloading their guns, at every house about town, and assured the Federal commander, that in case there came on another fight, they would all assist the Federal troops." Texas Bostonians did not want their attitude "misconstrued in consequence of the acts of one who is not their countyman, and with whom they have neither alliance nor sympathy."[40] The citizens also desired the soldiers' removal.

Most Baker writers have suggested that the soldiers did not perform well when confronted with the desperado. Kirkman reported, however, that the "non-commissioned officers and men did their duty bravely" in trying to arrest him. In Kirkman's estimation, what made an encounter with Baker so terrifying was that his "life appears to be of no value to himself." Deeply sorrowed at the lost of Titus, the Boston agent immediately had to request two replacements; one for Titus and another to relieve a corporal whom Kirkman had seen "under the influence of liquor several times." He re-

October 8, 1867, AC, LR, K-14, all in Texas, BRFAL, RG 105, NA. See also Richter, " 'The Revolver Rules the Day!' " 310.

39. Albert E. Titus, Compiled Military Service Record; Titus, Enlistment Papers, both in RG 94, NA. Another soldier was wounded in the affray. Kirkman was indeed a compassionate man. He later requested twenty dollars from headquarters to have the grave of Titus properly enclosed and covered with sod. There is a suggestion that Titus was disinterred and reburied in the National Cemetery at Alexandria, Louisiana; WGK to C. E. Morse (AAAG, DT), May 26, 1868, DT, LR, K-74, Box 11, USACC, RG 393, NA.

40. *Texas Republican* (Marshall), August 3, 1867, p. 2. For the hostility to the Bureau exhibited in this section and on Kirkman's performance as an agent, see Crouch, "To Die in Boston (Texas, That Is)," in his *The Freedmen's Bureau and Black Texans,* 69–101.

quired dependable men. Kirkman also specified that when the replacements traveled to Boston, they should wear "citizens clothes."[41]

Though pro-Baker chroniclers have presented many exaggerated and obviously false stories about how Baker made fools of Kirkman and the military in general, prior to July, 1867, Baker had apparently caused the army no concern. Rather, in the first years following the war, he was involved in his feud with Orr. Nonetheless, Eason, Taylor, Breihan, and others take apparent delight in describing how Baker stymied the army. These descriptions supply no chronology but provide many tales that are clearly based on folklore. They have little documentary base or connection to actual events. Occasionally, specific Baker attacks on the military are mentioned, but most of the material consists of invented accounts showing how Baker outwitted the Federal forces.

After the Boston fracas, Kirkman naively believed Baker could be found and brought to justice if the state offered a large reward. He had been informed that Baker had raised a crop on a farm in northeastern Cass County the previous season. Baker had sisters living there as well, one of whom Kirkman had seen. Kirkman thought the women had harbored Baker after he escaped from Boston. The Boston agent described the condition of the area Baker inhabited as "bad." Because of Baker's terrorizing activities, Kirkman believed that additional troops were required to preserve the lives of the innocent, but his request for more soldiers from three army posts in the region went unheeded.[42]

Kirkman enlisted Governor E. M. Pease's assistance in establishing an official reward for Baker's apprehension. Legal requirements had to be met. State law required that the arresting individual have a certified affidavit accusing the guilty party of a specific crime. In lieu of the affidavit, Kirkman needed a certified copy of the indictment and a sworn statement that the

41. WGK to Latchford (Commander, Post of Jefferson), July 26, 1867, pp. 16–18; August 20, 1867, pp. 32–33; WGK to Kramer, August 1, 1867, p. 18, all in Vol. 67, Texas, BRFAL, RG 105, NA.

42. WGK to Griffin (AC, Texas), August 22, 1867, AC, LR, K-8; Latchford to WGK, August 4, 1867, pp. 14–15; Allanson to WGK, August 5, 1867, p. 12; Kramer to WGK, August 11, 1867, pp. 16–19; September 18, 1867, pp. 20–21, all in Vol. 66; WGK to Clafflin, July 25, 1867, pp. 13–14; WGK to JTK, July 25, 1867, pp. 14–16; September 4, 1867, pp. 43–44; WGK to Latchford July 26, 1867, pp. 16–18; August 20, 1867, pp. 32–33; WGK to Richardson, November 13, 1867, pp. 108–111; WGK to Kramer, August 1, 1867, p. 18, all in Vol. 67; WGK to Allanson October 8, 1867, AC, LR, K-14, all from Texas, BRFAL, RG 105, NA. See also Richter, " 'The Revolver Rules the Day!' " 310.

criminal remained at large. Kirkman immediately began collecting affidavits. He received orders to have the sheriff or another official compile the necessary information to offer a reward. He recommended setting the bounty at $2,500. In mid-October, 1867, Governor Pease issued a proclamation establishing a reward of $1,000 for the delivery of Baker's body to the Bowie County sheriff.[43]

Baker had finally created enough havoc in the tri-state region to attract the notice of the District of Texas headquarters. The district's commander, Major General Joseph J. Reynolds, who also served as Assistant Commissioner of the Freedmen's Bureau, issued special orders for Baker's apprehension. The military had reportedly received reliable information that Baker, "a notorious desperado," was at large in Titus County (outside his normal area of activity); and they called upon all citizens to "arrest him, or to give such information" to military authorities that might assist in his capture. Any person harboring or abetting Baker would be "held responsible for all violations of law committed by and traced" to him while he remained at large.[44]

Baker, an absolute "terror" (Kirkman's word) to blacks, loyal whites, and the Union army, thrived on death. An Arkansas Bureau agent described him as "a notorious Texas desperado who has killed several soldiers in the adjoining county to this in Texas and boasts that he has killed an hundred negroes." The agent also believed the government should offer a reward and "levy a tax on the citizens of his county to meet it for allowing a highwayman and murderer to 'run the road' with impunity, and harbor him from justice because he confines his depredations to soldiers, union citizens and ne-

43. WGK to Griffin, August 22, 1867, pp. 34–35; WGK to Roberts, September 27, 1867, p. 67, both in Vol. 67; Allanson to WGK, August 5, 1867, p. 12; Thad McRae (Private Secretary; Governor Pease) to Roberts, September 13, 1867, pp. 28, 30; Roberts to WGK, September 23, 1867, pp. 28–29; Endorsements, Vernou, June 8, 1868, p. 177, all in Vol. 66; WGK to Reynolds, May 27, 1868, Vol. 68, pp. 88–89, all in Texas, BRFAL, RG 105, NA Smith to Bennett, November 30, 1867, AC, NR, LR, S-1593, Box 11, Arkansas, BRFAL, RG 105, NA. Watlington wrote that the reward eventually totaled $7,500; R. H. Watlington, "Memoirs" (Typescript in TSL), 82. For background on Watlington and his view of Baker, see Jean Elizabeth Lovil, "Cullen Baker," *The Junior Historian*, VII (November, 1946), 25–28.

44. Special Orders, No. 204, District of Texas, Austin, November 14, 1867. Adjutant General Reconstruction Records, Box 401/860, Folder 8, October–November, 1867, TSL; C. S. Mower (AAAG, DT) to Starr, November 16, 1867, DT, LS, Vol. 4, p. 476, M1165, Reel 6, USACC, RG 393, NA. The army also sought the fugitive John Duty of Red River County, who was likewise described as a notorious desperado.

groes." Baker's hatred seemed boundless and, according to Kirkman, he concentrated it against the government.[45]

Baker and his gang soon struck again. In September, 1867, near Linden, the outlaws (twelve of them) attacked a squad of four soldiers from the garrison at Jefferson, who guarded a wagonload of supplies destined for Kirkman's 20th Infantry escort in Boston. The band killed one soldier, mortally wounded another, and slightly injured the remaining two. The bandits carried off the mules, the wagon, and all supplies. What puzzled the Marshall Bureau agent, A. G. Malloy, was that Baker's "murderous exploits" had occurred within thirty miles of the Mount Pleasant post where two companies of the 6th Cavalry were stationed, which had not yet been summoned to assist in the search for the desperado and his men.[46]

Malloy also related that he daily received complaints from "Cass, Marion, Rusk and Panola Counties, of the bad treatment of the freedpeople by their employers." A poor cotton crop had been the year's result, so the employers were "anxious to get rid of their freedmen, and resort to every possible dishonorable means to accomplish it." A terror to the "well-disposed citizens" of these counties, Baker received support from a "certain class"—who were in the majority, according to Malloy—that rendered him "all possible aid," regarding him as a representative of the Lost Cause. Baker was useful to this class because he controlled their freedmen by inspiring fear, not hesitating to "shoot them on the slightest complaint made by their employers."[47]

Malloy realized what a demoralizing effect Baker had upon the local populace. He determined that a concerted effort should be made to capture Baker and "his desperate associates." Unless this were done, Malloy declared, other "desperate men" would follow his example, and "murder and rapine [would] be the order of the day." He was puzzled by the military's unsuccessful efforts to capture him, either by mounting a major hunt for Baker or by using their troops stationed at army posts throughout the region to advantage. Although they were not particularly useful in the field, Malloy did have a company of the 20th Infantry (forty-five men) with him at Mar-

45. V. V. Smith (Agent, Lewisville, Ark.) to Jonathan E. Bennett (AAAG), November 30, 1867, AC, NR, Lr, S-1593, Box 11, Arkansas, BRFAL, Rg 105, NA. WGK to JTK, July 25, 1867, p. 15; WGK to Latchford, July 26, 1867, p. 17, both in Vol. 67, Texas, BRFAL, RG 105, NA.

46. Malloy (Agent, Jefferson) to Charles Garretson (AAAG), September 30, 1867, Vol. 134, n. p., Texas, BRFAL, RG 105, NA; James Smallwood, "When the Klan Rode: White Terror in Reconstruction Texas," *Journal of the West*, XXV (October, 1986), 6.

47. Malloy to Garretson, September 30, 1867, AC, OR, M-46, Texas, BRFAL, RG 105, NA.

shall. But despite the presence of troops at Mount Pleasant and Marshall, Baker struck the military again.[48]

Kirkman firmly believed that Baker could be located and brought to justice, if the state offered a reward larger than $1,000 for his arrest. He also realized that Baker would attack again and that cavalry would be needed to stop him. After all, the cavalry's speed could somewhat compensate for Baker's knowledge of the terrain and his tactics of ambush, if an encounter occurred. Thus, the Boston agent requested that a mobile detachment from the Mount Pleasant post be ordered to Cass County as Baker's band reportedly numbered from fifteen to thirty. Although Baker committed depredations in Arkansas, he never ventured too far from where he grew up and frequently appeared back in Cass County.[49]

Nevertheless, all the available evidence suggests that the military failed to respond to Baker's threat to peace. He took full advantage of this failure. On Sunday, October 6, 1867, two miles south of the Sulphur River, the notorious outlaw and one or two other companions killed a teamster and a soldier, and wounded another soldier. One man from the escort escaped. The soldiers were members of the 26th Infantry, which was bringing rations to Boston. Baker and his cohorts ran the team off toward Douglassville or the Sulphur swamp. According to sympathetic writers, Baker distributed the supplies to neighbors. In return for his supposed generosity and "bravery," Jefferson citizens allegedly gave him two new revolvers and a shotgun.[50]

As soon as he learned of the wagontrain attack, Kirkman, "at a negro cabin near where the murder and capture took place," wrote a hasty dispatch on brown paper to the Mount Pleasant post commander, S. H. Starr,

48. *Ibid.*

49. Willis to WGK, October 4, 1867, Vol. 66, pp. 60, 62; WGK to Allanson, October 8, 1867, Vol. 67, pp. 76–77; WGK to Garretson, October 4, 1867, pp. 81–82; October 8, 1867, Vol. 67, pp. 77–78; WGK to Starr, October 7, 1867, Vol. 67, p. 80, all in Texas, BRFAL, RG 105, NA.

50. WGK to Allanson, October 8, 1867 and WGK to Garretson, October 8, 1867, AC, LR, K-14, Texas, BRFAL, RG 105, NA. S. H. Starr (Commander, Mount Pleasant Post) to H. A. Swartwout (AAAG, DT), October 18, 1867, Entry 5, LS, pp. 40–43; Allanson to Starr, October 7, 1867, and WGK to Starr, October 8, 1867, LR, all in Post Records of Mount Pleasant, USACC, RG 393, NA. N. B. Anderson to Charles E. DeMorse (editor, Clarksville *Standard*), October 7, 1867; C. S. Roberts (Agent, Clarksville) to Starr, both in DT, LR, S-144, Box 3, USACC, RG 393, NA. The identity of Baker's companion on this raid is not certain. He may have been Ben Griffith, Wild Bill Longley, or Matthew "Dummy" Kirby. See also Orr, *Life of the Notorious Desperado*, 120–21; Triplett, "Cullen Montgomery Baker," 456. Sensational and unreliable accounts are presented in Bartholomew, *Cullen Baker*, 57; Breihan, "Cullen Baker," 79–80; Taylor, "Swamp Fox of the Sulphur," 53–55.

which the latter received at 8:30 P.M. on the evening of October 7. Shortly after sending the notice to Starr, Kirkman and four soldiers started in pursuit of Baker and his companions. To reinforce his earlier message to Starr, the Boston Bureau agent dispatched two of the soldiers to Mount Pleasant. Kirkman and the two remaining infantrymen found the body of the teamster. Returning to Boston, Kirkman soon received six additional soldiers for protection, as Baker had threatened to kill him.

Finally—and much of the credit for this is due Kirkman—the military bestirred itself to take steps to capture Baker. By this time, the military commander at Mount Pleasant (who had cavalry at his disposal) was being bombarded with information about Baker and his exploits. After he received Kirkman's message, Starr immediately made preparations to send a detachment into the field. Meanwhile, additional information about Baker's activities came to Starr from the Clarksville Freedmen's Bureau agent C. S. Roberts and from Lieutenant John S. Allanson of the 26th Infantry, who was stationed in Jefferson. Allanson had been tracking Baker's attacks. It had been his two men whom Baker killed when he ambushed the wagontrain.[51]

On October 8, under orders from Starr, First Lieutenant Moses Wiley of the 6th U.S. Cavalry left the Mount Pleasant post in Titus County at 3:00 A.M. with four men (one non-commissioned officer and three privates) and proceeded toward Boston. Wiley's orders were to capture Baker and arrest any of his cohorts. The five soldiers traveled in civilian dress so that they might "mingle with the citizens and obtain information" about Baker. The army should have realized that any outsider or stranger would immediately become the object of suspicion. Baker's network was fairly extensive, and the movements of the military always concerned him.[52]

Starr learned soon after Wiley's departure that Baker's gang consisted of approximately fifteen men. On the afternoon of the same day, Starr also detached Lieutenant Jeremiah C. Wilcox with nine men with the hope that this group would coordinate its efforts to apprehend Baker with Wiley's expedition. Starr wrote that he feared they would "have no success, though two small parties cooperating will have a better chance than *one* large one." Amazingly, neither Wiley nor Wilcox was informed of the other's mission.

51. S. H. Starr (Commander, Mount Pleasant) to H. A. Swartwout (AAAG, DT), October 18, 1867, Entry 5, LS, pp. 40–43, Post Records of Mount Pleasant, USACC, RG 393, NA.

52. Starr to Swartwout, October 18, 1867, pp. 40–43; Starr to Charles E. Morse (AAAG, DT), November 8, 1867, pp. 46–47, *ibid.*

Starr had not as yet been able to formulate an effective plan to entrap Baker.[53]

Wilcox returned to Mount Pleasant on the afternoon of October 13 after having captured one of Baker's gang, a man named John Kelley. Kelley was imprisoned. Wilcox had neither communicated nor cooperated with Wiley. He had learned, however, that Wiley had reached Boston. Based upon Wilcox's information, Starr sent one noncommissioned officer and three privates to reinforce Wiley and to warn him that "there is great fear that the murderers will learn that you are awaiting them at Boston" and thus avoid the town. If Starr's suspicion proved true, Wiley was directed to find "a guide and hunt [Baker] up in [the] Sulphur Swamp, or wherever he most probably is. Spare no horse flesh, and persevere as long as there is any hope of success."[54]

If Wiley did not capture Baker—and Starr realized that the prospects of capture were not good—then Wiley should learn all he could of Baker's haunts, his sympathizers, and his sources of supplies: in short, all the information possible about the leader and his band. Starr received numerous communications from Wiley between October 9 and 17, keeping him apprised of the lieutenant's field progress. Starr presumed that headquarters records would show several other acts of hostility against the United States, including murders of its soldiers, committed by this "noted brigand." By this date, Baker had clearly become the nemesis of the army in northeast Texas.[55]

Upon his arrival in Boston, Wiley conferred with Kirkman. He learned that a man named Barnes had told Kirkman that Baker had threatened to kill him (Barnes). This man desired a gun with which to defend himself, but he also claimed he was well acquainted with the neighborhood in which Baker operated and would be willing to act as a guide for the detachment. Believing Barnes to be one of Baker's gang, Wiley arranged a private meeting in an attempt to judge his honesty. Wiley represented himself to Barnes as a friend of Baker's and charged Barnes with having threatened to kill Baker. After the Wiley meeting, in a surprise move, Barnes immediately approached Kirkman, informing the agent of what Wiley had said.[56]

53. Starr to C. S. Roberts (Clarksville), October 9, 1867, *ibid.* Wiley later learned that Wilcox had been dispatched from Mount Pleasant to cooperate with him.

54. Starr to Swartwout, October 18, 1867, pp. 40–43; Starr to Moses Wiley (6th U. S. Cavalry), October 13, 1867, pp. 39–40, *ibid.*

55. Starr to Wiley, October 13, 1867, pp. 39–40; Starr to Swartwout, October 18, 1867, pp. 40–43, Entry 5, LS, Post Records of Mount Pleasant, USACC, RG 393, NA.

56. Wiley to Post Adjutant (Mount Pleasant), October 20, 1867, DT, LR, W-46, Box 2, USACC, RG 393, NA.

Now believing in Barnes's honesty, Wiley issued him a gun and promised to pay fifty dollars in gold for his services if they succeeded in capturing Baker. Engaged to survey Baker's neighborhood and to learn what he could about him, Barnes would then pilot Wiley and his group to where Baker might be. Barnes left Boston on the evening of October 9, and Wiley set to work to gather information about the country and the people in the area. Joining a party of three Cass County citizens in search of horse thieves, Wiley rode with them to Rondo, Arkansas. There he learned that Ben Griffith had passed through the town on the Thursday preceding the October 6 capture of the government wagon.[57]

While in Rondo, Griffith had inquired about Baker and declared he wished to join him. At this point, Wiley believed Griffith had accompanied Baker in the wagon seizure. Reported to be a "desperate character," Griffith fled from Richmond, Arkansas, because troops stationed at Rocky Comfort pursued him. Returning to Boston on October 12, Wiley waited two days for the arrival of Barnes. Barnes uncovered nothing important except that Baker might be in his own neighborhood. He had discovered that the mules Baker had taken in the raid were killed at Evans on the Douglassville and Line Ferry road. On October 14, Wiley received Starr's communication, delivered by the corporal and three other men sent to reinforce him.[58]

To avoid observation, Wiley left Boston at 11:00 P.M. the same night with Barnes and the detachment. Proceeding through the woods and fording the Sulphur River at Knights Bluff, they waited in the swamp until the next evening, when they approached the house of L. R. Rollins, a friend of Baker's, whom Kirkman had previously investigated. They found no one there. After searching several other homes that night, they eventually camped overnight in the Sulphur bottom. Barnes had previously met a freedman named Moses Connelly, who informed him that Baker often stayed in the swamps at Horseshoe Bend, especially when troops looked for him. Baker took his meals at the house of Jack Bell, who lived close to this area of swamps.[59]

Hoping to surprise Baker at Bell's, the group arrived there at 7:00 A.M. on October 16. They found only Bell's wife and children at home. Bell had gone to Bright Star. They proceeded to Baker's home and searched the premises, finding only his sister. Wiley confiscated a double-barreled shotgun and some ammunition. After checking several other houses in the vi-

57. *Ibid.*
58. *Ibid.*
59. *Ibid.*

cinity, the detachment returned to Boston. As no leads on Baker surfaced, they went back to the Mount Pleasant post on October 19. Barnes agreed to keep a vigil for Baker and report to the military if the outlaw returned home. Moses Connelly and Frank Johns, another freedman who lived in Baker's neighborhood, promised to furnish any relevant information they gathered.[60]

The well-known destruction of Baker's wife's belongings, which many writers refer to as the basis for Baker's hatred of the military, may have occurred during Wiley's attempt to find him in mid-October, 1867. This, as far as we know, is the sole occasion presented in the army records on which the military found Baker's place of residence and what personal effects it contained. A military report would not necessarily include an account of a violation of a citizen's rights, but in the report in question there is no hint of such conduct. The soldiers may have violated Baker's private treasures, but the evidence for this alleged offense is only second- and third-hand corroboration. Anyway, Baker may only have been using such an offense as an excuse to carry out his vendetta against them.

Baker always seemed to find out whenever an army detachment was "secretly" dispatched to capture him. Friends often saved him from the Federal authorities. In the case of Wiley's pursuit of him, a Bowie County resident named James McQuotter provided Baker with information. Suspecting that the army was up to something, he rode to Baker's house declaring that soldiers were coming. This forewarning was relayed back to Kirkman through a black man (no name given) who heard McQuotter inform Baker. Baker went to the house of a man named Maxie, where he hid until the danger had passed. On learning what happened, Kirkman asked his superiors whether Rollins, Crawford, McQuotter, and Maxie should be arrested.[61]

While Kirkman investigated Baker's support from the community, Wiley, in the field chasing Baker, believed that Jack Bell (not Ben Griffith) had accompanied Baker when they captured the wagon on October 6. During that incident, Baker had compelled a freedman who lived near the scene to drive the wagon several miles. (Thomas Taylor reports that his name was Charles Johnson.) Wiley talked with this freedman, who described the man with Baker as a "little man" with "one eye." Barnes, the hired guide, confirmed the description. Wiley lists the members of Baker's gang; they included Rollins, Ben Griffith, Lee Rames of Bright Star (the census has

60. *Ibid.*

61. WGK to Richardson, November 13, 1867, Vol. 67, pp. 108–11, *ibid.*

"Raines"), and John Kelley (who had earlier been captured by Wilcox and imprisoned at Mount Pleasant), John Cooke of Cass County, and Bell. Wiley ascertained that Baker, Griffith, Rames, and Elisha P. Guest (another well-known desperado from the Clarksville area) had captured the wagon.[62]

According to Wiley, Baker had a "great many friends," and "those not friendly" were "afraid to speak of him." He exercised "*a species of terrorism* over every one within his reach, and owing to the successful manner in which he has fought the troops the respect for Gov[ernmen]t authority is very much depreciated in the minds of all the citizens." Wiley recommended that forty men be sent through Bowie and Cass Counties to arrest everyone suspected of having aided the Baker gang and to "*counter-act his terrorism* with terrorism from the troops, and for the sake of peace the people will of themselves root out all such characters." Those "not actually in with him, hold themselves as neutral spectators of what is going on."[63]

Wiley understood better than most Baker's elusive nature. After extensive contact with Baker's neighborhood, talking to county citizens and surveying the terrain, the lieutenant realized that he faced a daunting task. He believed that it would be "almost impossible" to capture Baker alive. Wiley represented the Swamp Fox as a desperate man who would "fight to the last against any odds." The recent altercation in Boston, Texas, with United States soldiers, including Kirkman, went "far to prove his character in this respect," observed Wiley. To Wiley, like Kirkman, the offer of a "large reward for [Baker] *dead* or alive" was the "most practicable method of ridding the country of this desperado."[64]

Wiley reported to Starr that Baker frequently lingered in the neighborhood of his own home but did not stay at any fixed place. The house, located on the Sulphur Fork of the Red River, was about three miles above Line Ferry. Close by was the Sulphur bottom: a swamp, an "immense jungle" about twelve miles long and five miles wide, interspersed with hog paths, where Baker often hid and where he took the stolen wagon. As a deserter during the war, Baker had availed himself of the labyrinths of the swamp and managed to elude all pursuit.[65]

---

62. Wiley to Post Adjutant (Mount Pleasant), October 20, 1867, DT, LR, W-46, Box 2, USACC, RG 393, NA.

63. *Ibid.* Italics ours.

64. Wiley (1st Lt.; 6th Cav.) to Starr, October 13, 1867, DT, LR, S-144, Box 3, USACC, RG 393, NA.

65. *Ibid.*

The field military understood what they were up against. Starr realized Baker had long been "a terror to the people of the several counties through which he roam[ed]." Baker entertained a "special hostility" to the army, and many sympathized with him "for that reason." All capture efforts had proved unavailing; Starr saw no hope of success. The unfavorable influence of Baker's "crime and hostility" to the army, his success in "beating off small parties sent against him, and his impunity thus far," had produced disaffection in the "minds of the people." Starr judged that it was of the "first importance for the interests of the United States" that this man's "career be ended without delay."[66]

Starr recommended, like Kirkman and Wiley, that a large reward be offered for Baker dead or alive. He suggested eight thousand dollars, "as a smaller sum . . . would be useless." A proportionate amount should be offered for the capture of each of his band, payable on conviction by a military commission. The country over which Baker ranged was densely wooded, with swamps, ravines, and abundant hiding places. Troops sent after him were recognized instantly by their garb, allowing sympathizers and confederates to immediately convey information of their presence. Many rejoiced at the trouble and annoyance he caused the "damned yankees." They expressed the opinion that Baker did right in killing the soldiers and capturing the wagon.

Opposition existed among the citizens against "delivering up to the authorities, any man for a reward, and the sum must be large to induce any to act in opposition to this prejudice." It was thought that whoever earned the reward "must be prepared to abandon everything, and leave the country, for his life would be in imminent danger." To promote this scheme, Starr suggested that handbills be distributed in all the northeastern counties of Texas, in the southern portion of the Indian Territory, and in southwest Arkansas and northwest Louisiana. The government should honor obligations for guides, such as the one Wiley entered into with Barnes, and pay in gold in case the military's enterprise should be successful.[67]

Starr claimed there were two ways to limit or crush Baker's effectiveness. First, soldiers should be stationed at Douglassville. "This little village and neighborhood is one of the worst" in this section of the country, he wrote. Cass County freedmen were "worse off by far than before emancipation;

66. Starr to Swartwout, October 18, 1867, Entry 5, LS, pp. 40–43, Post Records of Mount Pleasant, USACC, RG 393, NA.
67. *Ibid.*

they are more subdued, because their lives are of no value in the estimation of the people, and are taken on the least pretext." Second, Starr reiterated that the reward offered by Governor Pease was too small. A substantial reward, along with the soldiers, would have a "most beneficial effect, in subduing the turbulent, lawless and hostile spirit of this section."[68]

Starr had little patience with the citizens of this region. Even when they appeared before him complaining of attacks against the freedmen and freedwomen and problems with desperadoes like Baker, they refused to assist the military in ending the chaotic conditions. When an individual reported the wounding of several former slaves, Starr said he would attempt to capture the perpetrators if the complainant identified and pointed them out. "I am a little disgusted with those who cry so loudly," he told headquarters, "and yet will not lift a finger for their own protection, or give reliable information to lead to the capture and punishment of the villains against whom they complain."[69] Ultimately, Starr misjudged them.

Starr summed up his understanding of the impact of Baker's activities on local Reconstruction efforts. He had killed and wounded U.S. soldiers, captured one government wagon of subsistence stores as well as its team, defied national sovereignty, and threatened to attack the Mount Pleasant post. "He has brought contempt upon the troops of the United States by defeating and intimidating, on two occasions . . . single handed, detachments sent after him, and by eluding every attempt at his capture," wrote the post commander. The "inability of our troops to catch him," Starr said, "and the ignominious defeat and flight of small parties of soldiers sent after him, is bringing the troops into contempt and encouraging lawlessness in this section."[70]

Even Starr was amazed that Baker continued to receive such substantial support throughout the area. The distressed post commander claimed that Baker had killed many other individuals, both white and black, and continued to terrorize "all well disposed citizens." Nobody seemed willing to organize a group to eliminate Baker's troublesome presence. On October 21, a black man had been waylaid while returning to the post with a letter for the commanding officer. The waylayer, who claimed that he was a member of the Baker gang, tied the freedman to a tree and robbed him of the public

68. *Ibid.;* Starr to Morse, November 8, 1867, Entry 5, LS, pp. 46–47, *ibid.*

69. Starr to Morse, November 8, 1867, Entry 5, LS, pp. 46–47, *ibid.*

70. "Report of Lieut. Wiley of Expedition to Capture C. Baker, Highwayman"; Endorsement, Starr, October 23, 1867, LR, W-46, DT, LS, Box 2, USACC, RG 393, NA.

horse he was riding, along with the saddle, the bridle, a Spencer carbine, and a revolver. As long as Baker remained at large, the section would remain unsettled.[71]

But Kirkman constantly attempted to keep track of Baker, whom he reported to be within thirty-five miles of Mount Pleasant in late October, on his mule, which he attempted to trade for an iron gray horse. He intended, wrote Kirkman, to propose fair terms for the release of Kelley, whom he claimed was innocent. If these terms were not met and Kelley not freed, Baker would "let him out." Kirkman warned Starr that if Baker had not yet appeared, he soon would. Baker's plan might consist of capturing some of the soldiers when they were "in the bushes or off their guard, and propose an exchange." Baker did not appear at Mount Pleasant to reclaim Kelley, but he nonetheless remained on Kirkman's mind.[72]

Kirkman enlisted the assistance of Hiram F. Willis, the Rocky Comfort, Arkansas, Freedmen's Bureau official, whom Baker later murdered. Kirkman had information that some of Baker's gang were on the Arkansas side of the border. Willis, who with his twelve-soldier detachment had not yet encountered Baker, presumed he was a "desperate character" and agreed to assist Kirkman in arresting him. Willis, in turn, desired Kirkman's aid in arresting Ben Griffith and a man named Burke, two other desperadoes. Burke had fired four shots at Willis. The two agents searched for Griffith and Burke, but these men had left the immediate vicinity. Kirkman and Willis did discover a block house that the outlaws had recently inhabited.[73]

Whether it had been Baker or Ben Griffith, or the two in tandem, who had attacked the supply train, Kirkman and Willis believed they both had to be suppressed. Cooperating and using an old plan of Willis', Kirkman and a half-dozen soldiers in civilian clothes crossed the Red River and joined the Arkansas agent. Led by local blacks, they searched for Griffith's hideout. Like Baker, Griffith was a consummate escape artist. He had learned of the planned attack and departed in great haste, leaving clothing and food behind. Kirkman continued to share with Willis information on

71. *Ibid.;* Starr to C. S. Roberts (Clarksville), October 9, 1867, pp. 38–39, *ibid.;* Starr to Swartwout, October 18, 1867, Entry 5, LS, pp. 40–43, Post Records of Mount Pleasant, USACC, RG 393, NA.

72. WGK to Starr, October 17, 1867; Allanson to Starr, October 14, 1867, both in DT, LR, S-144, Box 3, USACC, RG 393, NA.

73. Hiram F. Willis (Agent, Rocky Comfort) to WGK, October 4, 1867, pp. 119–20; Willis to Bennett, November 30, 1867, p. 163, both in Vol. 177, Arkansas, BRFAL, RG 105, NA.

the Texas activities of Griffith until the latter's death at the hands of a Bureau agent.[74]

According to sources, the peculiar topography of the tri-state region and the Indian Territory involved helped account for the desperadoes' elusiveness. The bottoms of the Sulphur and Red Rivers contained almost impenetrable canebrakes that provided them with perfect cover. Although Kirkman and Willis scoured the countryside in search of clues as to where Baker and his confidantes might be hiding, no positive evidence could be gleaned about Baker's whereabouts. The agents discovered that reliable information on Baker's background, his personal status, and especially his whereabouts was nearly impossible to obtain. Local inhabitants were either too afraid of or too sympathetic to Baker to disclose anything.[75]

Neither Bureau headquarters nor the army responded effectively to Baker's initial depredations. Clearly, a Bureau agent in northeast Texas could do little against Baker's ilk without military support. The army's lackadaisical response was partially due to the yellow fever epidemic in Galveston, which claimed Charles Griffin, the Texas District's army commander. Griffin was head of the Bureau in the area and briefly the chief of the Fifth Military District. At the Fifth Military District office in New Orleans, changes in personnel hampered efforts to establish a basic strategy or a consistent policy. With Griffin's death, Joseph A. Mower assumed command of the New Orleans office at the same time that Joseph J. Reynolds became head of the District of Texas and of the state's Freedmen's Bureau.[76]

Several other bureaucratic problems impeded Kirkman and his fellow agents in northeast Texas in their efforts to capture Baker. From mid-1867 until late 1868, Texas Bureau chiefs and army commanders considered this region under the jurisdiction of the Louisiana military, so it remained in a

74. Willis to WGK, October 4, 1867, pp. 119–20; Willis to Bennett, November 30, 1867, p. 163, both in Vol. 177, Arkansas, BRFAL, RG 105, NA. Richter, " 'A Dear Little Job': Second Lieutenant Hiram F. Willis, Freedmen's Bureau Agent in Southwestern Arkansas, 1866–1868," *AHQ*, L (Summer, 1991), 193–94; " 'The Revolver Rules the Day!' " 303–32.

75. WGK to Garretson, October 26, 1867, p. 89; WGK to Starr, October 17, 1867, p. 82; October 20, 1867, p. 84, all in Vol. 67, Texas, BRFAL, RG 105, NA.

76. Richter, *The Army in Texas During Reconstruction, 1865–1870* (College Station, Tex., 1987); Richter, *Overreached on All Sides*; Robert W. Shook, "Federal Occupation and Administration of Texas, 1865–1870" (Ph.D. dissertation, North Texas State University, 1970). Shook summarized his ideas in "The Federal Military in Texas, 1865–1870," *Texas Military History*, VI (Spring, 1967), 3–53. James E. Sefton, *The United Army and Reconstruction, 1865–1877* (Baton Rouge, 1967).

state of limbo. Kirkman and other regional Bureau officers were often ignored when they requested cavalry. Many troops stationed in this area were
infantry; thus, mobility was limited. (The cavalry was at headquarters for
"show".) Richter, who has studied the army most intensely, concludes that
the commanders "failed to comprehend the dedication and viciousness of
the white opposition in northeastern Texas" to the Bureau and blacks.[77]

Ultimately, the Texas military gained the support of their superiors to follow the reward strategy to eliminate Baker. Joseph J. Reynolds told Starr to
continue to make every effort to capture Baker, but he knew the military's
dismal record in regard to the desperado. He now implemented the reward
scheme based upon recommendations from the field—recommended despite the opinion of those in the field that the small amount of money appropriated by the state to be offered as rewards for the arrest and delivery
of murderers could be of little assistance. The governor had established a
one-thousand-dollar bounty for Baker, dead or alive. This fact had been
communicated to the Clarksville Bureau agent with the governor's suggestion that it had "better be not published," though the field men could use
their "discretion on this point." Despite the governor's request, military
headquarters felt that if such a paper were distributed throughout Titus,
Red River, and adjoining counties, it would lead to the apprehension of
Baker and other desperadoes, or eliminate their presence entirely. In this
presumption, they were wrong. Cavalry and mobile forces would ultimately
be required to capture Baker.[78]

Two other organizational problems confronted the United States Army in
its efforts to capture Baker. First, there were several army posts in the region whose commanders often ignored Baker's presence. Lacking coordina-
tion, the expeditions sent against Baker did not prevent the Swamp Fox
from eluding capture. Second, district headquarters complained that a
shortage of funds shackled their efforts. They had pleaded with the Fifth
Military District commander to provide the extra money needed to pay for
special detectives and police service. The desperadoes could not be "effectually broken up or dispersed by the military force alone."[79]

77. Richter, "'This Blood-Thirsty Hole': The Freedmen's Bureau Agency at Clarksville,
Texas, 1867–1868," *Civil War History*, XXXVIII (March, 1992), 73.

78. C. M. Mower (AAAG, DT) to Starr, November 16, 1867, p. 476, DT, LS, Vol. 4, p. 457,
USACC, M1165, Rg 393, NA; Mower to George L. Hartsuff (AAG, 5MD, New Orleans), November 16, 1867, DT, LS, Vol. 4, pp. 476–77, *ibid*.

79. Mower to Starr, November 2, 1867, Vol. 4, p. 457, USACC, M1165, RG 393, NA;
Richter, *The Army in Texas During Reconstruction*, 52–53.

After Baker and his various outlaw cohorts engaged the Bureau and the army from July to October, 1867, they suddenly ceased their attacks. Kirkman supplied no information about what Baker might be suspected of doing or planning, and other Freedmen's Bureau agents and post commanders in the region were silent as to his whereabouts. He might have gone to Young's place in Perry County or he might simply have hidden himself closer to home, where he could observe what the Bureau and military were doing, and where he remained in familiar territory near his supporters. But Baker's absence could only last briefly before he began to yearn for action once again.

Baker appeared in Bright Star, Arkansas, on Christmas Day, 1867, where he joined some of his comrades. They bought a large amount of whiskey and proceeded to drink heavily. Heading off in the direction of the Sulphur River about two hours after dark, they made their way to the Howell Smith place. Smith had recently employed a family of freedmen, who lived in one room of his house until a cabin could be erected. To complicate matters, Smith had grown daughters, and black men residing in a household with white women was, as Eason notes, "in direct contrast to the accepted conventions of the community." Rumors began to circulate in the neighborhood that one of the black men had somehow offended Smith's neighbors.[80] Local gossip also had it that Smith was sleeping with a black woman.

None of these rumors about Smith's household can be substantiated, although some Baker aficionados have used them to justify what occurred that Christmas night at the Smith farm. James Smallwood believes the "outlaw's motives were racial." One Baker defender has theorized that the citizens desired to "correct a situation which was abhorrent to the whole community." Others see the event as a vigilante action meant to uphold traditional southern values and the honor of white society. Whatever impelled Baker—alcoholism, racism, vigilantism, or brutality—his actions that night were murderous.[81]

80. Eason, "Cullen Baker," 11; Breihan, "Cullen Baker," 80; Bartholomew, *Cullen Baker,* 57–58; Taylor, "Swamp Fox of the Sulphur," 63–64, 68; Triplett, "Cullen Montgomery Baker," 457; Johnson, "Cullen Montgomery Baker," 235. Vestal, *The Borderlands,* 72–74, accepts Taylor's rendition. Eason's discussion implicitly justifies what Baker did in the Smith affair on the grounds that blacks lived in the household. Orr, *Life of the Notorious Desperado,* 38 and 42, wrote that "rumors were immediately circulated by Baker's friends, stating that the family was of a low grade; that they were having a negro party at the house, and the girls were taking a part in the dance." He also claims the girls had good reputations and were upstanding members of the Missionary Baptist Church.

81. Smallwood, "Swamp Fox," Pt. 2, p. 40; Orr, *Life of the Notorious Desperado,* 39–40.

Howell Smith was a sixty-six-year-old farmer at the time of his confrontation with Baker and his desperadoes. South Carolina born, he resided in Georgia before settling in Arkansas. Smith, his wife Centha [Cynthia], and their children were neighbors of the Fosters, Baker's former in-laws. The Smiths had four daughters and three sons; how many of whom lived at home at the time of the attack is unknown. A man of more than modest means, owning real estate valued at $1,800 and personal property valued at $625, Smith attempted to make his farm a success; that effort may have entailed hiring freedmen for labor.[82]

What really occurred on December 25, 1867, and did Baker make the miraculous escape so often attributed to him by his sympathizers? Orr affirms that it was "a nightmarish brawl" that "ended in bloodshed and death." Although somewhat biased, the best contemporary source is a report by Captain N. B. McLaughlin, commander of the Jefferson post. Not until two days after the melee did a Cass County citizen inform McLaughlin that on Christmas night, Baker, the "highwayman and outlaw, together with sixteen others," attacked Smith's house, "firing some thirty shots into it killing two persons and severely wounding two more, all colored." The gang then charged the white people and beat Smith, "fracturing [his] skull to such an extent that he has remained insensible ever since and will probably die."[83]

Two daughters (Emily and Sally) who attempted to rescue their father were severely stabbed—one in three places, the other once—and beaten "with pistols until nearly dead." The desperadoes set fire to three beds, hoping to burn the house and its inhabitants. Fortunately, the fire did not spread and the residents escaped this horrible fate, "the old man however having his foot very badly burned." In the altercation, Baker was seriously wounded in the right thigh by his own men. Unable to walk by himself, Baker demanded the two women help him to mount his mule. They supposedly complied, and he managed to ride to the home of his former father-in-law, William Foster. Foster tended the wound while Baker told him what had occurred at Smith's and that he and his gang needed assistance.[84]

On Saturday morning, December 28, McLaughlin began pursuit of Baker with twenty men. They marched forty-five miles to the Smith house and verified the facts of the attack. McLaughlin learned the names of sev-

82. MCR, Eighth Census (1860), Lafayette County, Arkansas, p. 59, RG 29, NA.
83. N. B. McLaughlin (Commander, Post Jefferson) to Lt. Col. W. H. Wood (Commander, Department of Louisiana), January 2, 1868, DT, LR, Box 5, USACC, RG 393, NA.
84. *Ibid.*

eral of Baker's party and discovered they were camped only eight miles away. Moving at 2:00 A.M. Sunday morning to the vicinity of Baker's camp, the soldiers surrounded it, and when dawn came they charged but found that it had just been vacated. They returned to Foster's house, where McLaughlin questioned him and several neighbors. McLaughlin wrote that these people "were all anxious for the capture of Baker," but none dared guide the soldiers "in the swamps and forests for fear of his finding it out and killing them, the whole country being in mortal fear of this man."[85]

However, McLaughlin "compell[ed] every man in the settlement" to accompany him "with his gun." All retraced their steps to Baker's previous camp, ascertained that he had one horse and two mules, discovered a new trail, and followed it for three miles. At this point, one of the guides found a new camp and opened fire. McLaughlin charged the camp "as rapidly as possible" but had to cross the Black Cypress River to reach it. Three men who had remained with Baker fled, "leaving behind them Baker's battery consisting of one fine double-barrelled gun, and four six-shooters all heavily loaded, about fifteen pounds of pistol balls and buck shot, and plenty of powder and caps," plus blankets, saddlebags, provisions, and a "very fine mule."[86]

McLaughlin took possession of the property, but Baker and his cohorts escaped with a horse and a mule and "got over the hill and out of sight into a dense thicket." The hunters scoured swamps and woods for two days but "could find no tidings of them." They did capture one man who was present at the Christmas killing, Meredith McAdams. He was sent to the guardhouse. McLaughlin had used his "utmost endeavors to arrest several of [Baker's] confederates but they could not be found." Nonetheless, "by pressing in all the citizens in the vicinity," McLaughlin felt that the "most certain move has been made towards the capture or destruction of this band, as they now feel that unless destroyed Baker and his gang will waylay and murder them all."[87]

The military detachment searched for the gang until Tuesday, December 31. Apart from McAdams, McLaughlin identified Baker, Lee and Seth Rames, Joe Courtney, John Kennedy, and John and Henry Nichols (two brothers) as the Smith farm culprits. He disposed of the captured property, except the shotgun, at public auction and turned the proceeds over to the

85. *Ibid.*
86. *Ibid.*
87. *Ibid.*

Smith family, whom the gang had so abused "they [were] in the most destitute circumstances." He gave the gun to his "company for its use, and as a reward for their good conduct during the scout." The citizens promised McLaughlin to "assist in [Baker's] destruction," and he believed that "for their self-preservation they will not relax their exertions until success has attended them."[88]

Local citizens did not disappoint McLaughlin and faithfully joined in the hunt. Even though they feared Baker, they attempted to capture him. John S. Jackson declared in an 1868 letter that people opposed to Baker volunteered in searching for him in their capacity as "Scott's Company," headed by Preston R. Scott. Jackson agreed with their desire to end Baker's mayhem following his killing of Howell Smith and the abuse of his two daughters. Fifteen or twenty citizens had appeared at Jackson's house and requested that he take up arms in defense of the "country." Jackson consented, claiming he did not have any personal feeling against anyone except Baker. Jackson remained with the party for twenty-one days, long after the military had left.[89]

The citizens apprehended Matthew "Dummy" Kirby, a Baker compatriot, but released him when they discovered he had been so drunk that he had passed out and thus did not participate in the attack on the Smith family. Six men—Jackson, John Williams, Bill Dunlop, Green Allen, Peyton Murph, and John Salmon—seized Seth Rames and aimed to "make the boy talk." According to Thomas Taylor, six heavily armed and "determined" men subjected Seth, "a frail stripling of a boy 15-years old," to "an improvised third degree." One story claims they cut off Seth's fingers, toes, and ears. Orr contends that he was executed because he participated in Baker's gang and alerted the outlaw to the arrival of Federal troops.[90]

Thus, myth and legend surround the murder of Seth (John Howard) Rames, who was named after his father. (They picked the nickname Seth for unknown reasons.) Born in Bowie County, Texas, in March, 1849, Seth was eighteen years old at the time of his death at the hands of the "famous six." His brother, Lee M., born in 1844, was also a prominent member of the Baker gang and was often referred to as the "first lieutenant." One story

88. *Ibid.*

89. John S. Jackson to Colonel R. P. Crump, [1868], LR, Box 2, Post of Jefferson Records, USACC, RG 393, NA.

90. Taylor, "Swamp Fox of the Sulphur," 74; Orr, *Life of the Notorious Desperado*, 41–42; Bowman, *The People of Cass County*, I, 225.

perpetuated by some writers favorable to Baker is that Lee avenged Seth's death by murdering five of the men who participated in his brother's killing. One of the six died before Lee found him.[91]

Most of the citizens who went in search of Baker do not appear in the 1860 and 1870 censuses or in other contemporary documents. Although they have been portrayed as cowards by those writers sympathetic to Baker's doings, it seems probable they were yeomen farmers like Howell Smith in the neighborhood where Baker had grown to manhood, and were outraged at his killing of an innocent man. (They may have even been stock-raisers and herders like John Baker.) There is nothing to indicate what political party they supported or how they felt about Reconstruction in general, but they did desire to end Baker's disturbance and bring peace to their particular section.

The basic facts of the Howell Smith affair seem well established, but a host of legends have arisen surrounding the attack. One of the more remarkable accounts was begun by Taylor and maintained by others. Lee Rames "stood off a company of U.S. soldiers and twice as many well armed citizens" with a "roaring voice" by warning the soldiers and citizens that they would be the beneficiary of Baker's "big-bore shotgun" if they came closer. Eason claims that "out of 300 men of trained soldiers and tough frontiersmen—not one man accepted the challenge!" Rames put Baker, whose leg was in a splint, on a horse with his brother Seth, and stood guard while the two men made it across the Black Cypress River to safety. Taylor says Baker swam the Cypress.[92]

The military report undermines the validity of the Cypress-crossing tale. McLaughlin was silent about Kirby and Rames, but it was the citizens and not the military who captured them, so the Jefferson post commander might have known nothing about these events. The assault upon the Smith household was perpetrated by drunken, vicious, and prejudiced men. It seems similar to many raids performed by the Ku Klux Klan motivated by the desire to maintain a distinct sphere for each race. Destruction and death followed in the wake of the klan. So too there is no question that

91. Rames family material in possession of the authors. Even after Seth Rames's date of birth was learned (it is also given as 1850), the family still reiterated that he was only fifteen when killed.

92. Taylor, "Swamp Fox of the Sulphur," 68–77, relies on "an eyewitness and participant" who is never identified. Eason, "Cullen Baker," 12; Orr, *Life of the Notorious Desperado*, 41–42; Triplett, "Cullen Montgomery Baker," 458–59; Smallwood, "Swamp Fox," Pt. 2, p. 45.

Baker's original attack was unprovoked and his use of violence extensive. What he was attempting to accomplish through these kinds of actions is unknown. Baker was so unpredictable, he may not have known himself.

By January, 1868, the citizens of Lafayette County, Arkansas, had suffered enough of Baker. "For some time," their petition to the governor read, he "has been committing acts of violence on peaceable citizens and persons in the service of the U.S. Government, and he and his accomplices have become such a terror to the citizens, that many of them are in constant dread of being murdered." Baker had killed as many as eleven soldiers and had gone to the house of a "respectable citizen," Smith, and killed him, a freedman, his wife, and child, and severely wounded Smith's daughters, "all without any cause and provocation," so far as they could learn. Concealed in the thick swamps, he could not be found and captured without a considerable force.[93]

The "good and Law abiding" residents desired military assistance. Baker and his accomplices should be arrested and punished, but the "difficult matter" centered upon getting "enough citizens together to capture them." If one "good company of soldiers" was sent to Lafayette County, "enough citizens would join them" to ensure that the outlaws were arrested or driven from the country. The citizens also suggested the propriety of offering a large reward. Unquestionably, Baker was a "notorious and bad man." To facilitate matters, a writ was required from the civil authorities. The Rocky Comfort and Lewisville Bureau agents were instructed to keep each other informed of Baker's doings and coordinate any action with the nearest post commander in Texas.[94]

No one knows precisely where the wounded Baker spent the next few months. One report is that Lee Rames took him to a hideout on Mush Island (in Bowie County) and later to Elliott's pasture on Elliott's Creek, where he nursed Baker back to health and guarded him. Another story, to Eason the "most creditable," had Baker going to Hot Springs, Arkansas, to "seek the curative powers of its famous springs in healing his grievous wound." Taylor writes that the "impression was broadcast over Bowie and

93. Citizens of LaFayette County to Governor of Arkansas, January 29, 1868, Box 3, Arkansas, BRFAL, RG 105, NA. In fact, the "citizens" were either government or local officials in the county. The signers were a deputy collector and assistant assessor of internal revenue, a weigh master of cotton, a Bureau agent, the sheriff, and the county clerk.

94. *Ibid.;* Endorsements, J. M. Mills (AAAG), February 6, 1868. It is an interesting fact that the petition ended up in the hands of the Lewisville Bureau agent, one of the original signers.

Cass counties that Baker had either died from his wounds or had left the country." Again, there is no evidence to suggest where Baker recuperated, but it may have been in Perry County at Young's.[95]

Baker was absent from the Reconstruction scene for six months. Even while Baker was harassing the army, as well as the Freedmen's Bureau agents and the newly freed blacks, the Ku Klux Klan—which had appeared in Texas as early as 1866, but not in Baker's realm—had established an organization in Bowie County. In addition, numerous other outlaws such as Benjamin F. Bickerstaff and Bob Lee continued their depredations, and the locally known desperadoes Elisha P. Guest and John "Pomp" Duty attracted the attention of the military and the Bureau. While Baker was disabled, these rogues continued to disrupt the social and economic life of the area and may also have joined the Klan. It was not until mid-1868 that Baker reappeared.

95. Eason, "Cullen Baker," 12; Taylor, "Swamp Fox of the Sulphur," 72; Breihan, "Cullen Baker," 80–81.

Drawing of the Swamp Fox
Reproduced with permission from Ed Bartholomew,
Cullen Baker: Premier Texas Gunfighter *(Houston, 1954)*

Gravestones of William and Elizabeth Foster, Baker's second set of in-laws (located
on private land near Doddridge, Arkansas)
Photograph in authors' collection

Gravestone of Thomas Orr,
Baker's unassuming nemesis
(located in Texarkana, Arkansas)
*Photograph courtesy Jerry
and Dorothy Orr*

Gravestone of the Swamp Fox himself (located in Oakwood Cemetery,
Jefferson, Texas)
Photograph in authors' collection

William G. Kirkman, the Freedmen's
Bureau agent whom Baker murdered

Reproduced from Charles M. Clark, The
History of the Thirty-Ninth Regiment
Illinois Volunteer Veteran Infantry . . .
(Chicago, 1889), 540.

The barn now standing on the spot where Baker was killed, near Doddridge,
Arkansas, according to S. G. Nichols
Photograph in authors' collection

The rifle used to dispatch Baker
Photograph courtesy Archives Division—Texas State Library

THREE

Baker, the Klan, Blacks, and the Bureau

DURING THE RECONSTRUCTION YEARS there developed a "life and death struggle for Southern white people to exist," wrote a distressed observer. The eminent historian of the South C. Vann Woodward has less sympathetically captured this postwar attitude when he declared that in the former Confederacy, the appropriate word to characterize the action "of the supposedly vanquished and helpless whites" was "'advance'—aggressive, determined, and ruthless advance of racial oppression and white supremacy." Long before Cullen Montgomery Baker appeared, before Congress assumed control of national Reconstruction and reinstituted military rule, and before Republicans became a factor in Texas politics, violence aimed at the freedmen and freedwomen was a problem.[1]

Reports from across the South after the war, and especially from Texas, depicted the former slaves as being violated in every manner. Blacks were killed for simply being free; and when they asserted an independent economic outlook, violence was used to force them to remain on the plantation in a form of peonage. Much of the violence was perpetrated by outlaws such as Baker and focused upon disciplining black labor. The implementation of a

---

1. Barbara Leah Clayton, "The Lone Star Conspiracy: Racial Violence and Ku Klux Klan Terror in Post-Civil War Texas, 1865–1877" (M.A. thesis, Oklahoma State University, 1986), 15; C. Vann Woodward, "Birth of a Nation," *New York Review of Books* November 20, 1980, 49. Woodward lamented in *Origins of the New South, 1877–1913* (Baton Rouge, 1951), 159, that the "South seems to have been one of the most violent communities of comparable size in all Christendom."

free labor system proved difficult in Baker's region. Employers bartered with him to police the area searching for blacks who demonstrated a diligent desire to succeed, who wanted to move to another farm when they completed their contract, or who succeeded in acquiring acreage of their own.[2] Accounts relate that from the middle of the Civil War Baker evinced an overweening hatred toward blacks. Various reasons have been presented to explain what impelled him to regard blacks as fit only for enslaved labor, abuse, or death. The published numbers of blacks he murdered during the conflict are certainly exaggerated, but enough viable hints suggest that he found satisfaction in dispatching blacks, no matter what their status, and in bringing misery to their lives. At first, Baker killed blacks indiscriminately. Later, when he murdered freedmen and freedwomen, his victims were largely those who demonstrated economic independence. Blacks who voted also provoked Baker.

Numerous examples abound in Baker literature of the Swamp Fox shooting down blacks singly or in groups for the pleasure of intimidation, and of his murdering black laborers who refused to be bound by the stringent rules of the planters. Except for blacks Baker allegedly killed during the war, it is impossible to ascertain from past Baker writings when many of these outrages occurred. One account has Baker visiting a Cass County settlement of freedmen (no particulars about the visit are divulged) laboring for a unionist planter. He reportedly gunned "several" of the laborers down because they refused to work on another farm.[3]

Stories exist of Baker's postwar "regulation" of the freed black population, but the chronology is often confused and circumstances as well as background are often absent. In other words, these tales sound repetitious and exaggerated. One of the widely repeated Baker disciplinary efforts apparently began in 1865 in Arkansas. In Al Eason's version, a "Dr." Willis Dodd, who was self-taught, lived near Bright Star. A unique character, he attended

2. *Report of the Joint Committee on Reconstruction at the First Session Thirty-Ninth Congress* (Washington, D.C., 1866), 35–162; Charles V. Keener, "Racial Turmoil in Texas, 1865–1874" (M.A. thesis, North Texas State University, 1971); Eric Foner, *Reconstruction: America's Unfinished Revolution, 1863–1877* (New York, 1988), 119–23; Foner, *Nothing But Freedom: Emancipation and Its Legacy* (Baton Rouge, 1983); Leon F. Litwack, *Been in the Storm So Long: The Aftermath of Slavery* (New York, 1979), 274–82; Nancy Cohen-Lack, "A Struggle for Sovereignty: National Consolidation, Emancipation, and Free Labor in Texas, 1865," *JSH,* LVIII (February, 1992), 57–98.

3. Smallwood, "Swamp Fox of the Sulphur," *True West,* XXXVIII (November, 1991), Pt. 2, p. 39.

to the medical needs of blacks in the antebellum years in return for their tending and harvesting his crop, his major source of income. After the emancipation, Dodd could get no help with his crop; weeds took over, and blacks refused to enter his fields.

Learning of Dodd's difficulties with the former slaves, Baker came to the rescue. "Flashing" into the neighborhood one day, according to Thomas Taylor, Baker informed the "'boss' Negro" that he would later return and expected then to find blacks at work in the doctor's field. He called out the "names to this bell wether among the negroes" and stated that if he did not find them laboring, there would be trouble. After waiting in the woods near the Dodd farm, watching to make certain they heeded his admonition, Baker rode up with a shotgun across his lap and "warned them to work the crop until it was 'laid by.'" "Old-timers of the area," Eason confides, "say Dr. Dodd's crop that year was the cleanest they had ever seen in Miller County."[4]

James Smallwood asserts that Baker "entered into the pay of area landlords whose Negro workers were running away out of fear." Known in the past for "chasing freedmen," Baker "now attacked them if they tried to leave northeast Texas." The freedmen found themselves caught in a violent dilemma. If they labored industriously, they lost their wages by being run off. If they attempted to locate better working conditions, they were regulated. The Lewisville, Arkansas, Freedmen's Bureau agent believed that there was collusion between local officials and desperadoes. There was "no doubt" in his mind that "an understanding" existed "between the civil authorities and persons who are thus defrauding freedpeople."[5]

---

4. Al Eason, "Cullen Baker—Purveyor of Death" *Frontier Times,* XL (August–September, 1966), 9; Yvonne Vestal, *The Borderlands and Cullen Baker* (Atlanta, Tex., 1978), 66–67. T. U. Taylor, "Swamp Fox of the Sulphur or Life and Times of Cullen Montgomery Baker," *ca.* 1936 (Typescript in ECBTHC), 23–25, believed Baker performed these deeds "to keep the negroes in order and render a service to his neighbors and country." None of the other Baker biographers mention the Dodd incident. Perhaps the reason Eason highlights this story is that Dodd was a relative. In Chapter 4 of the present study, we discuss a real person named "Parson" Jesse Dodd, whom Baker seemed to trust, but there is no indication the Swamp Fox murdered any of his laborers.

5. James Smallwood, "When the Klan Rode: White Terror in Reconstruction Texas," *Journal of the West,* XXV (October, 1986), 10; *Time of Hope, Time of Despair: Black Texans During Reconstruction* (Port Washington, N.Y., 1981), 61; "Perpetuation of Caste: Black Agricultural Workers in Reconstruction Texas," *Mid-America,* LXI (January, 1979), 19–20; V. V. Smith (Agent, Lewisville) to Jonathan E. Bennett (AAAG), November 30, 1867, Vol. 109, pp. 342–44, 347–57, AC, Arkansas, BRFAL, RG 105, NA.

According to one Bureau agent in Marshall, Baker, though often described as a terror to the citizens of the region, depended upon them to sustain his depredations. How extensively they supported him is debatable. The majority of a "certain class"—planters and employers of freedmen— rendered him "all possible aid" as a "representative of the lost cause." Moreover, Baker was very useful to this class of people in controlling their freedmen: he did not hesitate to shoot blacks "on the slightest complaint." Whenever a crop of cotton appeared to be poor, employers resorted to "every possible dishonorable means" to rid themselves of their black laborers, which meant using Baker to harass and kill them, said the agent.[6]

As we observed in the previous chapter, by late 1867, almost every Freedmen's Bureau agent or army official in northeast Texas and southwest Arkansas had commented upon Baker's active hatred of freed blacks. His name inspired fear and loathing among the former slaves. He did not want them to rise on the social or economic ladder. For instance, he had brutally murdered a freedman by putting five shots into his heart for working a small farm independently (*i.e.,* for trying to buy the land). William Kirkman had initially been told that Baker could be hired to "shoot a freedman for a few dollars." Throughout Baker's region of operation, Bureau agents and others confirmed that he represented the interests of white employers and of the "lost cause" they mourned.[7]

A. G. Malloy, in Marshall, Texas, joined Kirkman in attempting most insistently to convince both Bureau and military headquarters of precisely what kind of menace Baker represented. And the Marshall agent had corroborated many of Kirkman's observations about Baker. To Malloy, Baker possessed three roles. First, he served as an economic enforcer for employers of freedmen, whose duty it was to run blacks off the plantation without pay or, as previously noted, to "shoot them on the slightest complaint made by their employers." Second, he terrorized the "well disposed citizens." Finally, Baker served as a model for other desperate men to emulate. If he were not captured, surely "murder and rapine" would follow.[8]

In 1867, Congress enfranchised blacks and, according to a Bureau agent in Lewisville, Arkansas, the sight of former slaves voting especially enraged

6. A. G. Malloy (Agent, Marshall) to Charles Garretson (AAAG), September 30, 1867, Vol. 134, n.p., Texas, BRFAL, RG 105, NA.

7. See Chapter 2 of the present study.

8. A. G. Malloy (Agent, Marshall) to Charles Garretson (AAAG), September 30, 1867, Vol. 134, n.p., Texas, BRFAL, RG 105, NA.

Baker. In the Bright Star area, Baker "threatened the entire colored population, if their votes were polled in favor of the republican convention." White
employers vowed to discharge blacks for the same reason. Fortunately,
when Baker was not physically present, his threats had little effect. In
Lewisville and other areas of Arkansas within easy riding distance of Texas,
Baker's influence was not felt. On November 5, 1867, black and white voters cast their ballots in Arkansas. In all areas, except for Bright Star, wrote
the Bureau agent in Lewisville, they "polled a full vote."[9]

Even though the freedmen had cast their votes and quietly returned
home, Baker's threatened appearance left a pall over the area. His absence
on election day occurred only because he was planning to rescue a comrade,
John Kelley, from military custody at Mount Pleasant, Texas. The Lewisville
agent believed that action should be taken to stop Baker's disruption of the
legal and political process and his harassment of blacks. The "Government
should offer a reward for his head," the agent suggested, "and levy a tax on
the citizens of his county to meet it for allowing a highwayman and murderer
to run the road with impunity, and harbor[ing] him from justice, because he
confines his depredations to soldiers, union citizens and negroes."[10]

Hugh Sutton, who allegedly saw Baker at the Battles of Oak Hills and
Elkhorn Tavern, claimed that he encountered Baker two or three times after the war. Once, at Bob Woodward's grocery, north of Boston, Texas,
Baker declared he needed to use Woodward's flatboat as he and his men
were "going to raise hell over in Little River County," Arkansas. They
"broke up a Republican barbecue and killed several men." Later, they murdered "nine negroes on the Henry Hawkins place." Months later, Baker appeared at the Red River, where Sutton was a ferryman, hollering that he
needed to cross as the Yankees were after him. Sutton demurred, afraid
Baker would kill his black employees. He promised not to harm them. After
the ride, Sutton never saw him again.[11]

In the estimation of one Bureau agent in Arkansas, by early 1868, Baker
was the "only man" causing any disturbance; however, it was "impossible to

9. V. V. Smith (Agent, Lewisville) to Jonathan E. Bennett (AAAG), November 30, 1867, Vol.
109, pp. 342–44, 347–57, AC, Arkansas, BRFAL, RG 105, NA.

10. *Ibid.;* Smith to Bennett, November 30, 1867, NR, AC, LR-1593, Box 11, both in AC,
Arkansas, BRFAL, RG 105, NA; Randy Finley, "The Freedmen's Bureau in Arkansas (Ph.D.
dissertation, University of Arkansas, Fayetteville, 1992), 168. Smith also referred to Baker as a
"notorious Texas hooligan."

11. Taylor, "Swamp Fox of the Sulphur," 14–15; Vestal, *The Borderlands,* 36.

arrest him as he lives in the woods." When elections again approached, it was the "intention of certain [white] individuals to prevent the freedmen from voting if possible." The military appeared, and owing to their presence and the fact that all "desperate men" had left the county, no trouble occurred at the polling places. Nevertheless, Baker still posed a problem. He was "not supposed to be in the county" at election time, wrote a hopeful Arkansas agent. These northerners working for the Freedmen's Bureau continued to be amazed at how some members of southern communities lauded Baker because he killed blacks and soldiers and how they attempted to duplicate his actions.[12]

Baker does not seem to have devoted much time to curtailing the political organization or the suffrage of blacks, but his sporadic efforts cast a long shadow. As we have seen, he did exercise some influence in west Arkansas close to his Texas home, but other than one documented example of his threats almost nothing exists. The only time blacks voted in Texas while Baker was still alive, in February, 1868, Baker was recuperating from the serious leg wound he received in his gang's attack on the Howell Smith household. Perhaps as a result of Baker's inactivity, in the Texas election determining whether to hold a constitutional convention and elect delegates to the meeting, blacks favored the convention and selected their delegates. The election was relatively peaceful, but many registered black voters did not vote.

In Bowie, Cass (Davis), Red River, Harrison, Lamar, Titus, Upshur, Wood, and Hopkins Counties, the Texas election seems to have gone off rather quietly. If the Hopkins County experience is typical—and Baker had sometimes operated around Sulphur Springs—then the lack of his presence certainly led to a peaceful election. J.A.B. Putnam, the county judge in Hopkins, informed provisional governor E. M. Pease that 61 percent of the black registered voters and 33 percent of the registered whites came to the polls. No disturbance or quarrel occurred on any of the five days although "no troops nor special constables were present," wrote Putnam; the "voters with scarcely an exception came to the polls unarmed."[13]

12. Smith to Bennett, February 8, 1868, Vol. 109, pp. 383–86; Smith to Bennett, March 4, 1868, Vol. 109, pp. 392–98; Smith to C. C. Ballard (Commander Post, Washington, Ark.), March 5, 1868, Vol. 109, pp. 387–89; Willis to Bennett, February 29, 1868, Vol. 179, pp. 42–43; all in AC, Arkansas, BRFAL, RG 105, NA.

13. Election Returns, Secretary of State; J.A.B. Putnam (County Judge, Hopkins), February 15, 1868, Election Returns, Secretary of State, RG 307, TSL.

In the area of Jefferson, Texas, unionists felt threatened at election time. Don Campbell, a local Republican, wrote to the governor that they were willing to "bide" their time and trust "to the wisdom and determination of Congress to secure to Union men all that is due them and to render treason forever odious." Campbell confirmed that, "strange to say," the election in his county "passed off quietly and without the least disturbance," which was not the case in adjacent areas. Elsewhere, conservatives had boycotted the polls, and a few radicals were deterred from voting. Campbell claimed that a number of blacks were "discharged by their employers for supporting the "Radical ticket," and others were threatened and thus did not appear to cast their ballot.[14]

In Campbell's home county, Marion, blacks voted in favor of calling a convention and supported sympathetic candidates. In Davis (Cass) County, the election to hold a convention garnered 450 favorable and 75 opposing votes, and in Bowie County, 250 voters favored such action and approximately 100 opposed the convention. Baker's influence lingered even in these counties, however. The white unionists declined to vote in Cass and Bowie because "of their apprehension of personal violence from the rebel element." Their opponents "drove negroes from the polls, swearing that if they returned, they would blow their brains out." Campbell found it "amazing how defiant and outrageous these [Confederate] people have become." Blacks' temporary submission to cruel, racist whims seemed necessary to their survival.[15]

Even while Baker recuperated from his bullet wound, his reputation for violence lingered over these polling places. Campbell suggested as much in his letter to the governor, and statistics tend to bear out his claim. For example, in Cass County there were approximately 688 blacks registered to vote, yet during the five-day election only 58 percent cast their ballot on this first opportunity. In Bowie County the percentage was even lower: 54 percent of blacks voted, the same number that trekked to the polls in Titus County. However, in Red River County, where Baker may have occasionally appeared, a significant 76 percent of registered black voters went to the polls.[16]

---

14. D. Campbell (Jefferson) to E. M. Pease (Provisional Governor), February 15, 1868, Election Returns, Secretary of State, RG 307, TSL.

15. *Ibid.*

16. Election Returns, Secretary of State, RG 307, TSL.

Baker did not take much violent action against blacks who joined the Union League (the local arm of the Republican Party) and participated in the political process; he left the regulation of black political activities to another group. But those who desired to control the freedmen politically could always invoke Baker's name in a less than subtle attempt at coercion. R. H. Watlington, who lived in Boston, Texas, during the Baker era and met him twice, remembered a man who murdered blacks "for the mere sport of killing": the "bare mention of 'Baker and his clan,' brought foreboding of direful portent."[17]

Legend also has Baker overseeing the maintenance of community standards on race. When blacks transgressed the code of southern etiquette and honor, he enforced its unwritten provisions. Coke Stevenson's grandfather, who lived in Baker country, shared the following recollection. A northern man with two daughters had moved to the vicinity of Jefferson. One Sunday, two black men offered to escort the daughters home from church. Their father said that the "negroes were free, and the girls should accept." At that "instant," Cullen Montgomery Baker, the savior of white womanhood, appeared and killed both freedmen. Baker told the father that if he "ever again consented for his girls to go with a negro," he would die.[18]

The foregoing episode is probably fabricated. But so much compelling contemporary evidence (from citizens, government officials, and the army) shows how Baker terrorized the region's black population, so that exaggerated accounts, as in this case, cannot be ignored. Every pro-Baker writer has several versions of stories demonstrating how the Swamp Fox had no compunction about cold-bloodedly killing a black person. Clearly, Baker earned a reputation for his deadly conduct toward blacks. In distortions of this reputation, Baker appears as a violent enforcer commissioned to keep blacks in their place. This version of his reputation has endured.

Baker is even said to have conveyed his legendary hatred of blacks to his mule, Nell. Andrew Hall, who lived to be a hundred years old, claimed that he knew Baker and often fed his mule. Hall told of blacks whom Baker chased to force them back to landlords with whom they had completed their contract; their employers desired that they remain for another year. Nell assisted in tracking these fugitives. Hall called Nell the "most unusual mule ever known in Texas." With her "uncanny sense of smell," he ex-

17. R. H. Watlington, "Memoirs" (Typescript in TSL), 83.
18. Taylor, "Swamp Fox of the Sulphur," 84.

plained, Nell "could track Negroes like a bloodhound." Carrying his shotgun, which "looked like a cannon to the 'Freedmen's Bureau Negroes," Baker would yell, "Loose Nigger, Nell!"[19]

Freedmen in northeast Texas recalled how Baker spread fear among black communities. Alex Humphrey, born in Cass County, remembered his "people hiding out from a man called Cullen Baker." If "he was somewhere close by all the big fo'ks hid out in the bushes and left the chil'ren in the house. He was a bad man, but they say he wouldn't bother the chil'ren." Baker "killed Niggers like they was dogs"; if anyone wanted to put blacks "on the run," they would simply say he had been " 'seen in a neighboring community last night.' They'd hide out for two days." Francis Black stated she heard "white fo'ks in Jefferson talk 'bout Cullen Baker killing a pacel of Niggers." She assumed "he was one of the Ku Kluxers" whites talked about.[20]

Ransom Rosborough told an interviewer that after the war, Baker "wuz makin' it hot fer some of the Niggers. I would run my las' limit," he continued, "if I heard he wuz in the neighborhood." During those days everybody had rail fences. Rosborough explained, "I could fin' a crack in the fence heap quicker when I hear Baker wuz aroun'." He knew that Baker had hanged a black man by the name of Ike Duncan close to where he lived. Although other desperadoes plagued the black communities in Texas, Arkansas, and Louisiana, none ever seemed to be as feared as Baker. As a self-appointed regulator and terrorizer of "impudent and shiftless" freedmen, Baker enhanced his image among those who could not countenance an alteration in race relations.[21]

Whether Baker's frequent presence in Bowie and Cass Counties made the plight of blacks worse than it was in areas where desperadoes did not operate is uncertain. But the contemporary testimony of citizens, Bureau agents, army officials, and local politicians, in conjunction with the narra-

19. *Ibid.,* 63–64; Vestal, *The Borderlands,* 65–66.

20. George P. Rawick, ed., *The American Slave: A Composite Autobiography, Supplement, Series 2* (10 vols.; Westport, Conn., 1979), V, Pt. 4, p. 1823 (Humphrey); II, Pt. 1, p. 302 (Black). See also John A. Carpenter, "Atrocities in the Reconstruction Period," *Journal of Negro History,* XLVII (October, 1962), 234–47.

21. Rawick, ed., *The American Slave, Supplement, Series 2,* VIII, Pt. 7, p. 3363 (Rosborough); James Martin, *Texas Divided: Loyalty and Dissent in the Lone Star State, 1856–1874* (Lexington, 1990), 102–103; Taylor, "Swamp Fox," 23–25, 30, 54–55, 58–60. See also Herbert Shapiro, "Afro-American Responses to Race Violence During Reconstruction," *Science and Society,* XXXVI (Summer, 1972), 158–70.

tives of blacks, suggests that it did. Indeed, Baker's actions and reputation threatened black communities throughout the region.

The anecdotal evidence of Baker's campaign against blacks is substantial, but statistical support is equally compelling. In 1864, Bowie and Cass Counties had 4,138 and 5,189 black (slave) inhabitants respectively. By 1870, the number of blacks who resided in each of the two counties had declined by almost two thousand. Baker's activities could not completely account for this precipitous drop in the number of black denizens: the war and its aftermath also contributed to the falling numbers. Many blacks had been brought to Texas during the war in order to save slavery. After the war they returned home. Nevertheless, Baker's racist propensities undoubtedly forced blacks to leave the area.[22] In this way, he aided the group who actively regulated black political activities: the Ku Klux Klan.

When Baker began his racist guerrilla activities in mid-1867, the Ku Klux Klan had appeared in Texas but not yet in his neighborhood. After the war, organizations like the Klan, aimed at black suppression, began to emerge. At the same time, outlaws preyed sporadically on the former slaves. Throughout late 1865 and early 1866, over a year before Baker's racism became active, blacks suffered at the hands of these desperadoes. As long as the outlaws demonstrated that they could control the black population and harass the army and the Freedmen's Bureau, communities in Baker's region did not view Klan activity as a necessity. But the guerrillas could not be everywhere at once. Thus, a locally based organization that could continuously oversee community affairs was deemed necessary to counter the changes entailed in Reconstruction. When Baker temporarily left the region, the "Kluckers," as they were often referred to, acted on their belief that the attempt to elevate blacks to full citizenship was seriously wrong.

The origins of the Texas Klan help us to understand Baker's connection with that entity. The Klan flourished in Texas under various rubrics: the Knights of the Rising Sun, the Knights of the Golden Circle, the Knights of the White Camellia, and the White Caps. But as a whole, its motives were consistent. Before 1867, black males could not yet vote. Like Baker, the Klan first concentrated its intimidation in the social and economic spheres, focusing on black churches and black schools and the discipline of farm laborers. The Texas Klan first appeared in seven counties—Anderson, Collin,

22. Randolph B. Campbell, *An Empire for Slavery: The Peculiar Institution in Texas, 1821–1865* (Baton Rouge, 1989), 264.

Hays, Panola, Robertson, Tarrant, and Travis. No common characteristic unites these counties and accounts for the rise of the white-hooded organization in them. Settlement patterns, geography and topography, population figures, relative percentages of blacks to whites, and responses to the secession crisis in 1861 varied widely among these counties.[23]

The majority of chapters that the Klan formed in Texas throughout 1867 were located in areas adjacent to Baker's home county, Cass. Interestingly, Klan activity was reported in every county surrounding Cass, but not Cass itself. The organization of Klan chapters began slowly among that tier of counties in the northeast that bordered the Red River, but they soon received impetus from Baker and his marauding band. (Baker's gang may even have been the Klan without regalia.) Baker's depredations coincide neatly with the Klan's timetable as all of his postwar efforts against Reconstruction occurred from mid-1867 until the end of 1868. Then, as the presence of the Freedmen's Bureau expanded, increased Klan and desperado activity aimed to root out agents.[24]

Although violence against white unionists, blacks, and the army had occurred in northeast Texas before 1867, it had not reached the scale that

23. Clayton, "The Lone Star Conspiracy," 14–16; Allen W. Trelease, *White Terror: The Ku Klux Klan Conspiracy and Southern Reconstruction* (New York, 1971), 137–48. For the denial that a Texas Klan existed or assertions that it was a benevolent organization, see Guy M. Bryan to Rutherford B. Hayes, August 29, 1871, in "The Bryan-Hayes Correspondence," IV, ed. E. W. Winkler, *SwHQ*, XXVI (July, 1922), 61; Bryan to Hayes, December 8, 1880, XIV, *SwHQ*, XXVIII (January, 1925), 238; W. D. Wood, "The Klux Klan," *Quarterly of the Texas State Historical Association*, IX; (April, 1906), 262–68. A similar prewar organization is studied in Roy Sylvan Dunn, "The KGC in Texas, 1860–1861," *SwHQ*, LXX (April, 1967), 543–73. That it existed is confirmed in Trelease and K. O. W. C. [Knights of the White Camelia] Ritual, [September 16, 1867], George Rouser Papers, TSL. In addition, see Paul D. Escott, "White Republicanism and Ku Klux Klan Terror: The North Carolina Piedmont During Reconstruction," in *Race, Class, and Politics in Southern History: Essays in Honor of Robert F. Durden*, ed. Jeffrey J. Crow, Paul D. Escott, and Charles L. Flynn, Jr. (Baton Rouge, 1989), 3–34; Patricia A. Gozemba and Marilyn L. Humphries, "Women in the Anti-Ku Klux Klan Movement, 1865–1984," *Women's Studies International Forum*, XII (1989), 35–40; William D. Piersen, "Family Secrets: How African-American Culture Helped Shape the Early Ku Klux Klan," in *Looking South: Chapters in the Story of an American Region*, ed. Winfred B. Moore, Jr. and Joseph F. Tripp (Westport, Conn., 1989), 41–50; Jack Hurst, *Nathan Bedford Forrest: A Biography* (New York, 1993), 261–356; Brian Steel Wills, *A Battle from the Start: The Life of Nathan Bedford Forest* (New York, 1992), 318–54.

24. See Clayton, "The Lone Star Conspiracy,"; Barry A. Crouch, *The Freedmen's Bureau and Black Texans* (Austin, 1992); William L. Richter, *Overreached on All Sides: The Freedmen's Bureau Administrators in Texas, 1865–1868* (College Station, Tex., 1991).

would prevail under various desperadoes and the Ku Klux Klan. When Congress assumed direction of Reconstruction affairs, black men were enfranchised and the elected Texas government under James W. Throckmorton was removed. The Freedmen's Bureau made its presence known on the Red and Sulphur Rivers, an area that had never before seen a Bureau agent. Reports from these government officials, confirmed by citizen observations, began to relate tales of mayhem and brutality against the freed black population. It became virtually impossible to distinguish between the desperadoes and the Klan.

When Baker resumed activity on the Texas scene in mid-1868, he focused his attention upon Lamar, Red River, and Titus Counties, the latter two of which were directly adjacent to Bowie, Cass, and Hopkins. He ignored Kirkman's domain. These counties, which had slave populations similar to Bowie's in 1860, saw a sizeable influx of bondsmen and -women during the war. By 1870, whites in the area (except in Red River) had increased and surpassed in number the blacks who during wartime were forced to migrate there. The whites had originated before the war from the Upper and Gulf South; they consisted of slaveholders and nonslaveholders. The two classes may have argued as to how to regulate blacks. The former owners opted for violence, and Baker served them as a wide-ranging overseer.[25]

Before the expansion of the Freedmen's Bureau in early 1867, the northeastern region had been supervised from the Marshall office, which meant that little was done outside of Harrison County. But along with stationing Kirkman in Boston, the new Bureau director also appointed a civilian agent, Albert H. Latimer, to supervise Clarksville and the immediate Red River region. Latimer, a prominent area unionist who had signed the Texas Declaration of Independence and served in both the Republic's and the state's legislature, was probably too old to perform the arduous duties of an agent. Much to Latimer's dismay, his home area still evinced the same attitude that the victorious North had fought to eradicate.[26]

One Bureau inspector similarly found this region unrepentant: pandemonium reigned and rowdies exercised control. Besides Baker, numerous desperadoes such as Elisha P. Guest and John "Pomp" Duty ran roughshod

25. Francis A. Walker, *A Compendium of the Ninth Census, 1870* (Washington, D.C., 1872), 63–67; Campbell, *An Empire for Slavery,* 264.

26. See Latimer's perceptions in AC, OR, Texas, RG 105, NA; Walter Prescott Webb and H. Bailey Carroll, eds., *The Handbook of Texas* (2 vols.; Austin, 1952), II, 34; Richter, *Overreached on All Sides,* 198. Latimer married three times and fathered nineteen children.

over blacks and Union-leaning whites. Latimer never received military assistance and so resigned. The agent who replaced him, C. S. Roberts, thus described the region to headquarters: "God knows that there is no other region in these United States so cursed with crime, so filled with lawless men, who have done their lawless acts so unblushingly as in the North Eastern Texas." He recommended the area subdistricts be merged under the direction of Brevet Brigadier General James Oakes, commander of the Sixth Cavalry.[27]

Headquarters ignored Roberts' suggestion, and conditions worsened in the Red River section. The cry among law-abiding citizens and those blacks and whites who supported Reconstruction became, in Roberts' words: "Protect us, show us, and the bad men among us, that the arms of the Gov't are long enough to encircle, & strong enough to defend us." Throughout 1867, Roberts endured desperado attacks, humiliation, and debilitation from the "infernal Red River Miasma." (At this time, Baker was keeping Kirkman and the Mount Pleasant army post occupied.) Then the central Bureau office relieved Roberts and selected Charles F. Rand to replace him. The office also shuffled the subdistricts in the region and added another office at Paris, to be staffed by DeWitt C. Brown.[28]

As desperado and Klan violence crescendoed in 1868, agents Roberts, Rand, and Brown found their lives constantly in danger. While Baker recuperated, Rand faced numerous desperate characters. In Clarksville, John Henderson tried to kill Rand, and then Henderson joined with outlaws Guest and Duty to intimidate him further. His repeated requests for military support went unheeded. In mid-1868, as Baker made his resurgence, Guest, "Indian Bill" English, and Benjamin F. Bickerstaff appeared. In July, Rand, with assistance from the military, did manage to end the career of Ben Griffith (who had bothered Willis in Arkansas) by shooting him outside

27. C. S. Roberts to JTK (AAAG), August 12, 1867, AC, LR, R-129, Texas, RG 105, NA; William L. Richter, " 'The Revolver Rules the Day!': Colonel DeWitt C. Brown and the Freedmen's Bureau in Paris, Texas, 1867–1868," *SwHQ*, XCIII (January, 1990), 329; Richter, " 'This Blood-Thirsty Hole': The Freedmen's Bureau Agency at Clarksville, Texas, 1867–1868," *Civil War History*, XXXVIII (March, 1992), 61–63; Richter, "Who Was the Real Head of the Texas Freedmen's Bureau?: The Role of Brevet Colonel William H. Sinclair As Acting Assistant Inspector General," *Military History of the Southwest*, XX (Fall, 1990), 140–41. Roberts wanted the Bureau to combine the 37th, 52nd, and 58th subdistricts, which comprised the counties of Fannin, Lamar, Hunt Hopkins, Titus, Bowie, Cass, and Red River.

28. Richter, " 'This Blood-Thirsty Hole,' " 61–63.

of Clarksville. Rand was finally forced to leave in August of that year, accompanied by soldiers in disguise.[29]

Meanwhile, Baker's new depredations concentrated around the towns of Paris (Lamar County), Clarksville (Red River County), Sulphur Springs (Hopkins County), Mount Pleasant (Titus County), and as far west as Bonham (Fannin County). Although Baker and his new-found friends continued to harass Freedmen's Bureau agents and the army, they now also included Union men who supported Reconstruction, both black and white. Apparently encouraged by Baker's depredations and their psychological impact, the Ku Klux Klan then appeared. By fall, 1868, however, Baker and his desperadoes had moved on to another section. Baker now concentrated on ridding his home area of the presence of the Freedmen's Bureau. He succeeded.

In mid-1868, at the time Baker was returning to the Reconstruction scene, the Bureau agent in Paris reported that desperadoes from all over the northeastern section had begun to link up in a loosely knit organization. Baker, Bickerstaff, Bob Lee, Dick Johnson, Sam Dixon, George English, Dick Harper, and others banded together for the "purpose of killing negroes and Union men and running off the same from the country." On May 31, seven of these brigands (Baker, Bickerstaff, Lee Rames, two of the Marshall boys, and two unknowns) entered Bonham and pursued a Union man, whom they murdered. They proceeded east to "clean out" Bureau agent DeWitt Brown.[30]

A native of Dayton, Ohio, Brown had served mostly on garrison duty as a colonel in the Sixty-Fifth U.S. Colored Infantry during the Civil War. Sickness forced him to resign just before his regiment was mustered out in Louisiana in 1867. As noted above, he was with Kirkman in July, 1867, when the two men first encountered Baker. Brown moved to Texas and received a Bureau appointment as traveling agent in Grimes and Robertson Counties, and as an agent at Wharton and briefly in Tyler. Brown began his duties as head of the 37th subdistrict (Fannin, Lamar, and Red River Counties) in October, 1867. During the early months of Brown's subassistant commissionership, Baker was making life miserable for Kirkman in Bowie and Cass Counties.[31]

29. *Ibid.*
30. Richter, " 'The Revolver Rules the Day!' " 329.
31. *Ibid.*, 303.

After leaving Bonham, Baker and his associates had moved on to Paris, where they stayed within easy range of the town throughout June, 1868. Brown scoffed at the governor's reward proclamation. Even though it had been posted in the courthouse and in various other prominent places, no one offered to "take stock in that line of business," the agent informed headquarters. Brown believed that if the same conditions of the reward were applied to those who were loyal to the Union, the response would be entirely different. "If a Union man or a Negro had committed any crime," he stated, "there would be no lack of volunteers to go in quest of the criminal." Not only did disloyalty hide "a multitude of sins," but the revolver "ruled the day."[32]

Baker, a "cold blooded assassin," was a "big man" in the area, Brown concluded, "notwithstanding it is a known fact that he has murdered many women and children in this State." He intended, Brown stated, on "attending to the bureau business in this country," meaning the Red River region. Commanding "no less" than seventy-five "armed villains," Baker planned to eliminate the Bureau's presence. These desperadoes entered and left Paris at their pleasure, Brown wrote, and aimed to harass and kill those who supported the government. In particular, they declared they would "kill the Union men and leading negroes." Failing this slaughter, the desperadoes would "drive them from the country and disarm and dismount all the negroes."[33]

Brown, from his Lamar County perspective, reiterated what every other agent had previously asserted. "Something decisive should be done to render life and property more secure in this community," he wrote; only force would keep the inhabitants peaceful. The Bureau agent had no faith in the citizenry, declaring that "public opinion is and has been and will be corrupt." The majority were "either cowardly or restrained from committing crime for fear of losing their property or being driven from home." The people "seemed anxious" to have Baker enter the town and "rid them" of

32. Brown (Agent, Paris) to Vernou (AAAG), June 30, 1868, AC, OR, B-174; Brown to Vernou, June 8, 1868, AC, LR, B-157; both in Texas, BRFAL, RG 105, NA.

33. Brown to Vernou, September 2, 1868, AC, OR, B-225; Brown to Vernou, August 16, 1868, AC, LR, B-202, both in Texas, BRFAL, RG 105, NA. New York *Tribune*, September 29, 1868, p. 1. C. S. Mower (AAAG, DT) to W. S. Reynolds (Little Rock), July 7, 1868, LS, Vol. 5, p. 250; Mower to Commander (Post of Jefferson), January 28, 1868, LS, Vol. 4, p. 566, both in DT, LR, Box 5, USACC, RG 393, NA.

Brown's "obnoxious presence." The populace "encouraged" Baker to perform "deeds of violence which they are afraid to do themselves."[34]

Indeed, the citizens did desire that Baker eliminate Brown. In one instance, thirty-five armed men led by Baker tried to kill Brown near Rockey Ford on the Bois D'Arc River. In another, forty armed men came into Paris hoping to find the agent so that they could fill him with buckshot. After failing to locate Brown, Baker conferred with principal citizens to "get men to assist him in making another attack on the troops at Sulphur Springs." He then moved on to Clarksville. "It seems that these *desperadoes of the Ku Klux Klan* have a particular spite at me," Brown lamented, and the "citizens of this place are in confederation with them." He may have had an exaggerated sense of his persecution in this area, but the citizens did want Baker to eliminate him. In general, the "programme" was to rid the area of the Bureau and to "force the negroes into the Democratic ranks for protection."[35] Especially in Red River and Lamar Counties, Baker generally received stronger and more continuous support for his actions than he did in his home area of Cass and Bowie Counties. Perhaps people outside his neighborhood section were less familiar with his long history of nonpolitical, pathological acts.

As Baker and his comrades continued their depredations and the death toll in northeast Texas and southwest Arkansas continued to mount, the army was finally forced into action. To end desperado forays and bring a modicum of peace to this turbulent region, the national and state governments adopted a two-pronged strategy. First, they reiterated that rewards were being offered for the bodies of Baker and his cohorts, dead or alive. Second, they mobilized elite cavalry units and dispatched them into the affected counties. In addition, the Arkansas governor called out the state militia. In northeast Texas, where Baker had much support, some citizens nevertheless began to form groups to eradicate the desperado menace. These concurrent hostile actions would influence Baker's movements.

Bewailing the fact that there was "no law east of the Trinity River," Brevet Major General Joseph Reynolds, finally called out the cavalry to free northeast Texas of desperadoes and the Ku Klux Klan in September, 1868. Such action should have been taken a year earlier. Reynolds ordered a sweep of

34. Brown to Vernou, June 30, 1868, AC, OR, B-174, Texas, BRFAL, RG 105, NA. See also Richter, " 'The Revolver Rules the Day!' " 303–32.

35. Brown to Vernou, September 5, 1868, AC, LR, B-226, Texas, BRFAL, RG 105, NA.

the region at this time because his Bureau agents were in serious danger and the army seemed to be under constant attack from outlaws and the Klan. As Kirkman had earlier apprehended, poor communication and transportation facilities made cavalry essential. After the army's initial occupation, Texas never had more than 5,700 soldiers, most of whom were stationed on the frontier.[36]

Reynolds devised a scheme that coordinated military efforts to capture the various guerrilla bands. Captain A. R. Chaffee and Captain T. M. Tolman, each with a company of the 6th U.S. Cavalry, were ordered to Sulphur Springs, which had been frequently "under siege" by the desperadoes. They would be reinforced with an additional hundred men. They were directed to scour the area "until the bands of desperadoes commanded by Bickerstaff, Lee, English, Baker, or their confederates are broken up or driven from the country." Chaffee and Tolman were allowed to divide their commands into smaller parties for "special trips" to ferret out these individuals, but they knew they had to be cautious in separating their troops. Ambush was the favorite tactic of the guerrillas.[37]

The troops moved with as little equipment as possible, and Reynolds advised against taking any lives unless the members of the bands offered actual armed resistance. In addition, he asked that every precaution be exercised "to see that private property is not destroyed by the troops." Any outlaws arrested would be turned over "for safe keeping" to the most convenient post commander. They were not to target the guerrillas' civilian support, as was done in Missouri during the Civil War. Chaffee had the names of individuals upon whom he could call for information and assistance. All area post commanders had been directed to render necessary funds and supplies. Three thousand dollars had been provided to finance the expedition.[38]

36. James E. Sefton, *The United States Army and Reconstruction, 1865–1877* (Baton Rouge, 1967), 261–62; Richter, *The Army in Texas During Reconstruction, 1865–1870* (College Station, Tex., 1987), 93, 134, 153, 163.

37. C. E. Morse (AAAG, 5th MD) to A. R. Chaffee, September 1, 1868; Morse to S. B. Hayman (Commander, Fort Griffin), September 1, 1868, both in 1210.M.1868, AGO, Records of the AG, RG 94, NA. Organized for "special field service," the detachment would carry only the field allowance of "camp and garrison equipage," which amounted to thirty days' subsistence stores. The government wagons remained with Chaffee.

38. C. E. Morse (AAAG, 5th MD) to A. R. Chaffee, September 1, 1868; Morse to S. B. Hayman (Commander, Fort Griffin), September 1, 1868, both in 1210.M.1868, AGO, Records of the AG, RG 94, NA. See also Michael Fellman, *Inside War: The Guerilla Conflict in Missouri During the American Civil War* (New York, 1989).

The Fort Richardson commander, S. H. Starr, a former Freedmen's Bureau agent, received orders to prepare a detachment of sixty or seventy cavalry with government wagons, to reinforce Chaffee. In addition, W. B. Pease, a former Bureau agent who commanded Company D of the 17th U.S. Infantry (which came to Texas in July, 1866, and remained until May, 1869), was ordered to take charge at Sulphur Springs. Along with Company D, Pease would use the cavalry "to break up the bands of desperadoes now infesting that portion of the country." Pease claimed he commanded a post in "one of the most lawless and turbulent portions" of Texas, "in a region infested by several organized gangs of most notorious desperadoes, and proclaimed outlaws."[39]

One army historian of Reconstruction in Texas has suggested that Chaffee and Tolman may have done their job too well. Tolman imposed such a "brutal discipline" on his men and on the townspeople of Sulphur Springs (thumb-hanging and shooting those trying to escape) that he received a reprimand from Reynolds. Chaffee, equally unmerciful, led his men on a 1,000-mile, 3-month march that was quite successful. His unit earned the nickname "Chaffee's Guerrillas" for their severe actions. This military foray, which came too late, eventually eliminated Bickerstaff and Lee, but Baker managed to elude capture. Again, the army seemed always to be where Baker was not.[40]

Simultaneously, the Republican-dominated 1868 constitutional convention turned its attention to violence and attempted to buy the army's assistance. Believing that there existed all over Texas a "class of desperadoes engaged in theft, murder and robbery," the delegates declared that it was of the "greatest importance" that these brigands be arrested and brought to justice. They resolved to appropriate $25,000 to be placed at the disposal of the governor, which would enable him to offer "suitable rewards" for the apprehension of these outlaws and to hire detectives to ferret out their hiding places. The money could not be spent, however, unless the district army commander used military commissions to try the offenders.[41]

39. Court Martial Proceedings, Walter B. Pease, P. P. 728, Box 1577, Office of the Judge Advocate General, General Courts Martial, 1812–1938, RG 153, NA.

40. Richter, *The Army in Texas,* 146–47. Richter, *Overreached on All Sides,* 285, asserts that "reports listed suspects 'lost in the swamp' or 'shot while trying to escape.' Local farmers who misled troopers or refused to inform on outlaws were strung up by their thumbs."

41. Edmund J. Davis (Convention President) to J. J. Reynolds (Commander, 5MD), August 3, 1868, DT, LR, Box 6, USACC, RG 393, NA. Reynolds authorized $1,000 each for Baker, Bickerstaff, and Lee; *Texas Republican,* September 11, 1868, p. 2.

Baker moved out of the Red River region just as the military was begin-ning to mount a major expedition to rid the area of outlaws. Although the evidence is slim, Baker may have participated in yet another attack on an army supply wagon near his Cass County home. On September 2, 1868, masked desperadoes, who now appeared in the guise of the Klan, killed a teamster on the road between Jefferson and Marshall. Because they dis-robed before returning, "of course nobody knows who done it," wrote one observer. Only a detachment of cavalry that patrolled the roads at night would prevent these outlaws from "riding round themselves and disarming the negroes and killing and robbing them."[42]

Some unionists claimed that the few military officials in the area could not be depended upon, calling them "out and out Copperhead[s]." What sort of showing would the military provide then, asked Donald Campbell, a Republican officeholder and chief justice of Marion County. Conservative Robert Loughery, editor of the Marshall *Republican,* had praised the new military appointments in the highest terms. Campbell was frightened by this eulogy as he understood that letters of introduction had been brought to "some of the leading Copperheads of Marshall." When such officials had authority, they could "wink at the outrages that will be committed on the freedmen and loyal men and deal rigidly with Radicals."[43]

By fall, 1868, Bureau officials, the army, white unionists, and freedmen and -women faced an increase in violence and judicial difficulties from "Rebel" officials. While Baker kept Brown and Rand occupied—he eventually forced their removal or nullified their power—Kirkman may have frequently en-tered his thoughts. Kirkman had wounded Baker in their confrontation in July, 1867, and made several efforts to capture him. It is not surprising that Kirkman was the next Bureau agent Baker targeted. Before he and the Boston agent had their final encounter, however, Kirkman's cavalry escort was recalled, leaving him to defend himself. Moreover, while the Freedmen's Bu-reau in Texas was phased out, Kirkman faced a murder charge.[44]

42. D. Campbell (Jefferson) to C. Caldwell, September 3, 1868, GP (Pease), TSL; Webb and Carroll, eds., *Handbook of Texas,* I, 286.

43. D. Campbell (Jefferson) to C. Caldwell, September 3, 1868, GP (Pease), TSL. There is no evidence that southern sympathies among the soldiers ever hindered the pursuit of Baker, although it is certainly possible.

44. WGK to C. E. Morse (AAAG, DT), February 14, 1868, DT, LR, Box 5, USACC, RG 393, NA. In February, 1868, headquarters ordered that the three men from the 6th U.S. Cav-alry who served on duty with Kirkman at Boston be relieved.

A prisoner in Kirkman's custody had been shot while attempting to escape. Kirkman had observed the shooting but did not fire himself. The indictment disturbed Kirkman; and Nathan B. Anderson, the county clerk, worried about the agent's mental health. Anderson, a true friend to Kirkman, presents an interesting case study of a southern unionist (a "scalawag" to southern Democrats). He, too, suffered because of Baker's activities. A Tennessee native, in 1852 he settled in Sherman (in Grayson County), managed a hotel, and accumulated considerable real estate and personal property. During the war, a "notorious mobb began threatening and hanging Union men," and Anderson's house was robbed "of divers things." The "Secesh broke me up," said Anderson before he moved to Boston, Texas.[45]

Anderson survived the war with his unionism intact. He received a state appointment in July, 1867 (shortly after Kirkman's arrival), to enroll both black and white voters. He proved himself as a registrar and advanced to the Boston postmastership. But Anderson aspired for a more prominent position. Using Kirkman and local contacts, he campaigned for the county clerk position. He had no doubt that he could "fully satisfy" the military authorities, he told the provisional governor in late fall, 1867, yet he begged for the appointment. "I am a cripple," he wrote, "have no one to work for me now, have 2 small children[,] one a daughter." He assumed his new duties in January, 1868.[46]

45. WGK to N. G. McLaughlin (Commander, Post of Jefferson), December 23, 1867, Vol. 67, pp. 143–44; WGK to Roberts, September 18, 1868, Vol. 68, p. 130; WGK to Roberts, September 24, 1868, Vol. 68, p. 131; Receipt, Gray, September 26, 1868, Vol. 68, p. 134, all in Texas, BRFAL, RG 105, NA. For background, see Crouch, *The Freedmen's Bureau and Black Texans*, 92–94; Watlington, "Memoirs," 77–78; N. B. Anderson (County Clerk, Bowie County) to J. J. Reynolds (Commander, 5MD), September 13, 1868, AC, LR, A-38, Texas, BRFAL, RG 105, NA; Marriage Record (Anderson/Alexander), February 14, 1861, Grayson County Courthouse; Anderson to General [Charles] Griffin (Commander, District of Texas), August 11, 1867, Governor's Papers (Pease), RG 301, Box 56, Folder 6, TSL; MCR, Eighth Census (1860), Grayson County, Texas, p. 137, RG 29, NA; MCR, Ninth Census (1870), Grayson County, Texas, p. 26, RG 29, NA.

46. Anderson to Pease, May [31], 1869, AG, GC, RG 401, Box 388, Folder 11, TSL; Anderson to Reynolds (Commander, 5MD), May 27, 31, June 6, 1869, with all endorsements, LR, M1188, Reel 11, USACC, RG 393, NA; Anderson to Reynolds (AC and Commander, 5MD), September 13, 1868, AC, LR, A-38, Texas, BRFAL, RG 105, NA; David M. Jordan, *Winfield Scott Hancock: A Soldier's Life* (Bloomington, 1988), 200–12. See also Anderson to Griffin, August 11, 1867, GP, (Pease), RG 301, Box 56, Folder 6; Anderson (Sherman) to Pease, May [31], 1869, AG, GC, RG 401, Box 388, Folder 11; Pease to E. R. S. Canby (Commander, 5MD), February 3, 1869, GP (Pease), RG 401, Box 388, Folder 11; Anderson to Pease, May

After being absolved of all charges in early October, 1868, Kirkman saw his tenure in Boston coming rapidly to a close. The Freedmen's Bureau in Texas was being terminated. Assistant Commissioner Joseph J. Reynolds, Kirkman's commanding officer, had relieved the agent of his position, stating that his life should not "be imperiled further." Kirkman had warned for several months that he had been threatened and could be killed at any time. Bureau headquarters, or Kirkman, did not respond quickly enough to these threats, however.

Before leaving his office on the night of October 6, Kirkman consulted with William W. Bass until about midnight. Next door, Anderson, who was working on a power-of-attorney matter for Kirkman, also remained awake. It had been raining hard for two weeks prior to this night. At about 2:00 A.M., Kirkman was completing some final Bureau business in his office after Bass departed. He heard a noise outside (probably Baker calling him out) and went to investigate. The shots came from the shadows, around the corner of the building where the agent's office was located. In all, the killers fired sixteen rounds, Kirkman only one. Dead before he hit the ground, with buckshot and ball in the breast, shoulder, and side, and a revolver bullet through the head, Kirkman never had a chance. When the echoes of the gunfire ceased, someone shouted, "All is well."[47]

Anderson, who thought Kirkman had accompanied Bass back to the house, was suddenly awakened by a "loud firing of guns and pistols (about 17 shots)" twenty paces from his bedroom in the direction of Kirkman's office. Bass hollered down from upstairs, demanding what the "shooting meant." When Anderson had confirmed that someone had been shot and that Kirkman was unaccounted for, he asked a black man to determine what

---

[31], 1869, AG, GC, RG 401, Box 388, Folder 11; Anderson to General J. J. Reynolds (Commander 5MD), June 10, 1869, AG, GC, RG 401, Box 388, Folder 14, all in TSL. See also C. C. Brinkley (Sherman) to Pease, June 11, 1869, LR, M1188, Reel 17, USACC, RG 393, NA; Mower (AAAG) to Commander, Post of Jefferson, April 26, 1869, and endorsements, LR, M1188, Reel 13, USACC, RG 393, NA; WGK to McLaughlin, December 23, 1867, Vol. 67, pp. 143–44; WGK to Roberts, September 18, 1868, Vol. 68, p. 130; WGK to Roberts, September 24, 1868, Vol. 68, p. 131; Receipt, Gray, September 26, 1868, Vol. 68, p. 134, all in Texas, BRFAL, RG 105, NA.

47. WGK to Griffin (AC, Texas), September 25, 1867, Vol. 67, p. 63; WGK to Starr, February 22, 1868, Vol. 68, p. 37; WGK to Richardson, February 29, 1868, Vol. 68, pp. 48–50; Roberts to WGK, September 22, 1868, Vol. 5, p. 414, all in Texas, BRFAL, RG 105, NA. See also Smallwood, "The Freedmen's Bureau Reconsidered: Local Agents and the Black Community," *Texana*, XI (1973), 309–20.

the commotion was all about. Nearby, four men in a boardinghouse and two citizens of the town heard the gunfire but refused to take any action; no one would approach Kirkman's body. The alarmed townspeople were too afraid of "personal assault."[48]

Approximately forty-five minutes after the killing, while Kirkman's gun was still clenched in his hand, two assassins examined the body. They spotted the black man who waited to identify the corpse. The two men bluntly gave him a choice: either shoot or leave. The black man ran into the house but not before ascertaining who had been killed; he then told Anderson. The body lay where it had fallen into the early morning hours; everyone feared to investigate further. When Kirkman was later examined, the pockets on his trousers had been turned out, and three twenty dollar gold pieces, a small roll of bills, and a watch and chain were missing. In addition, the dead man's horse and revolver were gone.[49]

Later the same morning, Baker, Elisha P. Guest, and at least two unknown men—all carrying double-barreled shotguns and six-shooters—returned to make certain Kirkman was dead and to search his office. After

48. Statement of N. B. Anderson Relating to the Killing of W. G. Kirkman, October 15, 1868, Entry 2, LR, Records Post of Clarksville, USACC, RG 393, NA.

49. George Shorkley (Agent, Clarksville) to C. S. Roberts (AAAG), October 9, 1868, p. 1; October 9, 1868, Vol. 83, pp. 4–5; October 15, 1868, Vol. 83, pp. 9–13; Joseph J. Reynolds (AC, Texas) to Oliver Otis Howard (Commissioner), October 20, 1868, Vol. 5, p. 437, AC, LS; Reynolds to Howard, October 24, 1868 (telegram), Vol. 5, p. 445, AC, LS; WGK to Roberts, September 24, 1868, Vol. 68, p. 131; WGK to Reynolds, December 4, 1867, Vol. 67, pp. 134–35, all in Texas, BRFAL, RG 105, NA. See also N. B. Anderson to Editor, *Texas Republican* (Marshall), October 16, 1868, p. 2. Denton *Monitor,* November 7, 1868, p. 2, has an accurate account. In his last report, Kirkman stated that two revolvers constituted the only government property he possessed; WGK to Roberts, September 9, 1868, Vol. 68, p. 122, Texas, BRFAL, RG 105, NA. Taylor, "Swamp Fox of the Sulphur," 86–87, who had interviewed Anderson's son, stated his father examined the body after finding it lying beside the fence, with "several pistol holes through the fence where Kirkman had shot while on the ground." There is no contemporary evidence that Kirkman was able to fire his gun. Only one sentence on Kirkman's killing occurs in two sources: Ed Bartholomew, *Cullen Baker: Premier Texas Gunfighter* (Houston, 1954), 69; and Thomas Orr, ed., *Life of the Notorious Desperado Cullen Baker, from His Childhood to His Death, with a Full Account of All the Murders He Committed* (Little Rock, 1870), 42. Frank Triplett makes only passing reference to the murder in "Cullen Montgomery Baker," in his *History, Romance and Philosophy of Great American Crimes and Criminals . . .* (New York, 1884), 459. Two twentieth-century sources do not even mention Kirkman's death: Carl W. Breihan, "Cullen Baker," in his *Great Gunfighters of the West* (San Antonio, 1962); and Boyd W. Johnson, "Cullen Montgomery Baker: The Arkansas-Texas Desperado," *AHQ,* XXV (Autumn, 1966).

completing this task, they appeared at the Anderson house, and demanded of Anderson's wife her husband's whereabouts. Someone stated that they intended "to kill all d——d Radicals and negroes." She informed them Anderson was absent. (He may have been taking care of the inquest details.) They ordered her to produce Kirkman's trunk, and she complied. They opened it, found nothing they wanted, and rode away. With his family thus endangered, Anderson knew that it was time to move.[50]

In the language of the inquest, the bullets did "strike penetrate and wound" Kirkman in the right side of the head and of the torso, just under the arm, and in the right breast and shoulder. Kirkman had four mortal wounds six to eight inches deep with a breadth of one-half inch, by which he had "instantly died." The unknown men with pistols and guns "feloniously, wilfully and with their malice aforethought killed and murdered" the agent "against the peace and dignity of the State." Precisely who violated the peace and dignity of Texas in this instance can never be precisely determined, but all evidence points to Baker and an accomplice.[51]

After the inquest, Anderson, William A. Payne (a merchant with whom Kirkman dealt financially), a Mr. Morrow, and others made the funeral and burial arrangements. Escorted by soldiers and a large number of local citizens, they temporarily interred Kirkman in Old Peters graveyard. The eulogy described him as "esteemed by all good citizens who knew him as a man of most unswerving integrity, earnest, fearless, and faithful in the discharge of every duty." The Andersons spoke of Kirkman as a "gentleman, and a Christian." If he had been left to do his duty, "all things would have worked out best" for both races "as he went down to facts and meted out justice to the negroes as well as to the white Southerners."[52]

50. Anderson (Sherman) to E.R.S. Canby (Commander, 5MD), February 14, 1869, 5MD, LR, Box 6, USACC, RG 393, NA.

51. Transcript of Verdict; Jury of Inquest; W. H. Tilson (Boston), October 9, 1868, Texas, 5MD, LR, T-178, Vol. 5, USACC, RG 393, NA. According to one account, the outlaws rode out of town after making a few purchases, their visit generally having been "uneventful"; Shorkley to Roberts, October 15, 1868, Vol. 83, pp. 10 and 13, Texas, BRFAL, RG 105, NA.

52. Shorkley to Roberts, October 15, 1868, pp. 10 and 13; Shorkley to William A. Payne, November 10, 1868, Vol. 83, pp. 26–27; Charles A. Vernou (AAAG) to Shorkley, October 28, 1868, Vol. 83, p. 4; Reynolds to Howard, October 29, 1868, Vol. 5, p. 450, AC, LS, all in Texas, BRFAL, RG 105, NA. See also Taylor, "Swamp Fox of the Sulphur," 47 and 87. For an inventory of Kirkman's effects made in Anderson's presence, see Shorkley, October 13, 1868, LR, Post of Clarksville Records, USACC, RG 393, NA. The individuals who took care of Kirkman's remains were later reimbursed by the government.

The next day, October 8, Watlington, the Boston farmer and school-teacher, encountered Baker. Baker announced that he had murdered Kirkman and that his men, even now, were camped not far off. He intended to return to Boston and "clean up" the entire garrison. Calling for another bottle of whiskey and bidding farewell, Baker rode hurriedly past at the head of a dozen or more of his gang, "all heavily armed, and many of them evidently drunk or nearly so." Watlington was stunned. He "could hardly realize that this was the Baker of our first meeting of two years before." Alcohol and constant pursuit had taken their toll upon the Swamp Fox's mind and body. He clearly bore the marks of his outrageous life.[53]

Although many stories exist depicting Baker and his relations with Cass County inhabitants, few connect him with the killing of Kirkman. By today's rules of evidence, it might be argued that there is no conclusive proof that Baker assassinated Kirkman. However, local folklore and history of the Rames family (*viz.* that of Seth and Lee) support Baker's implication. A week after dispatching the Boston Bureau agent, Baker and his cohorts appeared at Akin's Creek across from Holmes Cemetery. Bryant Holmes, who had been a Confederate soldier and was a cousin to the Rameses, may have known some of Baker's band. Returning from a trip, Holmes was informed by his mother that Baker and his men were down at the creek and needed corn for their horses.

When Bryant confronted Baker, the outlaw stated, "My boys had to get some corn for their horses. We're down there on the creek. Federals been on our tail. We lost 'em in Sulphur bottom at Stone Bluff." Baker did not offer to pay for the grain as "it was not expected." The Rames family story emphasizes Baker's resistance to carpetbag rule and "its hated impositions." Baker told Holmes, "I'm gonna give you this" as payment, and "pulled a large gold watch from his pocket," which he said that he had "got off that Carpet Bagger I shot up at Boston last week." His victim was probably Kirkman. Bryant declined to accept the watch as he wanted to forget the war: if he had taken it, he would "always be recollecting." Baker mounted his "raw-boned pacing mule" and rode off.[54]

The unresolved investigation of Kirkman's death continued into 1869 although all sources agree that the major instigator was Baker. William Bass, the Boston citizen who had been with Kirkman the night of the murder,

53. Watlington, "Memoirs," 83–85.
54. Rames family material, in the possession of the authors.

connected Baker to the killing through Kirkman's horse. Bass declared that Kirkman had owned an iron gray horse of medium size that had no brand or mark. Bass had sold it to him for ninety-one dollars. The animal was stolen from the stable the night Kirkman perished. Bass had been informed by reliable sources that Baker traded the horse to John Rochelle, who lived about fifteen miles east of Boston, where it was believed to remain. Unfortunately, nothing ever came of Bass's information.[55]

Kirkman's murder had a ripple effect throughout the Boston community. Citizens felt that the life of anyone who had befriended Kirkman could not be considered safe. Anderson, who had known and supported the agent well, decided to leave the area after the assassination. He made contact with Kirkman's brothers and moved back to Sherman, "fearing personal violence if he remained longer in Boston." In fact, Anderson resigned his clerkship shortly after Kirkman's murder, stating that "he could not safely reside longer in Bowie County." Baker's actions and reputation deeply influenced Anderson's decision to migrate.[56]

55. Affidavit of W. W. Bass, March 3, 1869, LR, Box 2, Post of Jefferson Records, USACC, RG 393, NA; W. A. Payne (Boston) to Commander (Post of Clarksville), January 6, 1869, Endorsements, Entry 2, Vol. 2, p. 24; Endorsement, Shorkley (Commander, Post of Clarksville), January 9, 1869, all in Post of Clarksville Records, USACC, RG 393, NA; George P. Buell (Commander, Jefferson) to Secretary of Civil Affairs (5MD), June 25, 1869, LR, J-6, M1188, Reel 22, USACC, RG 393, NA; Sworn Statement of Lizzie Campbell, Sworn Statement of Henry Campbell, May 7, 1869, both attached to Buell to Secretary of Civil Affairs (5MD), June 25, 1869, LR, J-6, M1188, Reel 22; Buell to Secretary for Civil Affairs (5MD), June 3, 1869, LR, J-51, M1188, Reel 22, all in USACC, RG 393, NA; Affidavit of William Johnson alias William Glover, May 26, 1869, LR, Box 2, Post of Jefferson, USACC, RG 393, NA; Charges and Specifications Preferred Against Citizen Richard Tiller, November 13, 1868, LR, Box 2, Post of Jefferson Records, USACC, RG 393, NA; James Davidson (Boston) to B. F. Grafton (Post Adjutant, Jefferson), May 5, 1869, DT, LR, Box 19, USACC, RG 393; B. F. Grafton (Commander, Jefferson) to Davidson, June 8, 1869, LS, Vol. 1, p. 65; both in Post of Jefferson Records, USACC, RG 393, NA; Davidson to Grafton, February 28, 1869, LR, Box 2, Post of Jefferson Records; Davidson to Morse (Secretary of Civil Affairs, 5MD), June 21, 1869, M1188, LR, Reel 9; Davidson to Grafton, June 23 1869, M1188, LR, Reel 22, all in USACC, RG 393, NA.

56. Shorkley to Roberts, October 9, 1868, p. 1; October 9, 1868, pp. 4–5; October 15, 1868, pp. 9–13, all in Vol. 83, Texas, BRFAL, RG 105, NA; E. M. Pease to E. R. S. Canby (Commander, 5MD), February 3, 1869, GP (Pease), TSL. Copies of the reports of the events surrounding the agent's murder were sent to his brothers, Joel and Marshall; Vernou to Shorkley, October 28, 1868, Vol. 83, p. 4; Vernou to M. M. Kirkman (Chicago), November 5, 1868, Vol. 5, p. 456; Shorkley to M. M. Kirkman, November 29, 1868, Vol. 83, p. 29; Reynolds to Howard, October 27, 1868, Vol. 5, p. 447, all in Texas, BRFAL, RG 105, NA. JTK requested a leave of absence to remove the remains of his wife who had died in the 1867 Galveston yellow fever

The Freedmen's Bureau in Texas appointed George Shorkley to investigate Kirkman's assassination. An agent himself, Shorkley had headquarters in Clarksville (Red River County). Shorkley had originally intended to visit Boston on October 10, three days after the murder. But a local judge and other community members advised him to delay his inquiry, and he wisely followed their advice. However, local citizens remained in an excited state, still disturbed over the killing of the government official. Rumors about the murder floated about the town, creating further confusion. While the population desired the return of peace, local law enforcement officials did nothing to apprehend the killers.

When Shorkley made the journey to Boston on October 13, he hired a light two-horse wagon driven by a black man and "traveled as a citizen on business." He had compelling reasons for assuming this disguise, the most important of which was the protection of his life. Incognito, he first visited Anderson, who in fright was preparing to leave town. After Shorkley identified himself, Anderson urged him to continue to conceal his true background while in the area. According to the county clerk, it was not safe for any government officer, particularly a Bureau agent, to enter the town without a "sufficient force of men for protection" as Kirkman's murder painfully demonstrated.[57]

Although many reasons could be given for this frozen state of affairs in Boston, at this time Baker's presence was most responsible. Local individuals would not even mention his name openly, simply referring to him as "that man" or "he." Many of the inhabitants refused to speak about the assassination because they believed, and rightly so, that Baker had confederates living in the town. The whole county, Shorkley observed, whether black or white, lived in awe and dread of Baker and his gang. Some of the area freedmen who farmed for themselves had left, either going back for safety to their "old masters" or moving from the county.[58]

---

epidemic and WGK to the family cemetery in Morgan County, Illinois. Whether he did so is unknown; JTK to Roberts (AAAG, 5MD), November 1, 1868, LR, Vol. 5, M1193, Reel 2, USACC, RG 393, NA; D. D. L. Sweet (Secretary, Board of Trustees, Chicago YMCA) to E. B. Washburne, April 5, 1869, 5MD, LR Box 6, USACC, RG 393, NA. JTK was Sweet's nephew. For Marshall, who became a successful railroad executive and writer, see "Marshall Monroe Kirkman," *Dictionary of American Biography*, V, 434–35.

57. Shorkley to Roberts, October 9, 1868, p. 1; October 9, 1868, pp. 4–5; October 15, 1868, pp. 9–13, all in Vol. 83, Texas, BRFAL, RG 105, NA. E. M. Pease to E. R. S. Canby (Commander, 5MD), February 3, 1869, GP (Pease), TSL.

58. Shorkley to Roberts, October 9, 1868, p. 1; October 15, 1868, pp. 9–13, both in Vol. 83, Texas, BRFAL, RG 105, NA. Watlington, "Memoirs," 83–85.

The freedmen needed special protection, but Shorkley deemed it unwise to send a garrison for assistance unless the company could be stationed permanently in town. In that way, he argued, black and white law-abiding citizens would be influenced to take active measures in support of "law and order without the fear of future consequences." Shorkley hoped the government would be untiring in its efforts to visit upon the Boston agent's murderers the "swift vengeance of an outraged law," and he informed William A. Payne that he wished the merchant would continue to assist the county. The Clarksville agent was "most anxious to relieve the people in some manner acceptable to them."[59] Their relief later came through the citizens themselves.

Baker and his group appear not to have remained quiescent long. Shortly after sunrise on October 15, a band of mounted men coming from Arkansas, reported to number about fifty, attacked the Whitaker place, located about twelve miles from Jefferson but in Cass County. They killed seven blacks and wounded two or three others. After burning the gin house, which contained thirty-five bales of cotton, and the gristmill, with all its corn, they rode off. It cannot be proven that Baker either led or participated in this event, but the military suspected him. The Whitaker plantation was managed solely by prosperous freedmen and freedwomen. Baker and his desperado colleagues could not countenance a successful experiment.[60]

Moving back across the state line into Arkansas, Baker set his sights on another Bureau agent. Hiram F. Willis considered his Bureau position "a dear little job." Conscientious like Kirkman about his duties, he died performing them. If Baker was Kirkman's nemesis, for Willis it was Ben Griffith, a man with characteristics similar to those of the Swamp Fox. Griffith, according to William L. Richter, had a "personal quarrel with the aftermath of the Civil War." Willis called him a "great desperado" who was "a terror to all peaceable men and freedmen": he disarmed blacks, "beat them with his gun butt, made them roll in the dirt, and shot barely to miss

59. Shorkley to Roberts, October 9, 1868, Vol. 83, p. 1; Shorkley to Payne, November 10, 1868, Vol. 83, pp. 26–27; Reynolds to Shorkley, October 28, 1868, Vol. 5, p. 449, AC, LS; Anderson to Shorkley, November 4, 1868, Vol. 83, p. 8; Endorsements, Shorkley, November 27, 1868, Vol. 83, p. 7; Shorkley to M. M. Kirkman (Chicago), November 29, 1868, Vol. 83, p. 29, all in Texas, BRFAL, RG 105, NA.

60. H. Sweeney (Agent, Jefferson) to Roberts (AAAG), October 26, 1868, AC, LR, S-327, Texas, BRFAL, RG 105, NA.

them if they failed to respond quickly enough to his commands." He could be hired to kill any recalcitrant black.[61]

Griffith's reputation for racist attacks paralleled Baker's, and the two men worked both sides of the Red River. Griffith, like Baker, was elusive. Neither had a real domicile, but they had relatives and neighbors willing to assist them. They both preferred operating out of the swamps and river bottoms that dominated the landscape in that region. Some freedmen informed Willis that they had discovered where Griffith was staying and volunteered to lead the agent to the outlaw. But Willis was cautious, having already led one unsuccessful attempt to capture him. Willis had to maintain constant vigilance as Griffith had many friends and had promised to kill him on sight.[62]

When some individuals charged that Willis no longer stood with the freedmen, he responded that whites claimed he was too pro-black. Nevertheless, any favoritism shown toward blacks disgusted Baker, and he surely knew that Kirkman and Willis had previously cooperated to locate him. On October 24, Willis, a planter named Porter J. Andrews, and Little River County sheriff Richard H. Standel went to Andrews' farm to negotiate a settlement with the workers. Willis and Andrews rode in a buggy driven by a black man, and Standel traveled slightly ahead on his horse. First, Standel disappeared around a bend. Then when those in the buggy rounded the curve, they were shocked to see Standel standing beside his horse with his hands in the air.[63]

Standel, covered by a gunman, could do nothing. Six other men, pistols drawn, advanced toward Willis and Andrews, shouting for them to stop and disarm themselves. Willis drew his six-shooter, the attackers fired, and all three riders in the buggy died. Standel took an opportunity to bolt for the woods and escaped. In town, he discovered a company of black militia in the midst of drilling. They all returned to the murder scene and found three bodies; gone were the horses, buggy, and assailants. Later, a local denizen observed eight riders guiding three horses along the Red River bottom. He identified Baker as the leader. The Bureau commissioner in Arkansas characterized the slaying as "high-handed, cold-blooded murder."[64]

61. William L. Richter, " 'A Dear Little Job': Second Lieutenant Hiram F. Willis, Freedmen's Bureau Agent in Southwestern Arkansas, 1866–1868," *AHQ*, L (Summer, 1991), 191–92.

62. *Ibid.*, 192–93.

63. *Ibid.*, 193. Willis made an offhand remark to headquarters about the rule of mob law.

64. *Ibid.*, 196–97.

The Little Rock *Daily Republican* reported the "sad intelligence" of the killing of an "unknown Negro and two government agents" by Baker and "his damnable Ku Klux gang." It explained that, bushwhacked by "cowardly villains" at Walnut Bayou, Sheriff Standel had suffered a slight wound. This account contends that Baker and his outlaws had plotted to murder various other local politicians (names and positions not identified), but these officials, hearing rumors of an assassination attempt, had taken another route. On October 25, state officials proceeded to Rocky Comfort to begin garnering evidence of the murders. They had learned that Baker had about one hundred men and anticipated murdering more men connected with the state and national governments.[65]

After Willis' death, the governor of Arkansas declared martial law in this area and sent R. F. Catterson with five hundred men to restore peace. Catterson arrested Bud Griffith, the brother of Willis' nemesis, as well as two associates for complicity in the murder of Andrews, Willis, and the black driver. Tried and convicted, they were hanged at Rocky Comfort. (As noted earlier, Ben had been killed at Clarksville, Texas, by the Bureau agent Charles F. Rand.)[66] Gradually, through a combination of military efforts, citizen bands, and state cooperation, desperadoes were being eliminated. Outraged citizens saw to it that Cullen Montgomery Baker would be the next major outlaw permanently removed.

65. *Ibid.*, 197. Richter writes (199) that Willis' career "demonstrated how much an able man might do in a revolutionary social and political situation to chart the difficult path between the extremes. Yet even in his success there was failure. Willis was ever the outsider in Arkansas, an interloper who was to be endured, not welcomed." He further states (200) that the killing of Willis "showed how easily a well-intentioned, objective man could be defeated by his extremist opponents' appeal to the suspicions, confusions, and deceptions inherent in a period of rapid, uncertain, and unwelcome change like the Reconstruction." For additional accounts, see Taylor, "Swamp Fox of the Sulphur," 88–92; and Eason, "Cullen Baker," 12. One source states that Andrews was an assistant United States tax assessor. See also Richter, " 'This Blood-Thirsty Hole,' " 51–77.

66. Richter, " 'A Dear Little Job,' " 191–99; Johnson, "Cullen Montgomery Baker," 236; Powell Clayton, *Aftermath of the Civil War in Arkansas* (New York, 1915), 99–105; Orval Truman Driggs, Jr., "The Issues of the Powell Clayton Regime, 1868–1871," *AHQ*, VIII (Spring, 1949), 1–75, especially 14–30. A poor biography is William H. Burnside, *The Honorable Powell Clayton* (Conway, Ark., 1991).

FOUR

The Death of the Swamp Fox

BAKER ONLY LIVED a couple more months after murdering William G. Kirkman and Hiram F. Willis, among several others. He spent his remaining days attempting to settle old scores in the home neighborhood. Although the army continued its intermittent efforts to capture Baker, it was local residents who finally ended his violent career. He returned to Cass County, and death for whites and blacks followed in his wake. He focused his attention upon those who had participated in the manhunt for him in late 1867 and early 1868; his motive, revenge for the killing of Seth Rames. Baker's other primary target would be Thomas Orr, whom he still hated for marrying Belle Foster, sister of his second wife, Martha. But there would be other victims as well.

Little is known about Baker during these final months: what his exact movements were, how large the size of his band was, and who accompanied him after he and accomplices murdered the two Freedmen's Bureau agents and numerous blacks. It seems that he was impelled to return to his formerly complacent neighborhood, though residents there would no longer tolerate his presence. Baker had not been back in Cass County since the attack on the Howell Smith farm in December, 1867, and his subsequent wounding. Of course, some citizens in the vicinity would be willing to compromise and accept a form of truce with him in order to end his terrorism, but not all. But before Baker reappeared in that area, he decided to hunt down those who had earlier attempted to capture him or participated in killing Seth Rames.

The evidence suggests that once the Swamp Fox moved back into Texas, the number of his followers dwindled significantly. The estimated size of Baker's gang varies widely throughout the contemporary and secondary literature. A majority of the time neither the numbers nor the names of his comrades are specified. Rather, approximate numbers are given for Baker's followers, and the figures range from five to over one hundred; there is never any explanation given for this phenomenon. It may be that once Baker left Arkansas, many of his cohorts abandoned him because they felt unwilling to leave their own locales or refused to become involved in the mere settling of personal scores as opposed to attacks on the army or the Bureau.

It seems that Baker had between four and six men accompanying him when he returned to his old neighborhood in Cass County. Riding into the area, they spread a path of violence. The gang, writes Triplett, stopped at the farm of a Dr. Jones, where Baker represented himself as a militia officer in search of Cullen Baker. Several freedmen had earlier stated that "they intended to hunt up Cullen Baker and kill him," so he persuaded them to assist him. After he decoyed these blacks away from the plantation, he lined them up in front of his men, who opened fire. Six were killed and others wounded. At the home of Jones's brother, the group murdered another freedman.[1]

As Baker embarked on this final bout of murder, he and his desperadoes scoured the countryside for defenseless whites and blacks. Since the war's conclusion, those who had expressed their unionism in the face of southern defeat had always been suspect in Baker's eyes, but he never made any attempt to articulate his behavior publicly. Instead, he exhibited his ideology through harassment and murder, though no written word from him confirms this perspective. Every past account, however, makes much of his hatred for those who remained loyal to the Union during the war and for

---

1. Frank Triplett, "Cullen Montgomery Baker," in his *History, Romance and Philosophy of Great American Crimes and Criminals* . . . (New York, 1884), 459; Boyd W. Johnson, "Cullen Montgomery Baker: The Arkansas-Texas Desperado," *AHQ*, XXV (Autumn, 1966), 236; Carl W. Breihan, "Cullen Baker," in his *Great Gunfighters of the West* (San Antonio, 1962), 81; Al Eason, "Cullen Baker—Purveyor of Death," *Frontier Times*, XL (August–September, 1966), 44; T. U. Taylor, "Swamp Fox of the Sulphur, or Life and Times of Cullen Montgomery Baker," *ca.* 1936 (Typescript in ECBTHC), 110–13. James Smallwood, "Swamp Fox of the Sulphur," Pt. 2, *True West*, XXXVIII (November, 1991), 41, claimed that Baker "left their bodies to rot in the field."

the freedmen and -women. Ostensibly on a revenge rampage, in October, 1868, Baker and his gang rode to Sarah Taylor's plantation and killed several freedmen.[2]

Then, according to the army, on October 24, between 2:00 and 4:00 A.M., Baker appeared at the home of James Salmon (five and one-half miles east of present-day Atlanta, Texas), accompanied by two men. Baker believed that Salmon had "talked about him," had assisted the army in its search for him in late 1867, and was implicated in Rames's death. Intent on avenging the murder of Seth, the gang surrounded the Salmon house. Claiming to be Federal soldiers, they ordered him to come out and talk with them. They threatened to set fire to the house if he declined. This ploy succeeded, and when Salmon reluctantly opened the door, Baker "rushed in" and grabbed him. Salmon quickly realized the purpose of the visit.[3]

Orr, who surely heard about the attack on the Salmon household first-hand, wrote that at the Salmon farm, the Baker band "instituted a general carnival of plunder and robbery. Trunks were bursted open and searched for money, arms and ammunition; beds were plundered, out-houses ransacked, and everything of value to them was taken, including a very fine saddle-mule, rifle-gun, saddle-bags, saddle, bridle, etc., and a small quantity of money." Salmon well understood that Baker had come not for the plunder but for him. Perhaps Baker felt that if he murdered Salmon, the community would immediately feel forced to come to terms with him.[4]

Salmon's wife begged the desperadoes not to take her husband. They informed her that they did not intend to hurt him and would return in a short time. After taking Salmon prisoner, the gang secured a rope around his neck, tied his hands, and rode about a quarter of a mile from the residence. They "shot him very badly," killing him "almost instantly," a local newspaper reported. Mrs. Salmon heard the gunfire; she did not know "what mischief they were doing, but was very well satisfied that they were depriving her of her only pleasures and comfort upon earth." A few months later, a reporter

2. Johnson, "Cullen Montgomery Baker," 256.

3. Abstract of Crimes, 5MD, Office of Civil Affairs, Vol. 1, USACC, RG 393, NA; Eason, "Cullen Baker," 44; Johnson, "Cullen Montgomery Baker," 236; Breihan, "Cullen Baker," 81; Taylor, "Swamp Fox of the Sulphur," 110–13. The two men who accompanied Baker were George H. Robinson and George S. Franks, but nothing further could be discovered about them.

4. Thomas Orr, ed., *Life of the Notorious Desperado Cullen Baker, from His Childhood to His Death, with a Full Account of All the Murders He Committed* (Little Rock, 1870), 43.

for the Harrison *Flag* found her to be "feeble, delicate, and emaciated," her life a "great misery."[5]

The story that circulated through the neighborhood was that Salmon had promised Seth he would not be harmed but had been unable to save him. (Salmon's brother John was also on Baker's list to be exterminated and later received his visit.) Thomas Taylor has it that Lee Rames exclaimed: "Jim, you deserve the death of a dog. You betrayed my little brother to the Vigilant[e]s, promised him protection, got him to surrender his pistol and then had him foully murdered. He surrendered to you thinking you were one of his best friends, and you betrayed him. On account of the long friendship between your family and mine I do not intend to kill you myself but you are going to die." The other gang members made sure Salmon died "in his tracks."[6]

On October 30, the group proceeded to the home of Frank Scarborough, believed to have been one of the six men involved in the Seth Rames murder. In 1868, Frank (or D. F.) Scarborough was becoming a prosperous farmer. His personal worth influenced Baker's decision to select him. A recent emigrant from Georgia, where he and his family were all born, Scarborough was married with two children (aged two and three at the time of moving). In Texas, he would accrue real estate valued at $300 and a personal estate worth an impressive $9,150. Scarborough settled in an area about one and one-half miles west of present-day Atlanta, Texas, on land adjacent to the farm of Preston R. Scott on the west. It was alleged that Scarborough saved Kirby's life the night of the Smith attack.[7]

At Scarborough's farm, Baker and his gang killed two freedmen. Scarborough, after being assured three times that he would not be harmed, finally appeared. Breihan claims that Baker "persuaded" Scarborough to "promise that he would talk to [Preston R.] Scott and others to inquire if a compro-

5. *Weekly Harrison Flag* (Marshall) January 28, 1869, p. 2. A reporter found Mrs. Salmon to be a "miserable being" who did not believe she could survive many months. This writer surmised that she would "rather be dead than in her present situation."

6. Taylor, "Swamp Fox of the Sulphur," 110; Breihan, "Cullen Baker," 81; Breihan, "Cullen Baker—First of the Gunfighters," *The West,* VII (July, 1967), 45; Eason, "Cullen Baker," 44; Yvonne Vestal, *The Borderlands and Cullen Baker* (Atlanta, Texas, 1978), 80; Johnson, "Cullen Montgomery Baker," 236; Triplett, "Cullen Montgomery Baker," 459. Smallwood, "Swamp Fox," Pt. 2, p. 41, asserted that after riddling Salmon's body with bullets, they left him "in the road to rot as a warning to other Unionists."

7. MCR (Eighth Census), 1860, Cass County, Texas, p. 123, RG 29, NA; Taylor, "Swamp Fox of the Sulphur," 111.

mise could be arranged." In any event, the agreement he sought would not protect Seth Rames's killers. Lee Rames, said Eason, insisted Scarborough be put to death for the part he had played in the death of Seth. Because of a plea from Scarborough's wife and from Matthew "Dummy" Kirby, Frank survived. Moreover, if Baker had intended to kill Scarborough, he would not have sought his assistance.[8] It appears that, in his typically unpredictable way, Baker was seeking revenge against those involved in the killing of Seth Rames while simultaneously wanting the assurance that he could enter his old neighborhood with impunity. Perhaps the military's increasingly organized pursuit of him had heightened his anxiety to act on his personal vendettas.

Baker, according to Thomas Orr, extensively questioned Scarborough about Scott and others in the neighborhood who had joined in the search for Baker after the Howell Smith debacle ten months earlier. Particular about whom he intended to harass or to leave alone, Baker desired that Scarborough talk with Scott and Robert Spell with a "view to making peace and burying the hatchet." (Baker and especially Lee Rames only desired access to those men who had participated in the murder of Seth.) If they refused this request, Baker claimed "he would burn every house within forty miles" of the Scarborough place. Scarborough promised to talk with Scott and Spell, and, if possible, bring about a compromise.[9]

The next stop on the Baker revenge/compromise tour was Parson Jesse Dodd's farm, where, according to James M. Smallwood, the gang murdered another freedman. Held captive, Dodd finally agreed to try to effect an understanding between Baker and area citizens. Jesse Dodd may also have

8. Breihan, "Cullen Baker," 81; Breihan, "First of the Gunfighters," 45; Eason, "Cullen Baker," 44; Taylor, "Swamp Fox of the Sulphur," 110–13. Taylor states that of the two blacks murdered, one was a "young negro who discovered the approaching party, took to his heels and was shot down." The other, an "old servant" named Drayton, tried to escape "when he was shot." Taylor also related the story of Scarborough saving Kirby's life during the Howell Smith attack in December, 1867. Vestal, in *The Borderlands*, 80–81, repeats the same story. Ed Bartholomew, *Cullen Baker: Premier Texas Gunfighter* (Houston, 1954), has much extraneous material but nothing on the Scarborough encounter.

9. Orr, *Life of the Notorious Desperado*, 34; Eason, "Cullen Baker," 44; Smallwood, "Swamp Fox," Pt. 2, p. 41; Taylor, "Swamp Fox of the Sulphur," 111–12, from whom Eason obtained his information. Taylor also states (112–13) that "Lee Rames was claiming the death warrant on account of the death of his brother," but " 'Dummy' Kirby threw his influence in behalf of mercy and Baker over-ruled Rames and spared Scarborough's life. He remarked later that he did not have the heart to kill a man whose wife made such an eloquent appeal."

been a lay preacher, but he was essentially a cultivator and reasonably prosperous. He and his wife Martha were Georgia born, and they had five children by 1870; three girls and two boys, ranging in age from four months to
twelve years. Four of the children had been born in Arkansas, one in Texas.
It is not known when Dodd arrived in Arkansas or Texas, but he was able to
accumulate real estate valued at $2,800 and personal property worth $800.
Listed as a farmer in the 1870 census, he was certainly that and perhaps
much more.[10]

Frank Triplett theorizes that the lives of Scarborough and Dodd were
spared "on their promising to try and effect a compromise between [Baker]
and the citizens." They "very willingly" undertook this task, Triplett contends, "since they saw that all attempts at his capture seemed likely to fail."
Accordingly, Dodd and Scarborough scoured the neighborhood in search of
citizens willing to parley. Hence a day was designated for a meeting, which
in reality had an infinitesimal chance of ending the Baker menace. Available
contemporary evidence suggests that some kind of informal gathering and
discussion occurred. Terms of compromise and assurances of abiding by
them may have been proposed. Little is certain. We do know that Baker did
not attend the meeting with local citizens in person; he sent a negotiator.[11]

Baker was definitely in the area in early November, having been seen in
Jefferson "prowling about and taking observations" along with Ben Bickerstaff when he was not abusing or killing those he had chosen to eliminate.
One government official had seen him on the border between Cass and
Marion Counties, the latter of which contains Jefferson. Baker's desire to
conclude negotiations with local citizens implies that he might have feared
that they were losing patience with him and that at least a small and dedicated coterie would go to considerable lengths to banish him from the
neighborhood and end his influence there forever.[12]

One contemporary source of Baker's negotiations with local citizens was
James P. Brown, the new commander of the Jefferson post. This official

---

10. MCR (Ninth Census), 1870, Cass County, Texas, p. 86, RG 29, NA; Orr, *Life of the No-
torious Desperado*, 43; Taylor, "Swamp Fox of the Sulphur," 98 and 105; Smallwood, "Swamp
Fox," Pt. 2, p. 41; Triplett, "Cullen Montgomery Baker," 459; Breihan, "Cullen Baker," 81;
Johnson, "Cullen Montgomery Baker," 236.

11. Triplett, "Cullen Montgomery Baker," 459; Breihan, "Cullen Baker," 81; Breihan, "First
of the Gunfighters," 45.

12. H. Sweeney (Agent, Jefferson) to Roberts (AAAG), November 2, 1868, AC, LR, S-329,
Texas, BRFAL, RG 105, NA.

stated that on November 3, 1868, area citizens held a meeting at Scott's Mill. Baker sent a delegate and agreed to cease his outrages. In turn, the citizens would give no aid or information that would assist in his capture; he had "to fight it out with the Federals." Baker also offered to give a bond in the amount of $200,000 guaranteeing his good behavior (with the "best securities") henceforth. In addition, "all hostilities should cease and each side should drop all strife." Baker exacted a price for his proposed good conduct. He exempted three men whom he intended to kill: John B. Williams, John Jackson, and Bill Dunlop. The citizens asked these three intended victims to leave the county.[13]

Baker continued to search for the three men. On the night of November 4, with a gang of eighteen or twenty men, he rode into Linden, the county seat of Cass County. His gang surrounded the house of the county clerk, W. C. Loving, and ordered him to surrender, shouting, "Come out God damn you we hear you now" and similar exhortations. W. F. Connell, who lived near Loving, saw and heard this fracas as he hid in a field two hundred yards from Loving's house. Connell told the military that he knew Loving was home at the time, became fearful for his own life, and retreated to Jefferson, ignorant of Loving's fate. Baker apparently believed the county clerk would have information on the whereabouts of Dunlop, Williams, and Jackson.[14]

On November 5, 1868, Connell met with two other Cass County citizens (John H. and A. W. Salmon) who had not been part of the Scott's Mill parley. Tired of Baker's depredations, they called upon James P. Brown, the Jefferson post commander, seeking assistance. The three individuals were related by marriage and blood to the James Salmon whom Baker had previously murdered. They told Brown they had been obliged to leave their homes, as Baker was determined to kill them because of their previous as-

13. James P. Brown (Commander, Post of Jefferson) to AAAG (5MD), November 6, 1868, 5MD, LR, B-165, Vol. 5, M1165, USACC, RG 393, NA; Breihan, "First of the Gunfighters," 45; Breihan, "Cullen Baker," 81–82; Orr, *Life of the Notorious Desperado,* 43–44; Eason, "Cullen Baker," 12 and 44; Triplett, "Cullen Montgomery Baker," 459–60. Taylor, "Swamp Fox of the Sulphur," 98–99, confirms most of this and claims that Baker's delegate was Parson Jesse Dodd; however, he states that when Lieutenant Williams heard of the exception made of himself, "he swore vengeance against both sides," claiming that "Scott and his friends had sold his life to save their own hides." He resigned, threatened he would go to Missouri, raise a company, return, and clean out both sides. Nothing "further was ever heard of him." Baker had reportedly killed another soldier.

14. James P. Brown (Commander, Post of Jefferson) to AAAG (5MD), November 6, 1868, 5MD, LS, B-165, Vol. 6, M1165, Reel 2, USACC, RG 393, NA.

sistance to Brigadier General N. B. McLaughlin of the 4th Cavalry in pursuing Baker. They believed the military should be making a more concerted effort to apprehend him.[15]

Connell and the two Salmons were united in their appeal. They stated that if a body of cavalry should be sent after Baker with the understanding that it was not to return until he was either captured or killed, it would be supported and assisted by an unspecified number of citizens. They were chary of giving any support unless the army totally dedicated itself to his effective eradication. They requested considerable assurance from the army because those who had joined in the pursuit of Baker under General McLaughlin were now "paying for it with their lives one by one as opportunity occurs." Area residents attempted to protect themselves from Baker and his adherents in Cass County, even seeking the army's assistance.[16]

John H. Salmon knew that Baker sought his life, so, in addition to talking to the military, he sought the assistance of one of the leading compromise spokesmen. He wrote R. P. Crump, whom Baker respected, that "I do not *know*, and have no particular reasons to believe, that *he*, in his own person, has *anything* against me." The little intercourse that had existed between him and Baker in the past had been of a "friendly, and rather confidential character." In two instances, Baker had visited this Salmon brother at his home and requested assistance and services, which the latter cheerfully rendered. Although sick, Salmon had aided Baker in making a settlement with Bill Foster in Arkansas over some difficulty.[17]

Even before this last transaction, Salmon had frequently heard from various sources that Baker intended to kill him on "first sight." He had been advised "to hunt [Baker] up and kill him, and [these sources] would clear me by their testimony." Salmon stated he did not believe such stories and felt these individuals wanted him to murder Baker because they were afraid to attempt such a deed themselves. As regarding "raids and hunts made by the citizens and the party known as the Scott party, after Baker and his friends," Salmon emphatically asserted he had never had anything to do with such activities. He had never knowingly harmed any of the Baker party. Salmon claimed it was not his fight and that he and his other

15. *Ibid.* Brown believed that the character of his informants entitled them to military support.

16. *Ibid.*

17. John W. Salmon (Jefferson) to Col. R. P. Crump, November 7, 1868, LR, Box 2, Post of Jefferson Records, USACC, RG 393, NA.

brother, George, agreed on a general policy of remaining aloof from the conflict with Baker.[18]

John Salmon voiced his worry over his future in this letter. He had been informed that there was a "general prejudice" against him and that someone was "particularly" determined to have him killed. Salmon could not safely stay in his house or attend to business. He regretted the killing of Jim Salmon, but it was not his fight and he could not interfere. How did he now stand? Did the Baker party desire his death and "if so, for what?" What assurances would they give of his safety and the continued cultivation of the Salmon farm? Would he be allowed to live on it safely or must he rent it out? Notably, he asked, "Will negroes be allowed to remain there unmolested?" He wanted peace and wondered, "Can I have it?"[19]

At about this time, John S. Jackson similarly appealed to R. P. Crump for assistance. Jackson was a Georgia-born farmer who had become an established member of the neighborhood where Baker had previously roamed. Jackson, with a wife and three children (two boys and a girl), had migrated to Alabama for an uncertain length of time, where the oldest boy had been born, and finally settled with his family in Texas. He apparently did not own any land because the census taker listed no property that could be assessed. His personal estate was evaluated at eight hundred dollars.

Jackson had learned that he was accused by Baker and his cohorts of being one of the party who killed Seth Rames. He, along with Bill Dunlop, Green Allen, and John B. Williams, witnessed the murder. Jackson claimed he had no idea Rames would be executed, only that he would be closely questioned and turned over to the Federal authorities. Blaming Williams, Jackson said nobody else shot him and "if any man in the party is punished but Williams, it will be unjustly done." If he could not settle his affairs and peacefully leave the country, he wished that he and his family and their few effects be left alone. Jackson eluded Baker's clutches.[20] Too often, those who have written about Baker have ignored these men like Jackson whom Baker targeted.

Baker did not harm Connell or the two Salmons as his attention had turned to events in Sevier (now Howard) County, Arkansas. The day after the general election, November 4, Powell Clayton, governor of Arkansas,

18. *Ibid.*
19. *Ibid.*
20. MCR (Eighth Census), 1860, Cass County, Texas, p. 117, RG 29, NA; John S. Jackson to Colonel R. P. Crump, [1868], LR, Box 2, Post of Jefferson Records, USACC, RG 393, NA.

had placed the county under martial law and dispatched 500 troops under Brigadier General R. F. Catterson to restore order. Clayton stated that Baker's "perfect Ku Klux organization" (he reportedly had 150 guerrillas) was searching for weapons and concentrating its forces at Centre Point, where a supply of arms was cached. On November 12, Catterson's state militia dispersed the desperadoes after what amounted to a relatively bloodless and brief skirmish. Baker more than likely retreated after he realized his opponents' strength. The "insurgent forces" scattered, a few were captured, and the conflict ended undramatically.[21]

Unfortunately, we have been unable to find much background on this confrontation at Centre Point. Its outcome does suggest that when confronted by the military, a state government police organization, and willing citizens all united, Baker and his followers were not nearly as steadfast as previous writers have suggested. In fact, the pattern of Baker murders indicates that he and his followers generally attacked unsuspecting individuals, rarely killing anyone who was prepared or who was part of a sizeable group. Baker's gangs, whatever their size, could not withstand an organized force. Centre Point proved what could be accomplished through the cooperation of the state militia and an organized citizenry. Instead of being the aggressor, Baker became the hunted. The citizens finally became disgusted with the noncommittal military and the state, and acted to eliminate him themselves.

After the brief clash at Centre Point, and in the hope of receiving local assistance to end Baker's reign of terror, the United States government along with Governor Clayton increased the monetary reward for the outlaw's capture or death. Although Baker's name generally headed their list, government authorities also sought the removal of other prominent gunmen. General Joseph J. Reynolds, commander of the Fifth Military District, announced that one thousand dollars per gunman would be paid to an indi-

21. Powell Clayton, *The Aftermath of the Civil War in Arkansas* (New York, 1915), 110–13; Eric Foner, *Reconstruction: America's Unfinished Revolution, 1863–1877* (New York, 1988), 440; Allen W. Trelease, *White Terror: The Ku Klux Klan Conspiracy and Southern Reconstruction* (New York, 1971), 43–44, 155–79. For horror stories of what the militia did, see Virginia Buxton, "Clayton's Militia in Sevier and Howard Counties," *AHQ,* XX (Winter, 1961), 344–50; J. H. Atkinson, ed., "Clayton and Catterson Rob Columbia County," *AHQ,* XXI (Summer, 1962), 153–57. Triplett, "Cullen Montgomery Baker," 459–60, wrote in the nineteenth century that Clayton's Arkansas militia was "composed of 'mountain Boomers,' thieves and thugs, under the command of officers no more honorable than themselves," and had "rendered themselves obnoxious to the citizens by their thefts, insults and outrages."

vidual for the delivery of Baker or several others, dead or alive, to either the Austin or the Marshall post commander. Because of Baker's "various outrages" upon Arkansas citizens and the murder of Howell Smith, Clayton offered a one-thousand-dollar bounty for him.[22]

After the militia almost took him prisoner (Baker's companion Matthew "Dummy" Kirby was shot and wounded in the Centre Point encounter), Baker returned with Kirby to Cass County. Similar to other Baker chroniclers, Orr has Baker regrouping his gang, or those he could summon in that portion of the country, then leading them in the opposite direction away from Catterson's troops and back across the Red River. Baker allegedly informed those who remained with him that he had to go into Lafayette [Arkansas], Bowie, and Cass Counties for the "purpose of collecting the balance of his force," declaring that he could "command the entire country."[23]

Baker's influence had waned, but he still dared to satirize the Arkansas governor's reward. Although no contemporary evidence exists for Baker's ridicule of Powell Clayton, it is alleged that he reversed the reward announcement, declaring, "by the power in me vested and by virtue of my own authority," to offer five thousand dollars for Governor Clayton, dead or alive. Nailing the information to trees at river crossroads in the Sulphur bottom, Baker attempted to demonstrate how puny the government's efforts were to capture him. Baker played one-upmanship by making his reward five times the amount offered by the state of Arkansas and by vesting all authority in himself. This effort at humor notwithstanding, Baker's position was becoming precarious, and he now sought assistance from three prominent community leaders.[24]

In addition to the Scott's Mill meeting, Baker seems to have met later with three important residents of Bowie and Cass Counties on the Dave Moore farm in the latter county. Although this meeting's date is uncertain, it must have been in November, probably after the Centre Point debacle.

22. J. H. Barton (Private Secretary; Governor of Arkansas) to Commander (Clarksville), November 31, 1868, Entry 2, LR, Vol. 5, pp. 16–17, Post of Clarksville Records, USACC, RG 393, NA. Taylor, "Swamp Fox of the Sulphur," 78–79; Johnson, "Cullen Montgomery Baker," 235; Bartholomew, *Cullen Baker,* 69; Breihan, "Cullen Baker," 81; Clayton, *The Aftermath of the Civil War,* 115.

23. Orr, *Life of the Notorious Desperado,* 46.

24. Taylor, "Swamp Fox of the Sulphur," 80; Triplett, "Cullen Montgomery Baker," 459; Johnson, "Cullen Montgomery Baker," 235; William L. Richter, " 'The Revolver Rules the Day!': Colonel DeWitt C. Brown and the Freedmen's Bureau in Paris, Texas, 1867–1868," *SwHQ,* XCIII (January, 1990); 317–18.

Contemporary newspaper evidence suggests that Baker appeared in person, in contrast to Scott's Mill, and talked extensively with R. P. Crump, F. M. Henry, and R. M. Stewart. Crump's brother-in-law gave an account of the meeting to Frank Taylor. Crump had been a Civil War colonel; Henry was a prominent Linden lawyer who owned the future site of Texarkana and helped to settle the town; and Stewart was a county commissioner in Cass who owned a farm near Linden.[25]

Upon appearing at the Moore place, Crump, Henry, and Stewart were informed by the owner that Baker had not yet arrived but could be found. Moore "slid" into the woods and in about an hour returned with Baker. The Swamp Fox came within 150 yards of the Moore house but then required the four men to come out and meet him. Crump advised Baker as a "friend" that he (Baker) had made a "good [Civil War] soldier" but that his "career" made it impossible for him to stay safely in the area. Crump, and presumably the others, urged Baker to leave the region forever to avoid being killed. Baker promised to do so.[26]

Through the "good offices" of Crump, Henry, and Stewart, Baker "permitted" a friend to write the following letter for him, which appeared in various Texas newspapers. Its tone suggests that Baker may have become desperate because of the organized pursuit of him in Arkansas. "Permit me," Baker said, "to publish a statement in your paper in order to place myself right before the government and the people of the country." Disturbed because "various rumors" had "obtained circulation through the country" in regard to his "course of conduct," he believed many persons emulated his mode of action and committed offenses "against law and good order" on his "credit." These misrepresentations forced Baker to declare his "sentiments and intentions for the future."[27]

Baker's amanuensis scribbled that to Baker was attributed the assertion that "no civil officers should perform the duties of their offices in the counties" where Baker stayed. In reality, the letter claimed, he favored the strict "enforcement of the civil laws of the country by the legitimate authorities."

25. Taylor, "Swamp Fox of the Sulphur," 103.

26. *Ibid.*, 104; Eason, "Cullen Baker," 12.

27. *Texas Republican* (Marshall), November 27, 1868, p. 2; *Daily Arkansas Gazette*, December 2, 1868, p. 1. The letter is fully quoted in Taylor, "Swamp Fox of the Sulphur," 101–102; in Vestal, *The Borderlands,* 83–84; in Orr, *Life of the Notorious Desperado,* 44–45; in Breihan, "Cullen Baker," 82–83; and in "First of the Gunfighters," 45–46. Johnson, Smallwood, and Eason mention nothing about the letter, and Triplett provides a very brief summary.

(No doubt he assumed that Democrats were legitimate and Republicans illegitimate.) Henceforth, he promised, it would be his "steady purpose to *protect the quiet* citizens and his laborers, either white or black, in the pursuit of their avocations." Baker requested that "all good citizens" inform him of "all depredations committed by other persons" charged to have been committed by himself so that he could rectify the outrages by dealing out justice himself.[28]

As this region was his "native country," and his interests were "identical" with those of his neighbors, he hoped to remain in Cass, Bowie, Marion, and the adjoining counties. It would not be his *purpose to make war* upon the good and peaceable citizens or laborers," nor did he "intend to interfere in any way with the powers that be." As long as every white man or black man left Baker "alone and pursue[d] his peaceful and lawful business," he would be "perfectly safe."[29]

Those men who impersonated him, however, he would attempt to stop. For example, he happened, "by accident," to detect a party of five men "robbing and plundering the Negroes," on Colonel Hook's Red River farm. They took guns, ammunition, and every "small article of value" and boldly called themselves "Cul Baker, Bickerstaff and company." Baker claimed to have immediately arrested, disarmed, and relieved J. Sharp, J. Porterfield, George Robertson, and George and Tom Franks of their plunder and returned it "to the proper owners." He denounced them "as being beneath contempt" and "sent the scoundrels home." He would have carried them to Boston, Texas, and had them committed to jail by the civil authorities but he had heard there were no officers in the county in whose charge he could have placed them. After discharging the five individuals, Baker warned them they would be killed if he "ever caught them under like circumstances." He concluded that, as this conduct indicated, he was "not the great manslayer that scandal has made me—killing white and black wherever found."[30]

From this time forward, Baker pledged that he would do all the good he could for the "peaceable and quiet citizens" in his area. He claimed that he would publish the causes that led . . . to his "present difficulties" because he felt he should not be "deemed by a just community wholly to blame for

28. *Texas Republican* (Marshall), November 27, 1868, p. 2. R. H. Crump may have written the letter for Baker.

29. *Ibid.*

30. *Ibid.*

my actions in the past." The Swamp Fox contended that he was, as ever, "willing to submit the whole of [his] conduct to a decision of unbiased men of [his] country, and abide by their just verdict." Unfortunately, finding such unbiased men residing in Baker country was largely impossible. Nothing he said had the ring of truth about it.[31]

The *Weekly Austin Republican* sarcastically commented upon this alleged Baker pronouncement: "So Cullen M. Baker has assumed the protection of quiet citizens, . . . so may all apprehensive souls rest under the aegis of this thief and murderer!" How ludicrous were the claims that "he will see their wrongs righted," and that "they, black and white, will be 'safe' in his hands!" Baker's successful outrages, the newspaper continued, had "so inflamed" his vanity that Baker now imagined himself "a power in the State and condescends to be gracious." Seldom, the *Republican* told its readers, had it seen "a more melancholy instance of moral perversion than this manifesto."[32]

In addition, the *Republican* could not imagine what Crump and company thought of Baker "or of themselves." Other honest men in search of the desperado, "if as fortunate in finding him, would have bound him hand and foot, and would have left him at the nearest military post to answer for his manifold atrocities." Instead, Crump and his companions, after a "cordial interview" with the "outlawed felon," returned by themselves and endorsed "his word of honor!" Baker could not be trusted, and that these individuals believed he could be suggested extreme naïveté on their part.[33]

Baker may have pledged to uphold the peace, but he had no intention of keeping his promise. He was back in the Cass County area by early December, 1868, seeking revenge. Taylor and Eason, without a shred of evidence, blame blacks for sabotaging the agreement reached at Scott's Mill. Taylor speculates that the "only condition upon which the truce could have been made a success would have been the organization of Preston R. Scott and other leading citizens of a closely-knit band of vigilant[e]s who would have let it be known publicly that any violation of the truce by anybody, white or black, would meet with drastic treatment. But the action of the negroes the day after the meeting at Scott's Mill started Cullen Baker on another raid."[34] The following account is based on insubstantial evidence and in no way diminishes the ample evidence that Baker's nature was dishonest and

31. *Ibid.* Taylor, "Swamp Fox of the Sulphur," 48.
32. Quoted in Breihan, "Cullen Baker," 84.
33. *Ibid.*
34. *Ibid.*, 100; Eason, "Cullen Baker," 44.

unscrupulous. In providing it, we demonstrate the efforts of pro-Baker writers to exonerate their man.

Blacks in the area believed that the truce included them and that Baker was under obligation to keep the peace. They acted upon the assumption that Baker had no jurisdiction over them. A local black man, Jerry Sheffield (also written "Sherfield") supposedly boasted: "I knows whar Mistah Baker sleeps in a cotton gin and I shows any white man the place foah $5.00" (some said as high as twenty-five dollars). On Sunday afternoon, December 6, less than two miles east of Queen City, Baker's group caught Sheffield and riddled his body with bullets until it "looked like a pin-cushion." Then, to "exercise their marksmanship," they "ran their horses at full speed, making them jump the negro's body and firing into his head as the horse leaped into the air."[35]

Frank Scarborough and his family, dining with Parson Jesse Dodd, heard the gunshots. The two men went down the road and discovered Sheffield's body. Placing it in a wagon, they brought the corpse back to the Dodd residence. J. D. Scarborough, Frank's son, saw the body and announced that Sheffield's "head was shot to a jelly." (J. D. was reportedly the one who had heard Sheffield remark that he knew where Baker slept.) Taylor facilely concludes that as a result of the black man's foolish statement, the "truce and all amnesty proceedings were swept aside." Eason states that "Baker heard of the talk and assuming he would never be safe or at peace, swept through the country on raids of retribution against all who had opposed him in the past."[36]

The same day he killed Sheffield, Baker searched for but did not find Robert Spell, who lived near Scott's Mill. He did capture an old acquaintance, George W. Barron (involved in the school incident between Orr and Baker), who was "hung to a cross beam across his gate" because he had participated in the "great manhunt"; however, Lee Rames cut him down. They proceeded to the Jackson and Johnson homesteads but found

---

35. Taylor, "Swamp Fox of the Sulphur," 99–100, 114–16; Taylor tends to repeat stories, especially those involving blacks. Eason, "Cullen Baker," 44–45, suggests that Baker's "intention to become law-abiding was probably sincere and [that] it's possible the truce could have been affected but for all the ill-timed boasting of a Negro boy." When word reached the area freedmen that Baker had capitulated to the demands of the citizenry, "many of them took it as a license to act as they pleased." Sheffield, Eason states, "paid dearly for a moment of bravado."

36. Taylor, "Swamp Fox of the Sulphur," 99–100, 114–15; Eason, "Cullen Baker," 44–45. Vestal, *The Borderlands*, 85–86, parrots Taylor's version.

no one at either: all had fled. Orr believed this to be "almost a miraculous escape, for had they been captured, nothing less than death would have sufficed the blood-thirsty villain." Baker wrote a note to Johnson, ordering him and his family to "leave the State within ten days, and not stop in Arkansas."[37]

As darkness settled on the day of these rampages, Baker's band surrounded the house of a Mr. Dempsey. Several of the desperados, Orr exclaims, rushed into the house, searched it, and took all the weapons and money they could find. Apparently Mrs. Dempsey did not believe the Swamp Fox was really who he said he was, so Baker, the "hero of the west," rolled his pants above his knee and pointed out the wound he had received a year earlier in the Smith affray. He contended he had been shot from the house. Orr claims Baker lied because he was actually wounded "by some one of his own clan." When the gang approached the house of Dempsey's son a half a mile away, the son and wife escaped into the woods. Baker's men searched for guns and ammunition, then killed the couple's dog.[38]

This manhunt and larceny only formed a prelude to the search for Baker's real target, Thomas Orr. Despite all Baker's threats—and documentary evidence of them is conclusive—Orr did not leave the area. Yet Baker's instability surely concerned him. In 1867, Orr had married Belle Foster and he continued to teach in Lafayette County, Arkansas, eight miles northeast of Line Ferry, until the fall of 1868. That winter, the couple decided to live with the Fosters. Orr and Baker had not encountered each other in over a year, and only Baker had made an attempt to compromise their differences (in a very general way). Orr, however, according to his recollections, remained suspicious of Baker's motives and knew his life would be in danger as long as Baker lived.[39]

By the end of the first week in December, Baker ceased to focus upon those involved in the Seth Rames matter. On returning to his old haunts, he may have been deeply influenced in his actions by Lee Rames, his supposed first lieutenant. (The army and the Freedmen's Bureau simply identify Lee as a member of Baker's most intimate group.) It is not known why Baker concentrated at this time upon Orr and ignored the surviving men involved

37. Breihan, "First of the Gunfighters," 46; Orr, *Life of the Notorious Desperado,* 46; Vestal, *The Borderlands,* 96. Barron, it might be remembered, was one of two students who withdrew from Orr's school after the schoolteacher's initial confrontation with Baker.

38. Orr, *Life of the Notorious Desperado,* 46; Vestal, *The Borderlands,* 96.

39. Orr, *Life of the Notorious Desperado,* 45.

in the murder of Seth Rames. He evidently still resented being rejected by Belle Foster and her family.

On Monday, December 7, Baker acted on this resentment. The Baker gang rode through the neighborhood harassing, threatening, and stealing. About 10:00 P.M., they appeared before the Foster home, where the family had already retired. After surrounding the house, the gang broke down the door and demanded the family's surrender. Baker ordered his men "in a very imperative tone" to keep their posts and to burn the house if a single shot was fired. Orr described Baker's followers as a "company of savage indians" who could be heard all over the house and into the yard. These "cowardly villains" entered with cocked pistols and threatened to kill all within if the inhabitants resisted.[40]

Indignantly demanding the cause of this untimely visit, Foster expected a modicum of deference from his former son-in-law. He was answered, according to Orr, with "threats and oaths that could not be excelled by all the demons of the infernal regions." Baker bellowed, "We want Thomas Orr," and ordered his surrender. Orr complied, but only after receiving assurances from Baker himself that he should not be hurt. (Although he seemed bolstered by this guarantee, Orr certainly realized that Baker's word could not be depended upon.) Orr admits that he had no confidence in Baker's pledge, but that for the sake of saving the women from destruction he surrendered. One of the women was his wife, Belle.[41]

When daylight came on December 8, Baker sent a detail to fetch Joe Davis, whom Orr describes as an old gentleman living in the settlement. Why they wanted Davis is unknown, but he returned with them. Baker bound Orr and forced him to ride behind a boy, introduced as Baker's cousin, but whom Orr identifies as Alfred Elliot, no relation to Baker. Tying a rope around Orr's neck, Baker led the group (including the three prisoners) in a westerly direction, away from Arkansas. As they rode, Baker attached the other end of the rope to a dogwood branch and commanded the boy to ride his horse forward. Orr likened his experience to being suspended by the neck between heaven and earth.[42]

Baker then conferred with his men to decide the fate of the prisoners. They all agreed that Joe Davis should also die. Having no surplus rope,

40. *Ibid.*, 47.

41. *Ibid.; Texas Republican* (Marshall), January 15, 1869, p. 3; *Flake's Daily Bulletin* (Galveston), January 20, 1869, p. 5.

42. Breihan, "First of the Gunfighters," 46; Orr, *Life of the Notorious Desperado*, 47.

Baker ordered that Orr, the "executed wretch," be cut down and dragged out of the way to make room for the second victim. Lee Rames reportedly noticed movements in Orr's eyes and threw a coat over him so that Baker would not see the man was still alive. Baker asked Rames why he had covered Orr, and he replied, "Oh, just to keep the buzzards from pecking his eyeballs out." Although physically hanged, Orr had not broken his neck; the major threat to his survival was asphyxiation. If he passed out but could still breathe, even if only slightly, he could live. Lying on the frozen ground, he feigned death.[43]

Orr survived, and so did Joe Davis. It may have been about this time that Orr, Foster, and others began to plot a course of action to murder Baker. R. H. Watlington asserts that Foster had now borne all he could from the Swamp Fox, and with his willing aid and that of Orr, who also joined the conspiracy, they began to discuss what moves they would make upon Baker's return. According to Watlington, Baker continued to visit the Foster house at night. His first demand, invariably, was for liquor, which he compelled Foster always to have available. Watlington explains that, in expectation of Baker's return, a "jug of mean whiskey was obtained and with an excessive narcotic drug added." The jug was stored away to await Baker's arrival.[44]

Fortunately for the citizens, Baker's gang broke up around the time this scheme to eliminate Baker was conceived. A rumor circulated throughout the community that Baker's clan had disbanded, apparently over conflict concerning Lee Rames's treatment of Orr. But this news did not reduce citizens' fears, "for it was expected when Baker learned that Orr was still alive, 'rescued from a living death by one of [Baker's] own trusted followers,' there would surely be a terrible reckoning in the Camp of these notorious outlaws." When Baker discovered that Orr still lived, Watlington declares, "his rage and fury was terrible, and with awful oaths [he] swore that he would find the traitor and kill him on the spot."[45]

43. Breihan, "First of the Gunfighters," 47; Orr, *Life of the Notorious Desperado*, 47; Bartholomew, *Cullen Baker*, 81–82; Vestal, *The Borderlands*, 95–96. Vestal also writes that "Joe Davis' son, 'Little Joe' kept the dogwood limb Orr was hung on for many years and showed it to visitors." Taylor, "Swamp Fox of the Sulphur," 143, gives Matthew Kirby credit for saving Orr, not Rames. Orr described the scene this way: "He was left by Cullen, apparently, a lifeless form, but had recovered, and was still living" (48). J. K. Bivins wrote that, bent on killing Orr, Baker hanged the "crippled schoolteacher," but Orr was "cut down and lived to tell how it felt to be" lynched; *Memoirs* (N.p.: Privately printed, [1945]), 22–24.

44. R. H. Watlington, "Memoirs" (Typescript in TSL), 88.

45. *Ibid.*, 88–89.

Watlington observes that apparently this was Lee Rames's opportunity to settle many old scores. Backed by his "two daring brothers and others of the band, all armed," Rames "hastily drew his pistols." Then, in Watlington's colorful prose, "with oaths equally forceful and convincing," he informed Baker that he need search no more for Orr's benefactor: "he was the *traitor*, and defied him to do his worst, and that if he was not 'bluffing,' to draw his guns and get busy with the 'killing.'" Although more verbiage thundered forth from the enraged Rames, not a shot was fired. Baker refused the challenge, and at that moment the gang members had to choose to follow either Rames or Baker.[46]

With "sullen looks and mutinous expressions," all the men but one cast their lot with Rames. Baker now realized that he had a mutiny on his hands, that his leadership was no longer needed, and that a parting of the ways between himself and the others had arrived. Watlington states that "only one man remained with him," apparently Matthew "Dummy" Kirby. The memoirist refers to Kirby as the "vilest and most notorious cutthroat of the clan." (He probably liked alcohol as much as Baker did.) Although Watlington maintains that nothing was ever heard again of Lee Rames or his followers, numerous unverified stories actually circulated throughout the area about his activities after he left Baker.[47]

The Rameses are elusive characters. Local folklore has identified them and portrayed their background, but these details that have the force of legend may be more compelling than true. Not all previous Baker investigators have elaborated on the precise status and role of Lee and Seth Rames as Taylor has done. In fact, several make no mention of the two gang members. Such omissions hinder any careful scrutiny of Baker. Many others who rode with the Swamp Fox are often not identified or related clearly to him. In the present case, determining the role of the Rames brothers in Baker's career is complex and frustrating.

The Rames family had a tragic background. John Howard Rames, after whom Seth was named, died before the war, and his wife, Harriette, moved from Arkansas back to Bowie County, where all the children had been born. The family suffered more grief when Sarah Louisa, a daughter, died near the

46. *Ibid.*, 89; Orr, *Life of the Notorious Desperado,* 48–49. Eason, "Cullen Baker," 46, contended that "no one knows exactly what triggered the quarrel but all agree Rames cursed Baker roundly and invited him to a 'shoot-out' then and there. For some reason, for the first time in his life, Baker declined to fight."

47. Watlington, "Memoirs," 89.

end of the Civil War; William, another son, fell in Confederate service; and Seth was murdered for his affiliation with Baker. Taylor opines that the Rameses' "fidelity to their friends, their grit and stoicism" derived from their Native American roots: they supposedly had "one-quarter Indian Blood." Lee, the "spectacular member of the family," exemplified such fidelity when he nursed Baker back to health and swore vengeance against those who had killed Seth (Jim Salmon, Frank Scarborough, and two others).[48]

Although Lee Rames was an occasional member of Baker's gang, little if anything is known about him (including how to spell his name). According to the 1860 census, Lee M., who was then sixteen years old, lived with his sister (possibly Sarah Louisa) and her husband, W. M. White. White, a South Carolina native, had been able to acquire some land and personal property in Cass County. Before 1868, when Lee and Seth possibly participated with Baker in the attack upon the Howell Smith farm, some evidence suggests that Lee, but not Seth, had associated with Baker. Because the two men lived in the same area, they probably had had previous contact with each other. Nothing else is known about the Rames brothers. Taylor alone claims that Lee saved the lives of Orr and Davis.[49]

Throughout December, 1868, the military in the northeast area of Texas again began to take cognizance of Baker. Almost simultaneously with a change in command at the Fifth Military District, from Reynolds to E.R.S. Canby, the Jefferson post received a new head, General George P. Buell. Canby immediately directed him to use the cavalry at his disposal to apprehend Baker. Buell found a contingent of 630 men and wrote Canby that he depended upon the advice of reliable citizens. These suggested that past errors be avoided: that Buell could assist the good people of Cass and Bowie Counties by sending a sufficient force into the field that could maintain itself for more than a day or two before returning. The military could then hunt Baker for as long as there was any chance of success.[50]

48. Vestal, *The Borderlands,* 97; Taylor, "Swamp Fox of the Sulphur," 142–43.

49. MCR (Eighth Census), 1860, Cass County, Texas, p. 117, RG 29, NA; Taylor, "Swamp Fox of the Sulphur," 141. The census taker spelled the name "Raines."

50. George P. Buell (Commander, Jefferson; Lt. Col. 29th Infantry) to AAG (5MD), December 21, 1868, 5MD, LR, B-254; B. W. Grafton (Post Adjutant, Jefferson) to AAAG (5MD), December 24, 1868, LS, Entry I, Vol. 2, p. 25, Post of Jefferson Records, both in USACC, RG 393, NA. Breihan, in "Cullen Baker," 84–85, and "First of the Gunfighters," 47, claims that "several thousand troops were also on order to capture the desperado, while he himself had only a score of followers." The clashes between national, state, and local authorities over politics and economics is recounted in Nancy Cohen-Lack, "A Struggle for Sovereignty: National

On December 14, Buell ordered Captain Wirt Davis of the 4th U.S. Cavalry, with two officers and forty-six men of Companies D and F, to proceed to Cass and Bowie Counties for the purpose of capturing the band of desperadoes headed by Baker, who, he emphasized, "had long infested that country." Buell encouraged the citizens of "all color and clan" in the two-county area to assist Davis. Buell also requested the cooperation of Governor Clayton in Arkansas as well as General Catterson in the event that Baker should flee to that state. After five days in the field, Davis reported that the contingent had captured one of Baker's gang.[51]

The military force gained momentum on December 23, when Buell also dispatched Lieutenant Boehm of the 4th U.S. Cavalry with ten men to reinforce and cooperate with Davis in the search for Baker and his party. Then on December 24, some of Baker's neighbors, including John Chamblee, arrived at Buell's office, proposing to organize a party of local inhabitants to operate against Baker and whatever remained of his gang, provided they could be assured of the U.S. cavalry's support for a specified length of time. The locals needed this additional manpower for assistance in the vicinity of Baker's haunts. Buell assured the citizens that he would do all in his power to eliminate Baker and his gang from the region.[52]

However, Chamblee and Buell did not reach an agreement. When the military returned to the Jefferson post in late December after two weeks in the field, the disgusted citizens were left to strike on their own. In reaction to the military's failure to capture Baker, a few in the Cass County area informally banded together and began constructing a plan to do something about their "local" problem. Almost all of those who lived in the immediate vicinity of Baker's childhood home realized that he would return and again attempt to kill Orr. Some had profited by Baker's murdering of freedmen and -women, but others had suffered whenever Baker returned and killed or harassed those who opposed him. In short, the persistent threat of Baker's vio-

Consolidation, Emancipation, and Free Labor in Texas, 1865," *JSH,* LVIII (February, 1992), 57–98. Obviously, this effort at establishing sovereignty continued throughout the first five years of Reconstruction in Texas, as Buell's comments make evident.

51. Grafton to AAAG (5MD), December 24, 1868, LS, Entry I, Vol. 2, p. 25, Post of Jefferson Records, USACC, RG 393, NA.

52. Buell to Louis V. Caziarc (AAAG, 5MD), January 14, 1869, LS, Entry I, Vol. 2, pp. 36–37, Post of Jefferson Records, USACC, RG 393, NA. Buell mounted an additional fifty men to reinforce the original force in order to finally stop Baker. Unsettled circumstances had compelled the Cass County sheriff to abandon his post and leave the county in fear for his life.

lence had become unbearable. Thus motivated, the citizens would execute their plan to perfection.

As the soldiers searched and the citizens made plans, Baker managed to disappear briefly. Then, in the first four or five days of January, 1869, Baker and Kirby returned to the scene of the Swamp Fox's first killing, the Baily place, and took a Mr. Haynes hostage. Breihan provides the dialogue: "What do you know about Thomas Orr?" Baker asked. "I suppose he is dead," Haynes replied, as Baker had hanged him. Baker affirmed he had "hung" Orr but that the man was not dead. Leaving Haynes, Baker sent a messenger to Jim Clements, then bought a gallon of peach brandy and headed toward Foster's farm. Taylor believed that Baker went to the Foster home to "make a final settlement of finances with a view of leaving the country forever, but fate willed otherwise."[53]

Baker, however, had no intention of arranging yet another agreement with Foster, who by now was thoroughly disgusted with the conduct of his former son-in-law. Rather, Baker sought Orr. On the morning of January 6, Baker and Kirby arrived at the Lamar place, about three-fourths of a mile north of the Foster farm, where Foster, Joe Davis, Leonard Spivy, and Billy Smith were butchering hogs. Meanwhile, Orr remained at the Foster homestead, and Frank Davis was three-quarters of a mile east "digging a hog tunnel." Taylor contends that Orr, Joe Davis, Foster, Robert Spell, John Chamblee, and I. M. Dempsey were "the special vigilante committee of six" that was organized for the purpose of killing Baker when he came back to the area.[54]

Taking Foster captive, Baker headed for his former father-in-law's home. Mounted on a "good horse," with his big shotgun in hand, Baker set out with Foster forced to ride behind him and with Kirby at his side. Baker's horse jumped a rail fence and the shotgun broke a bottle of whiskey in his pocket, which leaked all over his clothes. Orr, at the Foster homestead, saw the three men approach, escaped out the back, and headed in the direction that Davis and his sixteen-year-old son Bill went (three-quarters of a mile away) to excavate the hog tunnel. Orr told them, "Baker is here," adding he would notify the others in the band. Frank Davis suggested he go directly to the Lamar farm and induce the men there to join his effort to subdue Baker.[55]

53. Breihan, "First of the Gunfighters," 47; Orr, *Life of the Notorious Desperado*, 48; Taylor, "Swamp Fox of the Sulphur," 129; *Weekly Harrison Flag* (Marshall), January 28, 1869, p. 2.

54. Taylor, "Swamp Fox of the Sulphur," 129–30.

55. *Ibid.,* 130–31; Orr, *Life of the Notorious Desperado*, 49.

The men at the Lamar place agreed to assist Orr, who returned and informed Frank and Bill Davis that "the hog killers" (Taylor's phrase), would join in the effort. Orr and the two Davises went to the Davis house, where Frank procured a gun and told Bill to give Orr his rifle. Orr, Taylor contends, did not know how to use this weapon, "it being an old fashioned Tennessee rifle with a double or 'hair' trigger." After receiving instructions from the younger Davis on how to manipulate the rifle, Orr organized the men. The party—then composed of Joe Davis, Frank Davis (no relation), Leonard Spivy, Billy Smith (son of Howell), and Orr—rode to the Foster home. According to Taylor, Orr was in charge.[56]

They arrived in the woods west of Foster's at about 10:30 A.M. During Orr's absence, Baker and Kirby had also been busy. Baker stated his intention to settle financial accounts with Foster; but first, he requested whiskey, which Foster retrieved from the house and gave to him. After drinking some of the liquor, Baker and Kirby "lay down by the draw-bars about forty feet west" of the Foster home. While Kirby ate a snack of spare ribs and bread, Baker slept. Taylor insists that the Swamp Fox had "decided to take a nap and he requested Uncle Billie Foster to sit down on the ground and let him put his head in Foster's lap."[57]

In the standard account of Baker's death, the group led by Orr had stationed themselves in the woods west of the house. Orr surveyed the scene. Foster flashed a sign to Orr, who misread it and retreated. He later checked for and received another signal from Foster, which signified he wanted to meet Orr. The two men reconnoitered some distance away from the two prone outlaws and discussed a plan of action. Foster had managed to secure Baker's big shotgun and indicated that the assailants could approach. Taylor claims that "accounts on all sides agree that Old Joe Davis shot Baker in the head with a rifle and that Billy Smith shot Kirby." Several more shots followed. Baker reportedly "never moved a muscle"; Kirby "slightly raised his head." The shooting occurred at 11:00 A.M. on January 6, 1869.[58]

Fifty-seven years after Baker's death, in 1926, Hubbard Foster, William's son, told Taylor and others gathered at a church an amended version of this story. He was about twelve years old and at home when Baker and Kirby were killed there. He saw his father fetch the whiskey and pour "a heavy dose of strychnine" in the liquor before giving it to the two men. Hubbard was "cautioned to keep quiet" about his father's ac-

56. Orr, *Life of the Notorious Desperado*, 49; Taylor, "Swamp Fox of the Sulphur," 131.
57. Taylor, "Swamp Fox of the Sulphur," 131–32.
58. *Ibid.*, 132–33. *Daily Arkansas Gazette*, January 22, 1869, p. 3; January 26, 1869, p. 2.

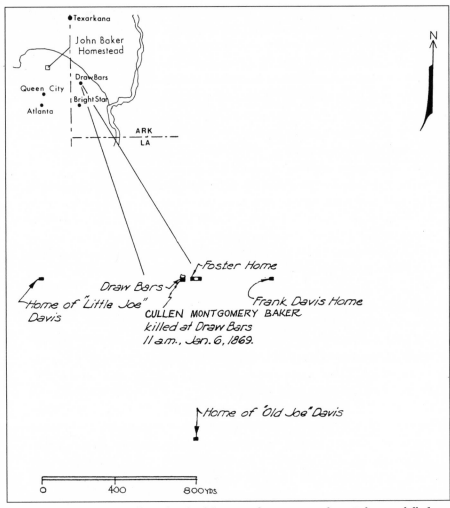

Adaptation of T. U. Taylor's sketch of the immediate vicinity where Baker was killed

Map by Keith Cheshire

tions. Foster gave Baker the poisoned spirits and then "took his head in his lap." Later, he got a pillow from his wife, which he placed under Baker's head. When Kirby said he was hungry, Foster gave him "spare ribs and other food," which he had sprinkled with strychnine.[59] This account receives indirect support from Watlington's claim that Foster had habitually prepared for Baker's arrival by adding a narcotic to a jug of whiskey intended for the outlaw.

A search of Baker's body revealed he was well armed when he died. On his person were a very large double-barreled shotgun, four six-shooters, three derringers, an unspecified amount of specie, twenty-seven keys of various makes and sizes, five or six pocketknives, and a clipping from the December 16, 1868, issue of the Louisville *Courier Journal*. Under a heading entitled "Southern news" ("carefully marked in pencil"), the newspaper article declared that "Cullen M. Baker, the Arkansas brigand, has left the State to join the Cuban expedition." If only, the account continued, Governor Clayton's Arkansas militia would follow Baker any place, whether Cuba or Halifax, the region "would enjoy peace and prosperity."[60]

According to Orr, who either performed or observed some of the search himself, Baker also possessed a "manuscript paper" at his death. It stated: "I, of my own free will and accord, and in the presence of Almighty God, do solemnly swear or affirm that I will never reveal to any one not a member ⊙ ⊙ by any nitus [*sic*], motion, sign, sintol [*sic*], word or act or in any other manner whatever, any of the secret signs, grips, passwords, or mysteries or purposes of the ⊙ ⊙ and that I am not a member of the same; or that I know any one who is a member, and that I will abide by the prescripts and edicts of ⊙ ⊙ So help me God. C. M. Baker." This Ku Klux Klan pledge strongly suggests that Baker had ties to that organization.[61]

On Kirby's body, the group similarly discovered one double-barreled shotgun, two six-shooters, a pocketknife, some ammunition, and an empty pocketbook. The last item deftly symbolized Kirby's life, both socially and economically. A drunk, much like Baker, he slavishly followed the Swamp Fox. Yet Taylor has praise for Kirby, who was "faithful to his chief to the very death." (It may be wondered if Kirby demonstrated faithfulness in the Howell Smith affair, when he became drunk, fell off his horse and passed out, all of which saved him from execution.) According to Taylor, Kirby

---

59. Taylor, "Swamp Fox of the Sulphur," 146–47.
60. Orr, *Life of the Notorious Desperado*, 49; Breihan, "First of the Gunfighters," 47.
61. Orr, *Life of the Notorious Desperado*, 49.

"simulated almost to perfection that he was deaf and dumb and would mingle with crowds and all the time he was drinking in and storing up each expression and word let fall." But Kirby himself profited little from this alleged talent.[62]

According to a newspaper report, W. A. Johnson, apparently a local resident, claimed that people frequently inquired about Baker and Kirby's situation: if they were asleep or drunk when shot, and who would get the reward. A man named Rogers told Johnson that they "were lying on the ground, by the side of a road[,] their horses . . . standing about ten paces from them." Whether the two men were drunk or asleep, he would "not attempt to say." They were dead, however, when he got to them. As to the monetary compensation, Johnson emphasized that Baker was not killed for the reward because "a million such rewards would have been no inducement to murder; it was done in a case of self defence, as well as to save our country from destruction."[63]

After the killing, Orr and his cohorts had to figure out a way to deliver the bodies to the army stationed at Jefferson. Taylor states they borrowed or obtained the two-horse wagon of Jess Sherman, who had a place about six miles southwest of the Foster home. Late on the afternoon of January 6, the men (number undetermined), having covered the bodies with corn stalks, began the venture to Jefferson, thirty-five miles away on the Line Ferry–Jefferson road. Passing near Queen City and Atlanta, they crossed over the Big Cypress Creek on a ferry north of Jefferson run by Edward Stevenson (the uncle of future governor Coke Stevenson). Stevenson checked the bodies (he had known Baker for many years) and confirmed their identity.[64]

62. *Ibid.*; Taylor, "Swamp Fox of the Sulphur," 144–45. There seems to be no extant evidence upon which to base an evaluation of Kirby's actual character. The "deaf and dumb simulation" is probably hearsay. Taylor states that Kirby appeared in Harrison County before the war and worked on the O'Neal farm near Atlanta. During the war, the impression was that he joined the Confederacy, but no trace of this fact could be found. After the war, he appeared in Linden and eventually hooked up with Baker. No evidence suggests that Kirby was as astute and observant as Taylor makes him out to be. According to Bivins, *Memoirs*, 22, Kirby was faithful to Baker until the very end. He was an "Irishman whose fidelity to Cullen Baker was like that of a dog to a kind master and who died side by side with him."

63. *Weekly Harrison Flag* (Marshall), January 28, 1869, p. 2.

64. Taylor, "Swamp Fox of the Sulphur," 133–34. Taylor states that after studying the life of Cullen Baker for many years, he could testify to the fact that Stevenson was "correct in his statement that the bat of Cullen Baker's eyes [after he was dead] would have put the whole crowd to flight."

The group arrived in Jefferson in the late evening on January 7 and immediately reported to General Buell. The bodies, reports Taylor, "were viewed by many hundred citizens in the U.S. Government barracks where they were fully identified." The Jefferson *Jimplecute* claimed that Baker "caused more excitement and committed more crimes than any other man of modern times." Without him, the newspaper added, the "country breathes freely once more." The Jefferson *Times* similarly said that "this great highwayman, who has not only been a terror to the soldiers and negroes, but also to white citizens of every political complexion in portions of Texas, Arkansas, and Louisiana, has at last met his fate, and that, too, at the hands of his own kinsmen and former neighbors."[65]

Only the question of the reward remained. Buell wrote that many area citizens who had known Baker and Kirby well identified the bodies, and he took affidavits from James F. Kirby, A. Glover, and W. P. Blalock to confirm the facts of the outlaws' death. He named John Chamblee of Cass County, Texas, and Thomas Orr of Lafayette County, Arkansas, as the individuals entitled to receive money offered for Baker. Buell had been informed that the state of Arkansas had also offered a reward for Baker's apprehension or the delivery of his body. The general gave credit to Davis and the men of his command for the energy displayed in their effort to execute the difficult duty assigned to them. The military's unsuccessful efforts to subdue Baker had forced the locals to kill him themselves.[66]

Buell, completing all the paperwork requirements, sent the necessary reports to Fifth Military District headquarters, stating that Chamblee and Orr were entitled to the reward. After Baker's body was taken to Little Rock and identified, a dispute ensued. As the reward for Baker was large, the military had requested instructions on the precise terms by which to pay it. Clayton had offered one thousand dollars, which would be paid "upon satisfaction" that he had been arrested and executed by the civil or military authorities of

65. Buell to Caziarc, January 14, 1869, LS, Entry I, Vol. 2, pp. 36–37; Buell to AAG (5MD), December 26, 1868, 5MD, LR, Vol. 5; Buell to AAG (5MD), December 26, 1868; Buell to AAG (5MD), January 6, 7, 1869, LS, Entry 1, Vol. 2, Part 5, p. 2 (telegrams), Post of Jefferson Records, all in USACC, RG 393, NA. Taylor, "Swamp Fox of the Sulphur," 134–36, 151. A summary of Baker's life, a semi-obituary, is given in the intriguing compilation of Ralph W. Steen, ed., *The Texas News: A Miscellany of Texas History in Newspaper Style* (Austin, 1955), May 1, 1870, p. 2.

66. Buell to Governor of Arkansas, February 5, 1869, LS, Entry I, Vol. 2, p. 56; Buell to Lt. L. V. Caziarc (AAAG, 5MD), January 14, 1869, LS, Entry I, Vol. 2, pp. 36–37, both in Post of Jefferson Records, USACC, RG 393, NA.

another state. Of course, as Orr and his group were not technically civil or military officials, the Arkansas military may have seen reason not to validate their claim to the reward. Perhaps as a consequence, Orr, representing the interested parties, experienced a long delay in receiving any information. Typical bureaucratic procrastination may have also contributed to this delay. Orr discovered that he had to submit to an extensive military process in order to claim the money that had been offered for the delivery of Baker's body.[67]

The bureaucracy moved cautiously. In February, 1869, the military prepared the necessary vouchers; but by August of that year the reward of two thousand dollars for Baker had still not been paid to the parties involved in his death. Writing from Jefferson in behalf of Orr and himself, James F. Davis suggested that the reward was actually three thousand dollars and should be "paid to the parties interested." They were "serious of knowing all the facts," and "when said money will be paid." Whatever legends may have been concocted by Baker's past and present admirers (they claim Orr did not kill Baker), there can be no question that Orr and Chamblee sought the reward.[68] The military paid them, but Texas responded slowly.

In late 1869, Orr contacted the Texas secretary of state, W. W. Philips, about the state reward. Orr had interviewed General Buell, to whom Baker had been delivered, and been informed that Buell had forwarded all the necessary affidavits to the district military office. Orr also included a certified deposition taken before justice of the peace M. T. Embree of Lafayette County, Arkansas, that he brought Baker's body to Jefferson. "Of course," Orr wrote Philips, "some parties assisted me in delivering him" to Buell, "but they forfeit all claims, as they *only* accompanied" him "in case of danger, but upon the reception of the military reward, I (after defraying expenses) distributed it among the entire band as my receipts will show."[69]

Orr decries the fact that "many persons have tried to debar me from procuring these claims" by circulating the rumor that Baker had been killed

67. Caziarc to Commanding Officer (Jefferson), February 6, 1869, LR, No. 27, Post of Jefferson Records, USACC, RG 393, NA; James F. Davis (Bright Star, Ark.) to Governor E. M. Pease, August 14, 1869, GC (Pease), TSL.

68. Clayton, *The Aftermath of the Civil War,* 114–15; J. H. Barton (Private Secretary, Governor of Arkansas) to George Shorkley (Commander, Clarksville), November 30, 1868, LR, Entry 3, Part 5, Post of Clarksville Records; Caziarc to Commanding Officer (Post of Jefferson), February 6, 1869, 5MD, LS, p. 289, M1188, Reel 1, all in USACC, RG 393, NA. James F. Davis (Bright Star, Ark.) to Governor E. M. Pease, August 14, 1869, GC (Pease), TSL.

69. Thomas Orr to W. W. Philips (Secretary of State), November 22, 1869, 5MD, Office of Civil Affairs, LR, Box 32, USACC, RG 393, NA.

several months previously by some of his friends. Philips may have seen a similar story in Texas newspapers, for "it has been published in nearly every . . . [one] as well as many others in different states." If Philips needed proof, Orr could appear in person or send a power of attorney, given in the presence of General Buell. John Chamblee, who had earlier been connected with Orr in claiming the military reward, had moved to Georgia and given Orr his power of attorney. Orr preferred the money in the form of a "donation" for "several different reasons," which he left mysteriously unexplained.[70]

To support his claim for the Texas reward, Orr sent the secretary of state an affidavit signed by six men: J. M. Davis, W. J. Smith, J. L. Spivey, Joel D. Walters, Henry Nichols, and J. Y. Lamar. They all deposed that on the morning of January 6, 1869, they saw Baker at the residence of J. Y. Lamar in Lafayette County. The same evening, they viewed Baker as "a corpse" after having observed Orr "shoot the said Cullen M. Baker." They had "fully recognized the features" of Baker; they affirmed that "it was the identical same Cullen M. Baker, who had so long disturbed the peace and quietude of South Arkansas."[71] Today, no evidence could be discovered that proves Orr received his money from Texas.

Baker's death elicited a sigh of relief from area newspapers, a fact that contradicts accounts by many of his biographers. For example, the *Texas Republican* of Marshall observed that Baker "had perpetrated many outrages directly traceable to him, and had the reputation for the commitment of many more of which he doubtless had no knowledge." The account explains that the outlaw was shot in the head during a drunken sleep, along with his friend Kirby. The latter, it qualifies, was "only notorious from his association with Baker." As Baker was a "bold, bad man," the newspaper could only "rejoice at his death."[72]

Contemporary newspaper accounts like this one portrayed Orr and those who assisted him in killing Baker in a much more sympathetic light than did Taylor, Eason, Bartholomew, and Breihan. Orr, with a few friends, declared one newspaper, "determined to kill [Baker] or sacrifice their lives in the attempt." *Flake's* in Galveston summarized, "Thus ends the career of a man who has kept a whole country in terror for months, and Mr. Orr deserves

70. *Ibid.*

71. *Ibid.* Taylor, who did not consult any original sources, claims (134) that all oral accounts confirmed that Davis shot Baker. Contemporary materials do not support his contention.

72. *Texas Republican* (Marshall), January 15, 1869, p. 3.

and will receive the thanks of mankind for his action in ridding the State of a man who had declared himself the enemy of his race."[73]

The execution of various outlaws and Baker's termination, Governor Clayton later wrote, "caused a panic and general exodus among the desperadoes who, as members of the Ku Klux Klan and under its protection, had carried on their nefarious operations 'without let or hindrance' in the southern part of the State." Geography had determined in large part the desperadoes' area of operation. Clayton reasoned that the location of their activities was "well chosen for their purposes on account of the ease with which they, if pursued by an officer of the law, could fly beyond the jurisdiction of Arkansas to the states of Louisiana, Texas, or the Indian Territory, which all cornered within a comparatively small area."[74]

After Baker died, information continued to surface about individuals who associated with him at various times. The military arrested Baker's cohorts throughout 1869 and into 1870, when Baker's influence was finally eradicated. Noteworthy Baker comrades such as Frank Rollins, whom William Kirkman had earlier encountered in his search for Baker, were captured and incarcerated.[75] Baker and his gang were finished. For almost a decade they had been a nemesis to the citizens in the tri-state region of northeast Texas, southern Arkansas, and northwest Louisiana. A thorn in the side of the army and the Freedmen's Bureau, they had at last been eliminated as a menace and nuisance. Baker's life hence passed into history and legend.

73. *Flake's Daily Bulletin* (Galveston), January 20, 1869, p. 5.

74. Clayton, *The Aftermath of the Civil War*, 115.

75. James Davidson (Post, Boston) to B. F. Grafton (Commander, Post of Jefferson), April 4, 1869, LR; Buell to Caziarc, January 17, 1869, LS, Vol. 2, Entry 1, Part V, p. 2; B. Burn to Caziarc, March 30, 1869, pp. 24–25; April 12, 1869, p. 30; Grafton to C. L. Orr (Bright Star, Ark.), July 8, 1869, p. 86; Grafton to Davidson, July 26, 1869, p. 97, in LS, Vol. 1; C. C. Morse (AAAG, 5MD) to Buell, April 14, 1869, LR, No. 51; James Davidson (Boston) to B. F. Grafton (Post Adjutant, Jefferson), April 4, 1869, LR, No. 40, all in Post of Jefferson Records; S. O. No. 48, April 3, 1870, Entry 4, Part 5, p. 49, Post of Clarksville Records; Buell to AAAG (5MD), April 12, 1869, DT, LR, Box 11, all in USACC, RG 393, NA. See also Galveston *Daily News*, March 26, 1870, p. 3. In late 1869, the army killed Bill Gray, who had allegedly committed twenty-five murders, and was reportedly a member of Baker's gang; *Weekly Austin, Republican*, October 6, 1869, p. 1.

Conclusion

———————◆———————

IN 1981, the Texarkana *Gazette* featured an article on the "favorite outlaw of Bloomburg, Texas," Cullen Montgomery Baker. If Baker had been alive to attend the Cullen Baker Country Fair, "a wingding of a fest," the newspaper rhapsodized, he "might wind up drunk and then plug somebody with the giant shotgun he always carried." This was the legend left behind by the Reconstruction guerrilla who cut a storied trail through northeast Texas and "probably killed more men than Wyatt Earp, Jesse James or any other gunslinger of the day" and who deserved a place in history comparable to the "James Gang and the Dalton Brothers." His murdering ways were of "silver-screen proportions."[1]

1. Texarkana *Gazette,* November 4, 1981, p. 3-A. Incredibly, the paper printed that Baker "won the nickname 'Swamp Fox' when, severely wounded, he swam the flood-swollen Black Bayou in 1887 under fire from some 200 pursuers." (Baker had been dead for eighteen years by their own account.) Bloomburg, a hamlet of 231 people in 1981, is twenty miles south of Texarkana. It did not exist in Baker's day. According to the newspaper, the fair in its eighth year featured a "flea market with some 150 booths, a quilting bee, lots of barbecue, a Little Mr. and Miss Cullen Baker contest, gospel music, an antique car show, a parade and the traditional 'Saga of Cullen Baker,' a play written by Ray Fults, a local writer." Fults allegedly had an unpublished 500-page novel about Baker, embellished only "slightly beyond what he was able to confirm through research." Movie producers desired to change the story considerably, "but Baker's legend is one that even Hollywood will have trouble topping," stated the newspaper. For a colorful account of this event, see Yvonne Vestal, "Bloomburg's Country Fair," *Texas Highways,* XXVII (November, 1980), 26–27.

Though Baker was an army deserter, the *Gazette* honored him for going to his grave "vowing to overthrow" Yankee forces and also terrorizing carpetbaggers who "infested the area." He is remembered for having won the "loyalty of countless law-abiding citizens" and "Civil War widows," who depended upon him for protection from the hated invaders and for sustenance. The paper gives tribute to the devious demeanor of this man for whom thousands of state and Federal troops hunted. His softer side is noted in the story that when his second wife, Martha, died, he constructed an effigy of her and talked to it for days, and killed several Yankee soldiers to "vent his grief." With apparent sympathy, it explains that Baker then courted her sister, but her "father married her off to a schoolteacher." It refers to the frequently circulated story that he had not been killed in 1869 but had instead escaped to Cuba.[2]

The passage of years brought apocryphal additions to the Baker legend. One of the most amazing and unfounded stories depicts Baker taking Belle Foster Orr with him to the Caribbean, where he subsequently "helped the Cubans win independence from Spain." (Not likely, considering his attitude toward blacks.) Baker allegedly "lived out his life there, but returned once a year to put flowers on Martha's grave." Baker's life, the *Gazette* concluded, "is the stuff of legends."[3] Even before Baker's death, newspaper articles embroidered upon his biography. The *Gazette* simply extended what had been an established nineteenth-century pattern that continued into this century. A majority of those who have concentrated on Baker have helped to fabricate a colorful if dubious version of his life.

Cullen Montgomery Baker's memory, periodically renewed, has survived in his community throughout the twentieth century. A brief exploration of this phenomenon is important for understanding the Baker milieu. Baker writings have been animated by a deep-seated racism, by a distortion of the Reconstruction years, and by a continued commitment to older viewpoints and characterizations of the postwar era that transform Baker into a southern Robin Hood. They portray the Federal army and the Freedmen's Bureau as running roughshod over their helpless victims and attempting to place blacks in control of local politics. In truth, Baker endeavored to stalemate their presence through his sporadic attacks and to enforce antebellum standards of etiquette and labor.

2. Texarkana *Gazette*, November 4, 1981, p. 3-A.
3. *Ibid.*

Perpetuated alongside this avenger image is the figure of a man whose loving mother had imbued him with Christian values; if Baker later became a bully, it was because of an encounter (not of his own volition) at a gristmill. In spite of his mother's effort, he emerged into young manhood as a heavy drinker and community bad boy. Although no reliable information on Cullen's mother exists, Orr has her whispering "good advice into the ears of a beloved son, whose heart had become dumb to her soft and motherly language, as the hearts of the antediluvian were to the divine preaching of Father Noah." An anonymous reminiscence later adds that Baker's mother taught him to "respect the Holy Bible": Baker "believed in a God and that man shall live again."[4] But Baker's religious principles, if he had any, are unknown.

Writers have made much of Baker's boyhood difficulties and his manner of dress. However, it is ludicrous to believe that his homemade clothes and one fistfight irrevocably determined Baker's life. Yet into the twentieth century writers have cited the gristmill incident as the single outstanding event that established Baker's skill and reputation as a rough-and-tumble fighter. Eason contends that Baker became thereafter a bully and that his role in the community "occupied much the same position as the 'fast gun' of the later cattle towns." Mrs. J. K. Bivins argues that Baker "came out [the] victor, an inflatus to his ego which never deserted him."[5]

Those who have been sympathetic to Baker's actions have invented various tales about his honesty, his romantic and humorous side, and his singing ability. Every aspect of Baker's life, from his caring mother to his deep affection for his wife and child, has been burnished by Baker biographers. Why Martha Foster's death should unhinge Baker as opposed to the death of Mary Jane Petty or that of his father (who probably died in 1862 or 1863) is never quite

4. Thomas Orr, *Life of the Notorious Desperado, Cullen Baker, from His Childhood to His Death, with a Full Account of All the Murders He Committed* (Little Rock, 1870), 6; Myreline Bowman, *The People of Cass County: Atlanta, Queen City, Texas* (Atlanta, Tex., 1973), I, 225; Mildred Mays McClung, *Caddo Lake: Mysterious Swampland* (Texarkana, 1974), 66. There is absolutely no evidence, either in his behavior or in his brief statements, that Baker believed in God or embraced Christianity. Mrs. J. K. Bivins, in her *Memoirs* (N.p.: Privately printed, [1945]), 21, dramatically remarks: " 'My son! My son!' Oh, Cullen, 'would that I had died for thee' was, no doubt, expressed by John Baker and his wife who loved their oldest son and indulged him in every possible wish."

5. Al Eason, "Cullen Baker—Purveyer of Death," *Frontier Times*, XL (August–September, 1966), 6; Bivins, *Memoirs*, 21–22; Jerry Arnold, "Cullen Montgomery Baker: The Swamp Fox," Marshall *News Messenger*, October 28, 1973, p. 8.

explained. In fact, in attempting to portray Baker in as respectable a light as possible, many of the accounts make him sound almost innocuous. He becomes, as one writer describes him, "like any other good citizen of his age," having fought "heroically for the cause he believed to be right."[6]

Even Thomas Orr is depicted in a demeaning way in order to promote Baker's reputation. Never bothering to investigate Orr's life before or after Baker was killed, those partial to Baker misrepresent Orr's origins and stress his anti-Baker stance; they attempt to discredit him by implying that he was from the North and supported that section during the Civil War. Orr may well have been a member of the Republican Party, but the term *carpetbagger* does not quite apply to him given that he was born in Georgia. Eason claims his own great-uncle, Lucillius E. Westerfield, knew Orr personally and stated that Orr was "a Republican carpetbagger and a liar to boot—that is, if he said he killed Cullen Baker."[7]

In addition to making unfounded comments on Baker's personal life, Bakerites have also emphasized the armor he carried. His weapons, in their revisions of his career, take on almost mythical proportions. Baker was often associated with a six-shooter and with a very large bore shotgun that had "unusual carrying power, [was] accurate in aim," and "did not scatter the blue whistlers." No one in Sulphur River country had seen a shotgun as large as this mysterious weapon. When asked how many buckshot he loaded in the gun, Baker replied that when he had time he loaded each barrel with twelve, but when hurried he would put in a handful and blaze loose. The shotgun figures dramatically in the Baker legend as Rames used it to cover Baker's retreat from the soldiers.[8]

A majority of the tales surrounding Baker focus upon the Reconstruction era. Among several local and regional historians, an older perception of this era has prevailed. In their writings, Baker fought evil outsiders and traitorous insiders to promote a noble cause. As late as 1992, a local essayist decried the appearance of the "hated Carpetbaggers," who arrived "like flies

6. "Cullen M. Baker, The Outlaw," *Flake's Semi-Weekly Bulletin* (Galveston), December 16, 1868, p. 4; T. U. Taylor, "Swamp Fox of the Sulphur or Life and Times of Cullen Montgomery Baker," *ca.* 1936 (Typescript in ECBTHC), 139–40; Yvonne Vestal, *The Borderlands and Cullen Baker* (Atlanta, Tex., 1978) 111; Taylor to A. L. Burford, July 19, 1926 (Taylor letters courtesy of Christine Woodrow of New Boston, Texas).

7. Eason, "Cullen Baker," 67.

8. Taylor, "Swamp Fox of the Sulphur," 148–150. Into the 1920s, local residents commented upon the weapon.

on fertilizer" and "hunger[ed] for political office." They included a "high percentage of misfits and never-do-wells out for 'profit.' " Their cohorts, the scalawags ("Texas turncoats"), "slithered into political puppet power, well aware of their favored legal protection" by the "Bluecoats," the occupation army who supported them and acted "tyrannical[ly]."[9]

Taylor perceived the South as helpless under carpetbag rule. In his account, Baker becomes the southern savior. "The negroes had the swell head, were impudent and shiftless." The Union League, formed by blacks to support the Republican Party, supposedly fostered impertinence and served to give the "thieving" freedmen "an exaggerated idea of their importance." Scalawags, the "most contemptible creature[s] that ever walked the earth," became "apostate[s]" to the cause of the South. Similarly, Bivins saw the South as "bled-white" and "devastated" under the cruel hand of the military and the Freedmen's Bureau. When on the war path, Baker righteously sought revenge for myriad wrongs and to rid the region of these insufferable influences.[10]

Ed Bartholomew, in his quaint way, takes the carpetbagger theme to new heights. He has Baker vowing the extermination of "Jayhawkers" and "yeller belies." In what Bartholomew terms the "Baker doctrine for 'Suppression of Carpetbaggerism,'" the description of a carpetbagger includes a "man who has no stock in the country beyond his satchel, and yet by the grace of reconstruction, he rules a black crook convention." Lacking "guts, red blood, starch in his back and a grain of brains," the carpetbagger was nothing but an exploiter. And Baker was a needed antidote to this exploitation. Yvonne Vestal contends that with the passing of the Old South and Reconstruction, there was no longer a "need for the 'Good Bad Man of the American West'"—someone like Baker—as there had been in the oppressive aftermath of war.[11]

9. Jim McMillen, "Reconstruction in Jefferson: The Best & Worst of Times," *The Jeffersonian*, XII (Spring/Summer, 1992), 8.

10. Taylor, "Swamp Fox of the Sulphur," 23; Bivins, *Memoirs*, 22; interview with J. C. Hutchinson and W. F. Endsley by T. U. Taylor, in Taylor material sent to the authors by Woodrow. For stories that belie the claim that Baker hated blacks, see McClung, *Caddo Lake*, 68; and Vestal, *The Borderlands*, 67. Louis L'Amour sounds a similar theme in his Baker novel, *The First Fast Draw* (New York, 1959), 54, 65.

11. Ed Bartholomew, *Cullen Baker: Premier Texas Gunfighter* (Houston, 1954), 42, 53, 55, 71. Bartholomew portrays Baker as opposing the division of Texas into various states. For more on this idea, see Vestal, *The Borderlands*, 118–19; and Ernest Wallace, *The Howling of the Coyotes: Reconstruction Efforts to Divide Texas* (College Station, Tex., 1979).

Combined with the myth of the helpless South plagued by outsider rule is the idea that Baker served countermeasures to the government's ruthlessness by making fools of the army and by murdering governmental personnel. He was unable to accept the Confederate defeat ("too bitter for him to take") or reconcile himself to the carpetbag regime. He could not (should not have, it would seem to many) tolerate the soldiers or the "free negroes roaming the country" who robbed and killed white people. "Disillusioned," Baker decided to "become a knight errant in his own right." Some say he began his heroic career by "killing negroes who became unruly and dangerous to white women in the community"; his neighbors never complained about him murdering "dangerous negroes." [12]

One of the staple beliefs of the local Baker legend is that Baker and the Ku Klux Klan had an important protective function. According to Chandler and Howe, the Klan "protected the people from the wrongs and indignities, and from trials without a jury; and from unlawful seizures" in the South. The Klan guarded families of dead Confederate soldiers from "unscrupulous carpetbaggers, undesirable men and vicious *negroes.*" From this prejudiced perspective, bloodshed was often *averted* by the Klan's nocturnal visits and threatening notices. When the soldiers left, it is claimed, these groups quickly disappeared. [13] It is dismaying that these myths still reign in the local literature despite the plethora of historical writing from the past three decades that has largely proven them to be false.

In fact, Texas was never ruled by the carpetbaggers on the local, county, or state level. Conservatives controlled the state for the first two years of Reconstruction and had considerable sway even when the Republicans briefly held power in the 1870s. Blacks did not control any convention or the legislature. Their legislative numbers remained quite low throughout Reconstruction, and they never held prominent appointed or elected state positions. It has been proved that the Ku Klux Klan was simply a terrorist organization that murdered largely defenseless blacks and unionists because of their political affiliation. And it was well supported: a majority of violence during Reconstruction was committed by whites sympathetic to the Klan and its desperado allies.

---

12. Walter Scott McNutt, "East Texas Outlaw During Carpet-Bag Days Buried Here," Jefferson *Weekly Jimplecute,* May 2, 1957, p. 3.

13. Barbara Overton Chandler and J. Ed Howe, *History of Texarkana . . . Bowie and Miller Counties Texas—Arkansas* (Texarkana, 1939), 36.

As for the scalawags, they only briefly dominated Texas government at all levels during congressional Reconstruction and under Republican control. They were natives of the South, just like the majority of white males in Texas. To blame them for civil distress, contends Randolph B. Campbell, "would mean admitting that not all white Texans were unified in opposing the evils" of the postwar years. It was easier to blame outsiders, such as the Yankees, for the corruption of those years. The conservatives asserted, however, that these southern unionists, like the carpetbaggers, "did not have the same high standards of honor as did the heroes of the 'Lost Cause.'" In truth, as Campbell explains, their rule was characterized by "extravagant spending, rampant corruption, ruinous taxation, and general mistreatment of ordinary white Texans."[14]

Cullen Montgomery Baker became a legend in the southwestern region of the former Old South because he challenged national and state sovereignty. Concentrating his attention upon the institutions that represented a Union victory—the army and the Freedmen's Bureau—he also aided planters in coercing excess labor from their newly emancipated laborers and harassed white unionists. Baker desired a return to the status quo antebellum. He simply could not condone or accept the South's postwar transformation. In his limited thinking, the only way to reverse the trend was through the use of organized violence, be it through gangs of desperadoes or the Ku Klux Klan. Baker engendered much of this type of activity in the tri-state region where he operated.

Two themes pervade the stories of Baker's encounters with the United States army. The first, which is substantiated by documentary material, is that Baker managed to elude the soldiers through his knowledge of the region and through details provided by his many informants, not necessarily because of the army's ineptness. The second theme is his dire hatred of these military men. Local material emphasizes Baker's sadistic pleasure in murdering troopers. In fact, some descriptions of how the Swamp Fox delighted in dispatching the hated occupiers rival those of his perverse pleasure in murdering the freed slaves whom he abhorred. Seen in this rather stark light, Baker's murderous intentions seem less political than irrational.

In one refrain, Baker kept "two six shooters concealed on his body and being a crack shot he thrived on killing Union soldiers." Popular mythology

14. Randolph B. Campbell, "Carpetbagger Rule in Reconstruction Texas: An Enduring Myth," *SwHQ*, XCVII (April, 1994), 594–96.

holds that Baker single-handedly captured Federal wagon trains, constantly goaded troopers, and cold-bloodedly killed soldiers; that he offered to capitulate if the army "left the South—[if] all rebels should be repaid for their losses during the war, and [if] the Southern Confederacy should be acknowledged." In this popular reconstruction of Baker's career, he then decided, because former Rebels had "submitted to the Yankees" and "dared to censure his acts," that he would "treat all alike" and spare no one. Baker assumed an air of bravado and defiance and intimidated his neighbors, "which," one writer ruefully observed, "he curse[d] with his presence." [15]

In pro-Baker lore, the most heinous crime committed by the army was the supposed desecration of Baker's home and the subsequent destruction of some belongings of his dead wife Martha. Nullifying the countless stories about Baker's derision and murder of military men, this story charges that soldiers found him unarmed one day and "beat and misused him." Moreover, when Baker later committed some kind of infraction, the military allegedly violated Baker's civil rights by searching his home in an attempt to capture him. Entering the house, they destroyed Martha's clothes, stole jewelry, and nailed her picture to a tree, using it for target practice. In response, Baker "went berserk." This story often serves to justify Baker's wanton killing of soldiers: they are responsible for provoking him into this way of life. [16]

The legends, myths, and local tales that represent the Baker/Kirkman confrontation in Boston, Texas, are numerous. Most focus upon the evils of the government and portray Kirkman as an intruder and Baker as the individual who removed the nemesis. (Kirkman's legacy has been chronicled elsewhere.) In general, a very negative depiction of the Freedmen's Bureau pervades the Baker material. Hal M. Simpson, for instance, argues that the Bureau "came under the influence of corrupt politicians and caused the people all over the South a great deal of grief." Mildred McClung said that the Bureau encouraged blacks "to commit deeds which cost many of them their lives, and Baker became known as a Negro hater as well as a Yankee hater"; the Bureau, by implication, was a Negro-loving, Yankee-loving institution. [17]

15. *Flake's Semi-Weekly Bulletin* (Galveston), December 16, 1868, p. 4. Flake's actually published four newspapers: the daily, semiweekly, commercial, and evening *Bulletin*.

16. *Ibid.* See also Carl W. Breihan, "Cullen Baker," in his *Great Gunfighters of the West* (San Antonio, 1962), 79; Eason, "Cullen Baker," 11; Boyd W. Johnson, "Cullen Montgomery Baker: The Arkansas-Texas Desperado," *AHQ*, XXV (Autumn, 1966), 235.

17. Hal Simpson, "A Brief History of Boston, New Boston, Old Boston, and Vicinity, Bowie County, Texas" (M.A. thesis, East Texas State Teachers College, 1950), 34–37; McClung,

Lemuel Dale Evans, a Tennessee-born Texas congressman who opposed secession, was a moderate Republican, and later became chief justice of the state supreme court, even subscribed to some parts of the Baker legend. Evans claimed Baker was "an old Texan" and a "union man in the political sense of that term."

Pointedly, Evans notes that Baker's house was robbed by soldiers after the war, so he retaliated and raised a party of desperadoes to assist him. They "killed several soldiers, white and colored, as well as peaceful citizens, whom they suspected of aiding the military in their pursuit." Evans laments that the outrages attributed to men of Baker's ilk had been "magnified to a most injurious degree against the people of Texas." Moreover, he contends, Baker only eliminated those people whom he thought were dangerous enemies to society.[18]

Although Baker's legend continued to be of local interest after his death, it was not until 1966 that his grave in Jefferson's Oakwood Cemetery was officially marked. Led by Bryan Hurt, relatives and other interested parties contributed to the purchase of a headstone. Hurt, who claimed that his grandfather J. W. Hurt had accompanied Baker's body to Jefferson, designed the marker. Two of Baker's relatives, Miss Eva Baker and Mrs. Jean Baker Foster, attended the ceremony of placing the headstone on the grave. Ninety-seven years after his death, the "notorious highwayman" received official recognition on his tombstone.[19]

The nineteenth century labeled individuals whose actions were not guided by discrimination between right and wrong "moral imbeciles." This phrase seems to aptly sum up Baker's character, personality, and attitudes. He may have assumed that the so-called southern code of honor gave him license to eliminate those whites who he felt challenged his manhood or those blacks who seemed to be moving up on the economic and social, not to mention political, ladder. Barring recourse to the category of moral imbecility, the burning question of why Baker became this murderous soul is inexplicable. Many have postulated theories—fallacious and otherwise—to account for his violence in this region during Reconstruction years. But in

---

Caddo Lake, 67–68. The origins of the Baker/Kirkman/Bureau myth can be found in R. H. Watlington, "Memoirs" (Typescript in TSL), 72.

18. *Texas Republican* (Marshall), January 15, 1869, p. 2; Walter Prescott Webb and H. Bailey Carroll, eds., *The Handbook of Texas* (2 vols.; Austin, 1952), I, 576.

19. Jefferson *Weekly Jimplecute,* April 21, 1966, p. 3. No contemporary evidence confirms that Hurt actually accompanied Baker's body to Jefferson.

truth, from his hatred of blacks to his irrational opposition to the concept of national sovereignty, Baker was a sociopath.

If the premise is accepted that Reconstruction was inherently evil, that the Federal army should probably not have occupied the South, and that the ideal of equal justice and equality before the law for blacks should never have been attempted, then Baker looks like a hero. But this premise, in it-self insupportable, eclipses the fact that the South lost the war and was de-servedly occupied. The number of gross exaggerations that infuse accounts of the era and Baker's life is appalling. Blacks did not run amok, nor did the army and the Freedmen's Bureau continuously oppress white people and violate their rights. All the most recent evidence, some of it even written by those who see Reconstruction as a disaster, proves that blacks and the two government agencies conducted themselves respectably during the postwar years.

A majority of writers have been favorable to Baker. Those who esteem him often mirror the interpretation of the postwar years that prevailed at the turn of the century. That interpretation is based on the belief that blacks should not have been allowed to participate in the democratic process and that all connected with that ghastly experiment were tainted. In this way they arrive at the conclusion that Baker defended the homeland against dis-ruptive outsiders and uppity freedmen and freedwomen. Since it is clear that this conclusion is invalidated by its faulty premises, Baker has to be considered in the context of the newer, less prejudiced and better docu-mented interpretations of Reconstruction. The present study has attempted such a reappraisal.

In debunking the Baker myth, we should also reevaluate past calculations of the number of murders he committed. In all that is said or written about the life of this outlaw, the question persists, how many men did he kill? Every past or present publication regarding Baker has provided at least a vague idea of the number of murders that should be attributed to the Swamp Fox. A definitive figure can probably not be ascertained because Baker murdered some individuals alone and because those whom he later dispatched as a gang member cannot all be accounted for. Like the num-bers of people allegedly killed by later outlaws, Baker's figures far exceed those attributed to more infamous bad men in American history.

Baker's murderous propensities received considerable attention even be-fore his death in 1869. *Flake's* stated that he had committed "upwards of forty murders." Bivins, like many others, risks a more excessive estimate:

"Cullen Baker's victims, souls whose life he had snuffed out with his deadly weapon, numbered more than fifty, not counting the part he performed in [the] War's program." According to McClung, who heavily relied upon Bivins, Baker was a confirmed Confederate "credited with killing as many as forty or fifty yankee soldiers during Reconstruction." McClung did not attempt to estimate how many neighbors, unionists, blacks, or Freedmen's Bureau agents he had murdered.[20]

A brief survey of reasonably verifiable Baker homicides, as opposed to the many undocumented murders that Bakerites attribute to their hero, should help clarify this issue. His first killing occurred in 1854 when he dispatched Baily, a white man. After an apparent hiatus in his life between 1854 and 1860, during which he may or may not have murdered again, Baker killed Warthan in 1860. During the Civil War, although he is credited with killing no one in battle, Baker is reported to have slain a black woman and savagely eliminated a black boy in addition to fifteen Arkansas unionists. However, there are no extant contemporary sources that substantiate these last figures. By the end of the war, Baker may have murdered five people.

After the war, Baker's murder credits reached astronomical levels. The number of blacks he slew is impossible to ascertain, but it seems to have been considerable. The secondary literature is replete with instances of Baker killing blacks both during and after the Civil War, but the documentary evidence for these actions is largely nonexistent. Based upon gleanings from all the material investigated, we estimate that during his life Baker murdered no fewer than seven nor more than twelve blacks, the accounts of which can in some manner be confirmed. This assessment is made difficult by the racist nature of the material and by the lack of precise information from primary documents.

There is no question that Baker either singly or with accomplices murdered four soldiers. Although the petition of the Arkansas citizens in January, 1868, claimed that Baker had killed eleven soldiers, these victims are not identified and their deaths cannot be confirmed. The available contemporary evidence does not contain any enumeration of soldiers Baker slew other than Titus and the two that were dispatched when Baker and his cohorts attacked the army wagon train along with one teamster. If all the stories that represent Baker killing soldiers should prove to be true, Baker

20. *Flake's Semi-Weekly Bulletin* (Galveston), February 19, 1868, p. 7; Bivins, *Memoirs*, 22; McClung, *Caddo Lake*, 67.

eliminated approximately seventeen troopers. The majority of these accounts are exaggerated, however, and based more on imagination or repeated hearsay than on any documented material.

In his Texas and Arkansas settings, Baker killed Baily, Warthan, and Rowden. He murdered government agents Kirkman and Willis, along with another Washington official, Andrews, a United States tax assessor. We cannot
ignore his killing of Salmon for the latter's participation in a citizen group's
search for him. He may also have eliminated one or two white unionists. It
is also possible that Baker murdered several individuals, both white and
black, in the other areas he roamed outside of Bowie and Cass Counties,
but the contemporary sources only allude to such acts and do not provide
relevant names, dates, or locations. But even with the paucity of information, Baker may be credited with a staggering number of slayings.

A compilation of all the murders committed by Baker as described by his
various chroniclers totals a staggering seventy-six. Of this truly exaggerated
killing total, forty-four, or 59 percent, were black. The remaining thirty-two
were neighbors, unionists, white soldiers, Freedmen's Bureau agents, and
other government personnel. The figure cannot be accepted. There is no
documentary support for such an inflated number. It will probably never be
known precisely how many individuals Baker killed. After combing the
available sources, we have concluded that the best estimate of Baker's murders, occasionally in league with cohorts, is fifteen men. (There is absolutely
no proof he ever killed a woman.) Fifteen largely innocent deaths constitute
the provable Baker legacy.

Beyond the number of murders Baker may have committed, our inquiry
must include something about his individual and community legacy. In fact,
Baker's most significant contribution may have been in creating a climate of
fear in his particular region, which retarded, and perhaps ultimately defeated, the implementation of the Reconstruction process. His negative
influence certainly hovered over the daily lives of those in this tri-state section, particularly if they had supported the Union during the war, become
free as a result of the war, or served in a governmental capacity to oversee
that change was implemented. In his guise as economic regulator, Baker seriously disrupted labor and race relations in the region.

Was Baker a social bandit? That is, was he one of those violent individuals
who arises in times of social tension and upheaval? Baker was regarded as
an outlaw whom the military and two state governments considered a criminal; but a large number of citizens considered him to be a hero, a champion,

an avenger, a fighter for justice, perhaps even a liberation leader. He was widely regarded as a man to be admired, helped and supported, whether for defending the traditional order of things (society before the war) or for desiring to restore it. More appropriately, he can be characterized as a social avenger, one of those individuals for whom "terror actually forms part of their public image."[21]

People of this type have been characterized as "public monsters." How are such monsters made? Baker, unlike his father, actually "lost the sense of the farm as an anchor, a place to love." At the same time, he observed rapid social change along with economic and class conflict. Not feeling rooted to his parents' homestead, he set his sights on the larger picture. He wanted to forestall the socioeconomic transformation that threatened his weak sense of himself. His vengeful tactics suggest how closely he identified himself with the fortunes of the Old South: he humiliated and vented his rage on those he believed to have oppressed others (the army and the Freedmen's Bureau). Baker and other social avengers were "heroes not in spite of the fear and horror their actions inspire, but in some ways because of them." They were "not so much men who right wrongs, but avengers, and exerters of power" who proved that "even the poor and weak can be terrible."[22]

Baker evinced a kind of duality: a self-motivated bandit, he also served the role of southern avenger. Consider those who followed Baker. The sources are often vague and there are few hints of who and how many composed his gang. Curiously, the group he led seemed to expand and contract rapidly. Did these fluctuations really occur, or did his contemporaries sometimes exaggerate his leadership? At times he seems to have been a mere outlaw with a handful of sidekicks; at other times, such as during the encounters with DeWitt C. Brown, the Paris Freedmen's Bureau agent, and the Arkansas militia at Centre Point, he appears to have been leading small guerrilla armies (rather than simply large outlaw gangs) that materialized out of who knows where.

In his raids, Baker demonstrated this dual role as freelance crook, thug and orchestrator of collective violence. The latter role involved Baker in social phenomena (even social movements) more complex than his random acts of murder, assault, and coercion. From mid-1867 until a month before his death, Baker's acts seem to fall into the second category. He regulated

21. Eric B. Hobsbawm, *Bandits* (New York, 1969), 58, 13, 15, 50.

22. *Ibid.*, 59 and 50. See also Hobsbawm, *Primitive Rebels: Studies in Archaic Forms of Social Movement in the 19th and 20th Centuries* (New York, 1959), 1–29.

blacks because they were free, could vote, and asserted a form of autonomy. Baker attacked army wagons to harass the boys in blue, apparently not profiting from these excursions. (He may have given the booty to supporters.) In short, Baker's later violent outrages always appear to have had a purpose: either he wanted to impede the process of Reconstruction and eliminate its agents entirely, and in the process regulate the social, economic, and political lives of the freed black; or he sought revenge against those who had aided the soldiers in attempting to capture him in late 1867 and early 1868. Although Thomas Orr apparently was not a member of the citizen group who searched for Baker or was involved in the killing of Seth Rames, Baker certainly detested everything about the man, especially when he married Belle Foster. This personal feud does not precisely fit into Baker's overall pattern of violence. Orr represented the very antithesis of Baker.

Baker never articulated his objective in eliminating local citizens, blacks, soldiers, and Freedmen's Bureau agents, but his actions demonstrate that he did not accept the final outcome of the Civil War. Yet he did not commit himself to the southern cause while his section was engaged in war. Nevertheless, he became an opponent of Reconstruction. Because Baker never explicitly expounded upon his motivation for murdering a variety of individuals, his reasons are difficult to explain. It seems rather clear from the brutality he evidenced in some of his killings that something had gone seriously awry in Baker's mind.

In sum, it is difficult to classify Baker psychologically and socially. Too many inconsistencies in his conduct and in the available evidence thwart a final categorization of him. Although he seems similar to Fellman's Missouri guerrillas, Baker does not exemplify the commitment of these Manichean avengers. In some ways Baker belongs to the class of social bandits and avengers described by Eric Hobsbawm, especially in light of his violent methods. And, given his affiliation with the Ku Klux Klan, Baker seems uniquely southern and racist in his manner of avenging the "Lost Cause."

The Baker portrayed here is not a likeable fellow. In his short and intense life, he was a killer (mostly of defenseless or unsuspecting individuals), a liar, a thief, a deserter, a drunk, and, in general, a derelict. Why he became this way or chose this path is open to speculation. Nevertheless, by simultaneously providing an analysis of how past writers have interpreted Baker and including our findings through manuscript material, we have attempted to create a comprehensive picture of him while exposing the exaggerations and fallacies falsifying earlier accounts of his life.

Although the Civil War's aftermath brought out the worst in Baker, with the result that several innocent and conscientious individuals died, the unsettled state of affairs during Reconstruction did not cause Baker's "moral imbecility." He exhibited this condition long before the North and South made war upon each other. Probably the times exacerbated Baker's dislike of outsiders and blacks, but his manner of acting on this hatred was exceptional. During the years from 1865 to 1869, he refined his deceitful techniques and managed to disrupt a large area of the South. It is difficult to sympathize with this man who murdered innocent people in the name of a lost cause and who attempted to forestall the extension of civil rights in America.

Essay on Sources

FROM HIS ENEMY Thomas Orr's 1870 biography through his great-great-grandson Robert W. Teel's 1995 narrative tribute, Cullen Montgomery Baker has attracted a wide variety of writers. Biographies, both published and unpublished, and biographical essays have appeared in 1870, 1884, 1936 [?], 1954, 1962 and 1967 (same author), 1966 (two different writers), 1978, 1979, 1991, and most recently 1995 (two different authors). Perhaps because of their divergent backgrounds and credentials, biographers of Baker have perceived their subject quite differently.

A biography of a regional legend like Cullen Montgomery Baker must include a study of those who have written about him, especially local authors. It is interesting to compare evaluations of Baker with what primary sources reveal about him. The myths, legends, and tales about Baker evolved over time and relate variously to the material disclosed in manuscript records. Indeed, stories about a specific Baker act can be quite dissimilar and only rarely cohere to form a consistent account. One major problem these sources have is chronology. A biography depends upon temporal structure, and from it flows much of the narrative; however, most previous Baker biographers refused to be bound by the logic of time.

Although no recent historian has tackled a full-scale biography of Baker, he has nonetheless been the subject of some scrutiny. Modern historians tend to take a more dispassionate view of the Swamp Fox than those who wrote about him in the past. Unfortunately, like their predecessors they have occasionally mixed fact and fiction; thus, a true or at least realistic portrait has not hitherto emerged. In reality, driven by psychopathic and sociopathic urges, Baker became a killer and a "local regulator." He reflected the values of a certain segment of nineteenth-century white southern society, especially in his penchant for dominating blacks and harassing government officials allied with them.

Little more than local legends, tales, and unsubstantiated information about Baker prevails. Because a mystique persists in coloring the memory of him, he is an ideal subject for a biographical novel. Perhaps that is why popular western writer Louis L'Amour used Baker's character as the kingpin of one of his fictions, *The First Fast Draw* (1959). Because of the confusion and controversy surrounding the Swamp Fox's life, it would be easy to elaborate the limited information on him into a novel, especially one that concentrates upon a romantic idea. L'Amour may have gleaned the idea that Baker initiated the "fast draw" from Ed Bartholomew, who had published his work *Cullen Baker: Premier Texas Gunfighter* (Houston, 1954) five years before *The First Fast Draw* appeared.

Perhaps surprisingly, after all that has been written about Baker, a basic source continues to be Thomas Orr's *Life of the Notorious Desperado Cullen Baker, from His Childhood to His Death, with a Full Account of All the Murders He Committed* (Little Rock, 1870). In its forty-eight pages, Orr has little good to say about Baker, who attempted to kill him. The intersection of Baker's life with his own appears to have astounded Orr to the extent that he found it difficult to conceive as having happened. Later Baker aficionados have relied heavily upon Orr's vivid account while simultaneously denigrating his efforts and accusing him of affiliations he may not have had. Orr may have been amazed by what happened to him and by the final result, but he nevertheless wrote insightfully about Baker's personality. No other writer knew Baker personally.

Fourteen years after Orr's biography appeared, Frank Triplett published "Cullen Montgomery Baker," in *History, Romance and Philosophy of Great American Crimes and Criminals* (New York, 1884), 434–63. His portrayal of the Swamp Fox was as unflattering as Orr's. Triplett painted an unredeeming picture of a bully, a coward, and a "fiend" (his favorite Baker appellation). He insisted that Baker had no characteristics worth emulation and that his life demonstrated how a boy could emerge from a good family and "go wrong." Triplett relied heavily upon Orr for his background material, but his essay does present some original observations regarding Baker's life. Many Baker writers have ignored Triplett's effort.

For a fascinating comparison of Baker biographers, Orr can be paired with T. U. Taylor, author of "Swamp Fox of the Sulphur, or Life and Times of Cullen Montgomery Baker," *ca.* 1936 (Typescript in Eugene C. Barker Texas History Center, Center for American History, University of Texas, Austin). These two nineteenth-century men wrote from vastly different vantage points. Orr, of course, lived around Baker; Taylor only learned of him through oral testimony. Their biographies come to nearly contradictory conclusions about the Swamp Fox, which makes an analysis of these works interesting. Orr does not refer to the so-called oppressiveness of Reconstruction, whereas this is Taylor's second major theme. Orr understood that Baker hated blacks and often killed them (he gives no reason why) but emphasizes that he had murdered whites long before he ever slew a black person. In contrast, Taylor conspicuously ignores Baker's early attacks on whites and places the blame on blacks for leading Baker down the path of violence.

A cache of letters in the possession of Christine Woodrow of New Boston, Texas, makes clear that Taylor, an engineering professor and dean at the University of Texas, began to amass material on Baker in the 1920s. A. L. Burford, a Texarkana lawyer, laid the groundwork for Taylor. Burford wrote to assorted newspapers that had supposedly published pieces on Baker; he collected names of old settlers who knew Baker and arranged interviews. For instance, Burford wrote to W. H. Foster (the brother of Baker's second wife) and stated that he wanted the "truth" about Baker: to learn "what he did and what he was trying to accomplish" and "whether he was a desperado or whether he thought he was trying to serve the country the best he could."

Securing a copy of Orr's biography, Taylor wrote to Burford that, "as expected," it was "very partisan" and "very one-sided." Particularly egregious to Taylor was Orr's cursory description of the Seth Rames killing, never mentioning Rames's age (he was seventeen or eighteen, not fourteen as Taylor contended) or the fact that he was "unarmed in a lonely wood, surrounded by six men all heavily armed and that he was killed because he would not squeal on his friends." Burford observed that if Taylor patterned his "life of Cullen Baker after the manner of Beveridge's Life of Lincoln," depicting "the social and economic conditions that moulded, if they did not create, his character," he would portray "the most tyrannical, mingled with one of the most romantic, periods in our history."

It is evident from Taylor's letters and typescript that he relied almost solely upon the recollections of local residents and Orr for his sources. For example, Taylor informed Burford that he "ripped out this morsel" from one of his interviews on June 23, 1926: "Old Tom Orr was a scalawag and was elected county judge by negro votes, because he claimed that he killed Cullen Baker"; as soon as the Democrats "redeemed the county from the scalawags," they "got him out of office." Taylor and his source were both in error here. Orr survived the political purge and won a disputed election in 1884 for sheriff on the Republican ticket in Miller County, Arkansas. Taylor's testament to the life and times of Cullen Montgomery Baker is largely composed of such dubious reminiscences.

Historians are influenced by the times in which they write. Baker's biographers exemplify this fact. Excluding Orr and Triplett, almost every Baker chronicler until the 1980s (and then in works whose primary focus was not Baker) has followed Taylor in blaming blacks for Baker's evolution into a killer and desperado. Of course, the rationale for this blame is never explained. And anyway, the facts belie this perception of Baker as motivated solely by racial hatred. Even according to those biographies' flawed chronologies, Baker did not murder a black person until 1863 or 1864. By that time he had already killed Baily in cold blood in 1854 and Warthan in 1860, among a host of other alleged slayings.

Taylor, however, makes race his central focus. The threat of blacks to the community and to white women in particular compelled Baker to become a killer. Taylor wrote at a time when the post–Civil War years were viewed as an era of corruption and of black, carpetbagger, and scalawag misrule. In this view, the villainous United States army had committed numerous misdeeds, and men like Baker were necessary to balance the equation. The army had superior numbers, but Baker had superior knowledge of the geography, giving him the power to surprise or to ambush. Taylor imbibed all these myths and found Baker, if not justified in his outlaw behavior, nevertheless serving a noble end. He elevated the Swamp Fox into a pantheon of individuals who were misguided and dissipated, but heroic.

Between 1884 and 1954, the majority of printed items about the Swamp Fox appeared in local newspapers. These columns are worth exploring briefly as they demonstrate that even on home ground, Baker was not always considered a positive influence. Indeed, they suggest that the original community division over Baker's actions persisted. Locales tend to preserve that aspect of history that is most likely to make them popular and attractive to tourists. Baker's haunts conform to this pattern, although not simply because of his exploits. His persona contributes to the lore local citizens consider worth relating about the area's exciting past. But like all past writings of Baker, these wonderful stories give no hint about original sources.

After Triplett, it would be seven decades before a published essay or monograph of Baker's life appeared: Ed Bartholomew's *Cullen Baker: Premier Texas Gunfighter.* After Bartholomew's work, a new publication focusing upon Baker, whether essay or small booklet, appeared about every twelve or thirteen years. Whatever the writers' predilections, they all perceived Baker as a fascinating and bizarre individual. If he exhibited freakish behavior, it was owing to the era, which wrung this conduct from some white southern citizens who could accept neither defeat nor the changed social order. The accounts vary widely in content. However, none attempts to discover Baker's family background or the facts of his escapades, but simply rely on previous reports while adding slightly varying twists.

Bartholomew concludes his "epic account" of Baker, which includes information on several other Reconstruction desperadoes, by declaring that "these men and their doings are little known today." They come before us "like wraiths now, the story they have to tell unbelievable." To Bartholomew it defies the human senses "to consider that these things could have happened at all, even in Texas in the early days." But happen they did, or at least some of them. All these men "lived and died for what they felt was their right," Bartholomew righteously observes, "so judge them not." But even judging them by the standards of their day, their actions in killing many innocent people must be considered despicable and cowardly.

Bartholomew waxes eloquent when he considers what might have been. "Baker was the fastest man of his day," he contends, and "had he lived to see and use the famous Colts cartridge single action revolver, he might have never been captured, or killed." Baker died, according to Bartholomew, "thinking that his beloved Texas had been partitioned into four states, that he was the only guerrilla left to fight the Unionists, and probably feeling that he had chased the army back into their forts all over east and northern Texas." With his death and that of Benjamin F. Bickerstaff and Bob Lee, only Wild Bill Longley of the famous "Baker's School of Six-Shooter-ology" remained to carry on "his old master's war."

Two other pro-Baker biographers came forth with their interpretations in the western boom of the 1950s and 1960s—which was also the civil rights era, when the bugaboo of federal intervention was once again experienced by the South. Carl W. Breihan offered two pieces: "Cullen Baker," in *Great Gunfighters of the West*, ed. Carl W. Breihan (San Antonio, 1962), 66–87; and "Cullen Baker—First of the Gunfighters," *The West*, VII (July, 1967), 16–19, 42–47. Al Eason published "Cullen Baker—Purveyor of Death," *Frontier Times*, XL (August–September, 1966), 6–12, 44–47, 67. These accounts are amusing rather than informative, having exciting and additional unverified background material, often so much that we lose sight of Baker himself. These writers, along with Taylor, have perpetuated the Baker saga, and local biographers accept their accounts as the truth and freely draw on them. Like Taylor's efforts, whom they rely upon, Breihan and Eason neither give us anything new about Baker nor present us with a more thorough or factual portrait. As a group, Bartholomew, Breihan, and Eason commonly display active imaginations. All three created careers writing about western outlaw history. Florid prose, inventive dialogue, and sumptuous background characterize their writings. Attributing dialogue to Baker and inventing circumstances that were always to his advantage became accepted conventions in this kind of writing.

An enduring myth of the Baker saga thus perpetuated is that Thomas Orr was a carpetbagger and unionist. It is true that he and Baker did not have an amicable relationship. But Bartholomew moves from contending that Orr "was an anti-Baker man" to claiming that "of course" Orr's book "was prepared from the Union point of view." Although Bartholomew duplicated many stories in Orr's account, the former attempted to write a more in-depth portrait of Baker during Reconstruction, "which for some reason or other had escaped his early biographer." Having made Baker the hero of his tome, Bartholomew needed a villain. Orr conveniently fills this role along with the army, blacks, Republicans, scalawags, and carpetbaggers.

It is fair to recall that Bartholomew's book appeared in the mid-1950s, before the decisive shift in Reconstruction historiography, and thus expounds all the old stereo-typical characterizations of the era and its individuals. But Bartholomew ingeniously ties the corruption of the carpetbaggers, scalawags, and Republicans in general, and the desire for their eradication, to Baker's so-called New Rebellion. Eason follows much the same line and refers to Orr as a carpetbagger. Until the 1980s, this viewpoint pervaded the Baker literature and was consistently used to justify the violence engendered by these turbulent times. As a result, Baker appeared to have assumed the mission to eliminate the influence of unscrupulous individuals.

Boyd W. Johnson added little to the Baker saga, although he interpreted with a trained historical eye. In "Cullen Montgomery Baker: The Arkansas-Texas Desperado," *Arkansas Historic Quarterly*, XXV (Autumn, 1966), 229–39, Johnson unearthed no new sources, relying instead upon Orr (though he has Orr's first name wrong). He argues that "it would have been extremely difficult" for Orr to have been objective because Baker was "Orr's worst enemy." He criticizes Triplett and Bartholomew for using "highly questionable newspaper accounts" and discredits the work of Arkansas governor Powell Clayton, whose viewpoint must have been colored by the fact that Baker was "an enemy of his administration." He rehearses some of the standard examples of Baker's prowess but judges him to have been a rather despicable character who disrupted the peace in the Arkansas-Louisiana-Texas region.

For over a decade (from 1966 to 1978), attention to Baker was dormant. During that period, no one challenged the vision of Baker constructed by the writings of Taylor, Bartholomew, Breihan, and Eason. The perspectives of the first biographers of Baker—Orr and Triplett—had been twisted and distorted. In effect, these two authors became villains themselves because they had dared to suggest that the Swamp Fox was an unsavory character. Then in 1978, new writers from the region decided to tackle the Baker saga again. These include Yvonne Vestal, Traylor Russell and Robert T. Russell, and James Smallwood.

The cover of Vestal's *The Borderlands and Cullen Baker* (Atlanta, Tex., 1978) calls the book "A True Story of 'Civil War and Reconstruction in Southwest Arkansas and Northwest Texas.' " Vestal wrote that Taylor, "whose avocation was Texas desperadoes," spent two summers during the 1920s in the Arkansas-Louisiana-Texas region interviewing men who had lived during Baker's era. She obtained a copy of Taylor's manuscript, to which a letter was attached written by Jessie Muriel Teel Cooter, Baker's great-great-granddaughter. Cooter wrote that "too many people have tried to write [Baker's] life story. Some have not spent enough time in research and hurriedly . . . printed his life—even changing the names of the family." Cooter contended that Bartholomew and Taylor were the only "two writers that the family recommends others to read." Both, of course, are ardent Baker sympathizers.

Vestal's small booklet is a local publication. It draws mostly on local resources for its information, supplemented by a heavy dose of Taylor. Pervading her interpretation of the Reconstruction years is an antiquated perspective similar to that of most previous writers, which has been thoroughly discredited in the past three or four decades. Even before Vestal's work appeared in 1978, the post–Civil War era was no longer seen as a time when the South suffered untold vicissitudes and blacks behaved irresponsibly. Vestal's justification for the necessity of the Ku Klux Klan and of men like Baker had already been demonstrated to be a considerable distortion of the actual events.

The Russells' 1979 essay, "'If I Had Killed Jesus Christ . . . ,'" in *Some Die Twice* (Waco, 1979), 1–21, is worth mentioning because the Russells label Baker a schizophrenic. Traylor Russell was born and reared in Titus County (separated from Cass by Morris County since 1875). When he completed his political career as a state representative in the 1930s, he chose history as his avocation. Before he turned to Baker, Traylor Russell had authored a book entitled *Carpetbaggers, Scalawags & Others* (Waco, 1973) and written about his home county of Titus. Like those of Taylor, Bartholomew, Breihan, Eason, and Vestal, the Russells' interpretation stresses the negative aspects of Reconstruction. Among their contentions is the idea that the imposition of black voting rights violated every precept of the white South. They judge Baker's response to be appropriate and even necessary.

One of the most recent contributions to the subject is James M. Smallwood, "Swamp Fox of the Sulphur," *True West*, XXXVIII (October, 1991), Pt. 1, pp. 20–23; (November, 1991), Pt. 2, pp. 38–41. Smallwood, a professional historian, has written extensively about Texas during the Reconstruction years and is the author of the standard work on black postwar history. That Smallwood knows northeast Texas is illustrated in his various articles. He has investigated Baker's background, his killing propensities, and his alcoholic and psychopathic tendencies. He has also tied Baker to the Ku Klux Klan and boldly suggested that he was in the pay of planters who desired to discipline their black laborers. The Freedmen's Bureau records, which Smallwood has mined, suggest that this connection existed.

Two 1995 works add nothing new to the Baker story: Billy Cox, "Cullen Montgomery Baker: Scourge of the Red River Country," *Old Time Chronicle* (June, 1995), 6–10; and Robert W. Teel (Baker's great-great-grandson), *Cullen Montgomery Baker: Champion of the Lost Cause* (Huntsville, Ala., 1995). Both paint sympathetic portraits of Baker.

Since the 1930s, regional and local writers have made contributions to Baker's legend. They have adopted much of the tone of the Taylor *et al.* school, which portrays southern life after the Civil War as disrupted by a series of governmental intrusions and black despotism. From their standpoint, Baker was merely performing his "proper" community vigilante role in challenging these twin forces of destruction. However, other sources suggest that the region did not require this kind of regulation and protection. This collection of area writers supplies the Baker legend with local folklore and perspective on Reconstruction in the region.

Baker's local ratings rose and fell depending on the writer. In the 1970s his reputation may have reached its nadir. A member of the "Jefferson Junior Historians of Texas," Joe Bailes declared that if current clinical diagnostic methods had been available in Baker's time, perhaps a "tragic tale" could have been avoided. Calling Baker deranged and comparing him to Lee Harvey Oswald, Charles Whitman, and "history's countless other sadistical personalities," Bailes contends that Baker led a life of "crime and violence, running and hiding from the guns of lawmen and citizens alike, and being feared by all!"

In effect, there are three schools of Bakerology. One views him as a lightning-fast gunslinger and an unreconstructed Rebel. To another, he appears as a type of social bandit or postwar guerrilla who defended and protected southern honor. These two viewpoints have often merged successfully. The third group depicts Baker as a psychopathic killer. Of the three images, the quick-draw artist and guerrilla who refused to accept southern defeat in the war has generally predominated in writings about Baker. Although he has been appropriated by writers of the western genre, he was originally claimed by those who believed he continued the Civil War in another form. There can be little question that Baker was a son of the Old South.

Reams have been written about outlaws, gunfighters, and western violence. A comprehensive starting point is Richard Maxwell Brown, "Historiography of Violence in the American West," in *Historians and the American West,* ed. Michael P. Malone (Lincoln, Nebr., 1983), 234–69. Also important are Ramon F. Adams, comp., *Six-Guns and Saddle Leather: A Bibliography of Books and Pamphlets on Western Outlaws and Gunmen* (rev. ed.; Norman, Okla., 1969) and his *More Burs Under the Saddle: A Second Look at Books and Histories of the West* (Norman, Okla., 1979), which led us to additional Baker material.

Two books by Eric B. Hobsbawm are significant: *Bandits* (New York, 1969) and *Primitive Rebels: Studies in Archaic Forms of Social Movement in the 19th and 20th Centuries* (New York, 1959). Richard White applies Hobsbawm's thesis to America in "Outlaw Gangs of the Middle Border: American Social Bandits," *Western Historical Quarterly,* XII (October, 1981), 387–408. William A. Settle, Jr., in *Jesse James Was His Name . . .* (Columbia, Mo., 1966), argues that the James-Younger gang must be viewed through their "Confederate-guerrilla origins" to understand their actions. This interpretation might also apply to Baker except that so little information about him exists for the war years.

One of the major efforts to interpret the mythology of the western frontier, its violence, and its enduring hold on the American imagination has been made by Richard Slotkin in three large volumes: *Regeneration Through Violence: The Mythology of the American Frontier, 1600–1860* (Middletown, Conn., 1973); *The Fatal Environment: The Myth of the Frontier in the Age of Industrialization, 1800–1890* (New York, 1985); and *Gunfighter Nation: The Myth of the Frontier in Twentieth-Century America* (New York, 1992). Slotkin has massively documented the aura of the frontier and its meaning for the American character. Using a variety of sources, he argues it has had a negative, violent influence.

Studies of Civil War guerrillas include Thomas Goodrich, *Bloody Dawn: The Story of the Lawrence Massacre* (Kent, Ohio, 1991), and *Black Flag: Guerrilla Warfare on the Western Border, 1861–1865* (Bloomington, Ind., 1995); and two earlier works by Albert Castel, *William Clarke Quantrill: His Life and Times* (New York, 1962), and *A Frontier State at War: Kansas, 1861–1865* (Ithaca, 1958). Richard S. Brownlee also treated this subject in *Gray Ghosts of the Confederacy: Guerrilla Warfare in the West, 1861–1865* (1958; rpr. Baton Rouge, 1984). Michael Fellman's *Inside War: The Guerrilla Conflict in Missouri During the American Civil War* (New York, 1989) is a psychological portrait. Its notes contain many other relevant and useful citations.

The argument that Reconstruction violence perpetrated by desperadoes like Baker as well as by the Ku Klux Klan differed quantitatively and qualitatively from that practiced in central Texas occurs in Richard Maxwell Brown, *Strain of Violence: Historical Studies of American Violence and Vigilantism* (New York, 1975). The fatalities from this violence far surpassed the number of frontier murders in other areas, including the later cattle towns, as described in W. Eugene Hollon, *Frontier Violence: Another Look* (New York, 1974), and Robert R. Dykstra, *The Cattle Towns* (New York, 1968). Dykstra provides an in-depth study of five Kansas cow towns during the height of the cattle boom.

Less has been written about Baker since the historiographical perspectives on Reconstruction changed. And few accounts of Baker and other Reconstruction desperadoes utilize the voluminous records in the National Archives. Admittedly, the latter sources are somewhat biased, given that they comprise records from the Freedmen's Bureau and the United States army. These organizations attempted to capture Baker in order to curtail his violence, which disrupted social, economic, and political life in the region. Nevertheless, these unpublished materials provide a more accurate account of Baker's activities and their ramifications than anything in print. In them, his links to the Ku Klux Klan quickly become evident.

In researching the present study, we scoured the National Archives, the Texas State Archives, the University of Texas Archives, and local depositories for any extant Baker material. In the National Archives we mined Record Groups 29 (censuses), 105 (Bureau of Refugees, Freedmen, and Abandoned Lands, for Texas, Arkansas, and Louisiana), and, significantly, 393 (military and post records for the region where Baker operated). Combining these sources with those in the Texas State Archives and those discovered in the courthouses of Grayson, Fannin, Lamar, Red River, Bowie, and Cass Counties made it possible to view Baker through a variety of perspectives. In the National Archives, we also rechecked the material that William L. Richter relied on for his analysis of Willis' murder. We attempted to locate all military records pertaining to Texas, and the army records that we reviewed are impressive. They include the District of Texas, the Department of Texas, and the Fifth Military District files (over two hundred boxes).

As for the secondary literature dealing with this region during the postwar years, we relied upon the most recent publications in the field, not ignoring local and regional works that might refer specifically to Baker or provide background on the locality where he was best known. Every county has some kind of local publication. Lay historians abound in these areas, and they have contributed significant accounts of their communities' historical development. Although these materials vary in quality, they were considered for the flavor they give to the Baker saga.

A professional who has often focused his sights upon Texas and its northeast area is the just-mentioned William L. Richter. We often cite his work in the notes although we disagree with many of his interpretations. Richter's two major efforts are *The Army in Texas During Reconstruction, 1865–1870* (College Station, Tex., 1987) and *Overreached on All Sides: The Freedmen's Bureau Administrators in Texas, 1865–1868* (College Station, Tex., 1991). Richter has also published a number of related articles in historical journals. He views Baker critically but judges those who attempted to implement the Reconstruction experiment equally severely. His research is impeccable.

Secondary state and local literature that is valuable for understanding the era includes Randolph B. Campbell, *A Southern Community in Crisis: Harrison County, Texas, 1850–1880* (Austin, 1983), a model study. For politics, see Carl H. Moneyhon, *Republicanism in Reconstruction Texas* (Austin, 1980). The efforts of the Freedmen's Bureau on the local level in Baker territory can be partially followed in Barry A. Crouch, *The Freedmen's Bureau and Black Texans* (Austin, 1992). How the freedmen and freedwomen fared during this era is addressed in James M. Smallwood, *Time of Hope, Time of Despair: Black Texans During Reconstruction* (Port Washington, N.Y., 1981).

There are three quite useful surveys of the literature concerned with the Reconstruction in Texas. The most comprehensive is Crouch, " 'Unmanacling' Texas Reconstruction: A Twenty-Year Perspective," *Southwest Historical Quarterly*, XCIII (January, 1990), 275–302; but also important are Campbell, "Statehood, Civil War, and Reconstruction, 1846–76," in *Texas Through Time: Evolving Interpretations*, edited by Walter L. Buenger and Robert A. Calvert (College Station, Tex., 1991), 165–96; and Ralph A. Wooster, "The Civil War and Reconstruction in Texas," in *A Guide to the History of Texas*, edited by Light Townsend Cummins and Alvin R. Bailey, Jr. (New York, 1988), 37–50.

Our viewpoint on Reconstruction has been influenced by two outstanding works: Eric Foner, *Reconstruction: America's Unfinished Revolution, 1863–1877* (New York, 1988), and Leon F. Litwack, *Been in the Storm So Long: The Aftermath of Slavery* (New York, 1979). These comprehensive historical studies provide fresh perspectives and extensive information on post–Civil War Arkansas, Texas, and Louisiana. The Baker myth reflects the fact that Reconstruction is still a controversial subject in these states where Baker operated. Where traditional views prevail, Reconstruction is described as a horrible experience, a perspective that in turn conditions interpretations of Cullen Baker's violence.

INDEX

Allanson, John S.: expedition against Baker, 81

Allen, Green, 94

Anderson, Nathan B.: background of, 121; and death of Kirkman, 122–23; and Baker, 123–24; forced to leave Boston, 126

Andrews, Porter J., 129

Aurora, Tex., 24

Baily, Wesley: background of, 35; killed by Baker, 36–38

Baker, Cullen Montgomery: birth of, 20; as teenager, 28–29; and alcohol, 31–32; marriage of, to Petty, 33–34; killing of Baily, 35–38; living in Arkansas, 40–41; killing of Warthan, 42; marriage of, to Foster, 42–43; in Confederate army, 43–45; origins of hatred for blacks, 46–48; and guerrilla activities in Arkansas, 48–52; returns to Texas after war, 53; and Robin Hood image, 53–54; and ferry business, 57–58, 62; confronts Orr at school, 63–64; and citizens, 64–65; dog-killing spree, 67–68; killing of Rowden, 68–69; killing a black man, 72; and shootout in Boston, 75; and soldiers, 76–77; various attacks of, 79, 80, 91–92, 120, 128; disciplining black labor,

102–104; in pay of planters, 105; and black voting, 105–109; as overseer of community standards, 109; forcing blacks to migrate, 110–11; 1868 Texas activity of, 113; and north-central Texas, 115; nullifying bureau power, 120; killing of Kirkman, 125–26; numbers in gang of, 132; offers reward for Clayton, 141; and Dave Moore farm parlay, 142–44; and killing of Orr, 146–48; split of, with Rames, 148–49; death of, 152–53, 155–56, 159–60; legends of, 162; and religion, 163; and Martha's death, 163–64; weapons used by, 164; and Ku Klux Klan, 166; and Reconstruction, 164–67; and Freedman's Bureau and army, 167–69; grave of, 169; as moral imbecile, 169–70; as hero, 170; numbers killed by, 170–72; individual and community legacy of, 172; as social bandit, 172–74

Baker, Elizabeth, 19–20

Baker, John: background of, 19; move of, to Texas, 20–21; land owned by, 25–26; assets of, 25–27; homestead of, 27–28

Baker, Louise Jane, 40, 41

Baker, Martha Foster: background of, 42–43; famous ride of, 52; death of, 60